"Haugen's great good news is that Christian compassion combined with down-to-earth professional expertise—in investigations and advocacy, case by case—are forcing essential law-enforcement reforms, and that more and more Christians are coming forward to help achieve that."

BOB ABERNETHY, *Religion & Ethics NewsWeekly*

"This book is quickly becoming a classic for folks who have seen the good news, and who have seen the bad news . . . and yet who still believe, in spite of all the ugly things happening in the world, that in the end love wins, life conquers death, grace triumphs over hatred, and the good news is more compelling than the bad."

SHANE CLAIBORNE, bestselling author, Christian troublemaker and recovering sinner

"People of faith have long been ambassadors for the poor and vulnerable in our world. Gary Haugen is a shining example, having worked on the front lines of injustice for more than a decade giving a voice to those who desperately need an advocate."

JIM NICHOLSON, former U.S. Ambassador to the Vatican and former Secretary of the Department of Veterans Affairs

"It's easy when confronted with the suffering of the world to be overwhelmed with guilt, despair and their nasty friend, indifference—but when you hear or read Gary Haugen, something altogether different happens. You're not just inspired, but you're empowered to do something, and that can make all the difference in the world, which, of course, is literally what it's doing."

ROB BELL, author, speaker and founding pastor of Mars Hill Bible Church

"Haugen has seen lives changed as a result of the action taken in the name of the God of justice, and his testimony will likely provoke you to question your own inaction. His book pulls no punches about how dark the world can be, but will leave you with hope as it exposes the authentic light of this holy and urgent calling."

FATHER JONATHAN MORRIS, news contributor and analyst, *FOX News*, and theologian

"When I read the stories and the successes of God's intervening justice on behalf of the abused and seemingly forgotten children created in his own image, I was aware of both eyes and heart opened afresh to the greatest truth of all—God cares for the forsaken, the abused, the oppressed and those countless numbers denied justice, and he is about making things right. . . . I highly recommend this book. It's a must-read!"

PHIL KEAGGY, Dove Award–winning recording artist

"Justice—the life-giving use of power in all relationships—is essential to God's joyful vision for human flourishing. *Good News About Injustice* points us toward this intention and hope, and motivates us to join God and one another in a passionate and urgent pursuit of this vision."

MARK LABBERTON, author of *The Dangerous Act of Worship*

"Few books deserve to be called 'life-shaping.' This book warrants that description! Through personal stories, biblical insights, humor and passion it makes God's call for us to 'do justice' accessible, attractive and compelling."

TIM DEARBORN, director of faith and development, World Vision International

"How so many of us Bible-loving disciples have missed God's passion for justice that is plain on innumerable pages of Scripture is a tragic mystery. God has used this classic to open the eyes of the blind and to ignite a movement of prayer and action to join him on his mission of releasing the oppressed. Read it and be changed."

DR. AMY L. SHERMAN, Senior Fellow, Sagamore Institute Center on Faith in Communities

"Gary Haugen is a prophetic voice to this generation. We are called to live courageously for the cause of Christ. *Good News About Injustice* will show you how. Prepare to be convicted, challenged and inspired."

MARK BATTERSON, author of *Wild Goose Chase*

"Gary Haugen and International Justice Mission have helped ignite an inspiring movement of Christians fighting oppression around the globe. In so doing they have recaptured the spirit of great saints such as Carey and Wilberforce, who saw the gospel as good news both for now and for eternity."

STAN GUTHRIE, author of *Missions in the Third Millennium*

"Gary Haugen tells us stories we need to hear about the injustices in the world, but he also convinces us that God is at work to counter these injustices, and invites us to be part of the struggle."

TONY CAMPOLO, Eastern University

"This is not comfortable, but it is essential reading for us all."

DR. CLIVE CALVER, former president, World Relief

"This book has opened my heart to a greater sense of compassion for those victims caught in the grip of severe persecution as well as given me newly directed passion to be a part of God's redemptive work surrounding human injustice. Be careful—the contents of this book will inspire us all to take action. It will change both the reader and the world."

DAN HASELTINE, lead singer, Jars of Clay

TENTH ANNIVERSARY EDITION

GOOD NEWS
ABOUT INJUSTICE

A WITNESS OF COURAGE
IN A HURTING WORLD

GARY A. HAUGEN

FOREWORD BY JOHN STOTT

IVP Books

An imprint of InterVarsity Press
Downers Grove, Illinois

Inter-Varsity Press
Nottingham, England

InterVarsity Press, USA
P.O. Box 1400
Downers Grove, IL 60515-1426, USA
World Wide Web: www.ivpress.com
Email: email@ivpress.com

Inter-Varsity Press, England
Norton Street
Nottingham NG7 3HR, England
Website: www.ivpbooks.com
Email: ivp@ivpbooks.com

Second edition ©2009 by International Justice Mission
First edition ©2009 by International Justice Mission

Gary A. Haugen has asserted his right under the Copyright, Designs and Patents Act, 1988, to be identified as Author of this work.

InterVarsity Press®, USA, is the book-publishing division of InterVarsity Christian Fellowship/USA® <www.intervarsity.org> and a member movement of the International Fellowship of Evangelical Students.

Inter-Varsity Press, England, is closely linked with the Universities and Colleges Christian Fellowship, a student movement connecting Christian Unions in universities and colleges throughout Great Britain, and a member movement of the International Fellowship of Evangelical Students. Website: www.uccf.org.uk.

All Scripture quotations, unless otherwise indicated, are taken from the Holy Bible, New International Version®. NIV®. Copyright © 1973, 1978, 1984 by International Bible Society. Used by permission of Zondervan Publishing House. Distributed in the U.K. by permission of Hodder and Stoughton Ltd. All rights reserved. "NIV" is a registered trademark of International Bible Society. UK trademark number 1448790.

Design: Cindy Kiple
Images: candle: Florea Marius Catalin/iStockphoto
        lit candle: Noel Powell/iStockphoto
        hands: Ted Haddock/International Justice Mission
        red gold wall: iStockphoto
        Gary in vehicle: Ted Haddock/International Justice Mission

USA ISBN 978-0-8308-3710-6
UK ISBN 978-1-84474-407-7

Printed in the United States of America ∞

Library of Congress Cataloging-in-Publication Data

Haugen, Gary A.
    Good news about injustice: a witness of courage in a hurting world
    /Gary A. Haugen; foreword by John Stott.—10th anniversary ed.,
    [rev. & expanded].
        p.cm.
    Includes bibliographical references.
    ISBN 978-0-8308-3710-6 (pbk.: alk. paper)
    1. Christianity and justice. I. Title.
    BR115.J8H388 2009
    241'.622—dc22
                                    2009021601

British Library Cataloguing in Publication Data

A catalogue record for this book is available from the British Library.

P   18   17   16   15   14   13   12   11   10   9   8   7   6   5   4   3   2
Y   24   23   22   21   20   19   18   17   16   15   14   13   12   11   10   09

For my father and mother

CONTENTS

PART 3: REAL-WORLD TOOLS FOR RESCUING THE OPPRESSED

FOREWORD

Gary Haugen's book is a powerful combination of narrative and Scripture, of dramatic storytelling and biblical reflection, of human injustice and the justice of God.

One moment we are in the Rwandan killing fields, watching with mute horror the genocide of Tutsis, or in the red-light district of a large Asian city, whose brothels hold young children captive, while the next moment we are deep in Scripture, exploring the character and the will of God. And the interaction between these two perspectives continues throughout the book.

On the one hand, we are introduced to injustice, which always involves the abuse of power, and to the wide range of its victims. We are confronted not only with the cruelties of bonded labor, enforced prostitution, rape, torture, lynching and the misappropriation of land, but also with the frequent failures of the law to bring the perpetrators to justice because they are protected by the establishment.

On the other hand, we are confronted in Scripture by the true and living God, who loves justice and hates injustice, whose anger is roused by evil and rests on evildoers, and who is moved with compassion toward all those who suffer.

What this book obliges us to do is to ask ourselves some basic and uncomfortable questions that living in a comfortable culture may never have allowed us to ask before.

First, what sort of God do we believe in? Is he concerned exclusively with individual salvation? Or does he have a social conscience? Is he (in Dr. Carl Henry's memorable phrase) "the God of justice and of justification"? How is it that so many of us staunch evangelical people have never seen, let alone faced, the barrage of biblical texts about justice? Why are we often guilty of selective indignation?

Second, what sort of a creature do we think a human being is? Have we ever considered the unique value and dignity of human beings, made in the image of God, so that abuse, torture, rape and grinding poverty, which dehumanize human beings, are also an insult to the God who made them?

Third, what sort of a person do we think Jesus Christ is? Have we ever seen him as described in John 11, where first he "snorted" with anger (v. 33, literally) in the face of death (an intrusion into God's good world) and then "wept" (v. 35) over the bereaved? If only we could be like Jesus, indignant toward evil and compassionate toward its victims!

Fourth, what sort of a community do we think the church is meant to be? Is it not often indistinguishable from the world because it accommodates itself to the prevailing culture of injustice and indifference? Is it not intended rather to penetrate the world like salt and light, and so to change it, as salt hinders bacterial decay and light disperses darkness?

To ask ourselves these questions honestly—about God, Christ, human beings and the church—and to answer them biblically, as Gary Haugen does, is to expose ourselves to radical challenge and change.

This book does not leave us in suspense or with the doubts, the cynicism, even the despair which the world's monumental evil provokes in many Christian people. Instead, we are given solid grounds for hope. We are reminded of God's character, of his purpose to work through his people and of some of the heroic social reformers of the past. We are not given utopian visions of a perfect society, but we are encouraged to expect some substantial success both in defending human rights and in bringing to justice those who violate them. Gary Haugen outlines practical ways in which his International Justice Mission has been at work since 1994 and in which members of the body of Christ can contribute their distinctive gifts and specialist ministries.

I heartily commend this book. It is well researched and well written. Its author faces the unpleasant realities of our fallen world and responds to them with a biblically developed mind and conscience. He has the sharp eye of a lawyer and the sensitive spirit of an authentic disciple of Jesus Christ. He pulls no punches. We need to learn from him, to know what he knows, to see (at least in our imagination) what he sees and to feel what he feels.

I defy anybody to emerge from exposure to this book unscathed. In fact, my advice to would-be readers is "Don't! Leave the book alone!"—unless you are willing to be shocked, challenged, persuaded and transformed.

John Stott

PREFACE TO THE
TENTH ANNIVERSARY EDITION

There is nothing quite as awkward as an enthusiastic but misplaced celebration. Indeed, I can vividly remember setting one off in the lunchroom of my elementary school as a small boy. Our principal had jammed all of us into the lunchroom for a special assembly and launched the festivities by asking the scores of squirming children if anyone had a birthday. Unable to wait for my shy best friend, Marty, to out himself as the day's Birthday Boy—I leaped to my feet and shot my hand in the air to share what I knew about Marty. Amidst the deafening clamor bouncing off the concrete acoustics of the lunchroom, our ever-eager principal blew past my stammering objections and immediately began leading the raucous throng in a rousing and seemingly endless chorus of "Happy Birthday" and "He's a Jolly Good Fellow"—to *me*. Needless to say, when all the whoops and hollers and applause finally died down, there I stood, all alone in the now-silent lunchroom, awkwardly pointing and explaining to a sea of staring classmates that, actually, no, it was not *my* birthday—but *Marty's*.

The generosity and enthusiasm expressed for me was kind enough, but it was all just too awkward when expressed by mistake. I just

wanted people to celebrate Marty—but I ended up disastrously di-
verting unwanted and misplaced attention to myself.

This is the awkward little memory that came to mind as I began
thinking about the tenth anniversary celebration of *Good News About
Injustice*. I am so very eager to celebrate the miraculous things that
the God of justice has done over this past decade, to honor the heroic
frontline work of my colleagues at International Justice Mission, to
testify to the valor of the victims we serve and to draw attention to
the amazing transformation that has taken place in the church over
the past decade since the book was first released. But obviously my
intentions have backfired before. So this time, right from the start, I
want to be very clear about whose day it is.

I am grateful for all the kind encouragement that has come my
way as the author of this book, but my own experience of the last
ten years has been one of riding a wave of much larger events and
forces that have left me feeling rather small—wonderfully small. It
is these larger events and forces that I hope draw wide attention and
grand celebration, because they offer very great hope for the future.
And that, after all, was the fundamental prayer behind the original
book project. As I wrote ten years ago in the original preface to this
volume: "My prayer will be answered if it conveys even a small measure of the hope and encouragement that the God of justice intends
for his people." Indeed, this book was meant to offer *good news*
about what is perhaps the most painful and discouraging reality of
human history—the aggressive, intentional, violent evil in our
world. And now, ten years later, I have seen more good news than I
ever imagined.

Here then, in four affirmations, is the testimony of hope that I—
along with my IJM colleagues—have witnessed with our own eyes
over this past decade.

1. There is a God of justice who is active in the world.
Our first affirmation of hope in a brutal world of injustice is simply
about the nature of God. Over the last decade we have found the
teachings of Christ and the Scriptures true and reliable—and we

have, at moments, literally staked our lives on the truth of these teachings. *Thousands of times* over the last decade, my colleagues at IJM have confronted brutal men of great evil and great power: rapists, murderers, slave owners, sex traffickers, torturers, thieves, kidnappers, thugs and sadists (many of them wearing uniforms of official authority and power). In desperation we have cried out in prayer to the God of justice, asking him to rescue the victims of abuse when we could not, to protect us when we were too weak, and to bring down the arrogant men of violence and lies when they were too strong. And we have seen God answer these prayers—more frequently, more reliably and more powerfully than I ever dreamed I would see. Surely there has also been heartache and disappointment and painful loss. And certainly others will find more mundane explanations for the miraculous events we have witnessed, but we have no appetite to dispute with others. Rather, for those of us *who were there*, we found in the crucible an experience of God. We found mysteries consistent with the ancient words of the Scriptures, of Jesus and of the prophets—an experience so convincing that we are doubling down our bets and heading out for more.

At IJM we carry in our archives the names of thousands of men, women and children who once were slaves, prisoners, dispossessed and abused. And now, quite simply, they are not. They are free, they are safe, they are restored. All we can say is what the blind man said in the Gospel of John when pressed by religious leaders to explain his healing from Jesus: "One thing I do know, I once was blind but now I see" (John 9:25).

Moreover, what my colleagues and I can very clearly affirm is that *we* could not have done this. I think I can safely speak for all my colleagues in saying that none of us have emerged from this remarkably powerful decade of justice with a convincing experience of our *own* power, ability, intelligence or courage. What is most palpably memorable from the experience for us personally is the way the confrontation with violent injustice took us to the limits of our own power and capacities—in a humbling and even humiliating way. In the confrontation with injustice, we have experienced (painfully many times) our own weakness, incompetence, folly and fear. But as the apostle Paul promised us: God's power is made perfect in our *weakness* (2 Corinthians 12:9). For us, this familiar proverb is not a nice, humble thing to say; it's a painfully glorious truth about the way the spiritual universe actually works.

After a decade on the front lines, I have found profound comfort and encouragement in the fact that our Lord, Jesus Christ, described his ministry this way:

> The Spirit of the Lord is on me,
>   because he has anointed me
>   to preach good news to the poor.
> He has sent me to proclaim freedom for the prisoners
>   and recovery of sight for the blind,
> to release the oppressed,
>   to proclaim the year of the Lord's favor. (Luke 4:18-19)

2. The Word of God has the power to change lives.
The second testimony of hope that we can affirm from this decade of struggle is about the power of the Scriptures to transform those who earnestly and humbly seek God.

Sadly, as we get older, it seems harder to hold out hope that people can really change. I know I get frustrated with my own stubborn weaknesses, fears and blind spots—and I imagine we all get discouraged by the obstinate habits, prejudices and insecurities that seem to shrivel and destroy the lives of so many people around us. It's hard not to grow cynical and resign ourselves to the fact that people don't really change; and if *people* don't change, then surely *the world* isn't going to change. This is bad news for those of us who so desperately want the world to change—to address the injustice, the violence, the abuse and suffering. We have a vision for the way the world might be changed if people cared, if they were willing to stand up, to be brave and to actually *do* something. But so many people clearly do not meaningfully care about injustice in our world, and it's just as clear that they are not doing anything about it. And worst of all, they are not going to change. How hopeless.

This discouraging narrative sounds realistic and right, but honestly this simply has not been our experience. On the contrary we have seen vast numbers of people actually change. When it comes to the struggle for justice, people have moved from apathy to passion, from obliviousness to responsible knowledge, from helpless paralysis to courageous action, from numb fear to liberating joy. We have seen thousands of people transformed in their minds, hearts and souls. And where has the change come from? From what I can tell, through an encounter with the Scriptures. People have come to the Word of God with what Jesus called "that good and noble heart" (Luke 8:15)—people "who hear the word, retain it, and by persevering produce a crop." They have rediscovered God's passion for the work of justice in the world, and they are changed. They see the way God cares about justice, and they see what he promises to those who *do the work* of justice. And the truth sets them free—free to actually look at the reality of injustice and to do something about it. We have indeed seen the truth that "all Scripture is inspired by God and is useful for teaching, for reproof, for correction, and for training in *dikaiosynē* [*dikaiosynē* being a Greek word for justice]" (2 Timothy 3:16 NASB).

Because the Bible teaches that "God loves justice" and calls his people to "seek justice, rescue the oppressed, defend the orphan and plead for the widow" (Isaiah 1:17 NRSV), pastors who hadn't preached on justice in twenty-five years now do; seminary professors who had never offered courses on biblical justice now do; missions committee elders who had never supported the work of justice now do; Bible study groups who had never studied justice now do; prayer warriors who had never prayed for the work of justice in the world now do; lawyers, investigators and social workers who found no calling in the work for justice among the poor now do; artists who had never rendered the truth about justice now do; students who never imagined they could free slaves now do.

We have seen the Bible's teaching on justice not only change people's minds and hearts but change *the way people live.* Moms and dads actually open themselves up to see what is happening to other people's children and allow themselves to weep. Families live on budgets to make sure they can pay for the rescue the poor cannot afford. Lawyers leave lucrative jobs and safe neighborhoods to stand with the oppressed in the darkest streets. Parents release and bless their children to seek justice in violent places. Decorated and accomplished criminal investigators reject a smooth path to professional ease and instead put their lives on the line one more time. Social workers who have seen a lifetime of trauma and pain return to the breach to train others in the steady stonework of healing. And now, because the Bible changes the way these people live, thousands of other people around the world get to live. The Word of God has the power to change lives.

Good News About Injustice is a story based on the Scriptures about the fallen world, the God of justice and his work of rescue and redemption through his people. The two books that followed over the next decade—*Terrify No More* and *Just Courage*—are mostly about the way that simple Bible stories change lives. And because the Word of God still has the power to change lives—there remains great hope for changing the world. For indeed, since the beginning of time, God has been transforming the world through transformed people—usually through very small bands of people—who manage to "turn the world upside down." And according to Jesus, "the gates of hell shall not prevail against it" (Matthew 16:18 KJV).

3. God redeems and restores the victims of injustice.

The third testimony of hope I would like to offer from our experience is the affirmation that good has the power to triumph over evil—even the darkest and most brutal evil. Again, this is not, for us, a thin slogan of wishful thinking. This is the miracle that my colleagues and I have witnessed in the lives of those who have endured unspeakable violence and abuse, and have been resurrected from death by the love of their Maker.

- We have seen a child scrawl Bible verses on the walls of the brothel where she was being serially raped, and pray to Jesus for rescue.

We have seen Jesus bring rescue and resurrect his child to life. We have seen her restored to her family, graduate from college and boldly speak before crowds of thousands in the public fight to end sex trafficking.

- We have seen a man rescued from nearly four years of illegal detention and police torture find his voice as a gentle, passionate poet and become a full-time community outreach director for justice.

- We have seen a police commander and the son of another police commander brought to justice after raping impoverished girls. And just as powerfully, we have seen both girls grow up as dignified young women who now lead a movement of former victims who provide hands-on mentoring for child victims of sex crimes.

- We have seen former slaves from rice mills, rock quarries and brick factories take their freedom in hand, build businesses to feed their families, proudly send their children to school and even help rescue others held in slavery.

- We have seen girls once curled up in fetal positions from abuse in brothels grow up to be young women of great dignity and beauty, get married, raise families and lead us on raids to rescue other children.

- We have seen destitute widows thrown off their land by bullies, restored to their homes, finding their dignity. We have seen them grow food for their children and run a school for the village—and even train the leaders in their community on how to protect other widows from violent dispossession of their land.

- We have seen a man maimed by police abuse and illegal detention rise up with an indomitable spirit of love, become a student of legal advocacy and return to his community to successfully bring rescue to the vulnerable in his neighborhood.

For those who look at the deep ravages of injustice and find themselves descending into despair, I do not have adequate words. In such dark waters, words can rarely do the required work. But I can usher you into the places where we have been over this last decade—into the holy spaces where we have met these survivors, by the thousands, and allow you to be awed by their stories. There is little about the agony and humiliation of evil that they do not understand, but in their harsh struggles they have also testified to the mysteries and mercies of God in a way that, to me, makes despair or cynicism seem like an indulgence, a lie and a dishonor.

4. Christians are embracing the biblical call to justice.
Our final affirmation of hope is a testimony to the historic movement of justice that we are witnessing in the Christian community in this era. What we have witnessed over the past decade is surely just the beginning of what is yet to come, but perhaps a better glimpse of the power and glory of what may yet unfold will emerge most vividly from an appreciation of what has already taken place. And for that, a bit of personal perspective may help.

First, the reason for writing *Good News About Injustice* was very simple: in 1999 there were very few articles about justice and a few chapters the on subject scattered in academic volumes—but there was no book-length treatment of the problem of injustice in the world, God's view of it and the role of God's people in addressing it. This seemed an absurd state of affairs considering the magnitude of the problem in the world (i.e., the number of people who suffer because of intentional abuse and oppression) and the massive portions of the Bible that address this problem. Imagine if we had no books on love, evangelism, grace, discipleship, mercy, compassion and so forth. Yet there can be no doubt that justice is just as fundamental an aspect of God's character and our calling as his people.

Moreover, discussions among Christians in the United States about the global challenges of violent injustice were relegated to a small number of Christian circles—religious liberty activists, mainline Protestant denominational offices, groups like Evangelicals for Social Action, Catholic social justice advocates and a few academic groups. There were a microscopic number of self-identifying Christians serving in the traditional human rights agencies and a few more Christians engaging human rights through the important but narrower cause of religious persecution. Certainly Christians who were talking about international issues of violent oppression and injustice ten years ago had a "prophet crying in the wilderness" experience.

In 2009, however, we must acknowledge that a sea of change has taken place. A transformation of stunning speed and breadth is altering the Christian community—a transformation that offers great hope for the body of Christ and the world. Discussions of biblical justice are bursting into the mainstream of Christian dialogue, church leadership and ministry. Mainstream evangelical movements like Rick Warren's Purpose Driven Connection, Willow Creek's Leadership Summit, InterVarsity's vast Urbana Student Missions Convention and Youth With A Mission's Discipleship Training Schools are giving a prominent place to the biblical call to the work of justice in the world. But this movement is also propelled by the commitment and passion of small neighborhood churches in suburban America, by Christians in the developing world, by mothers and fathers training their children in justice even as they teach them about mercy and love. Even a casual Internet search of Christian books, magazine articles, conferences, blogs, music and church activities will produce an avalanche of justice-related discussions, ministries, course and educational materials that did not exist a decade ago. *Christianity Today*, the flagship publication of evangelical Christian leadership, not only shows a significant increase in articles related to broad themes of justice over the past ten years but a more than 500 percent increase in the proportion of articles that discuss the specific problem of violent oppression and abuse in our world.

In many ways this transformation reflects the next great movement in the Christian community's understanding of mission. A hundred years ago Christian mission was largely understood as the *verbal proclamation* of the gospel—an outreach of Christian love through evangelism and discipleship that was meant to meet the needs of those who were alienated from their Maker. Then in the 1950s the Christian community expanded their vision to add ministries of *relief and development*—an outreach of Christian love that met the needs of those who were suffering from deprivation—to their work of evangelism and discipleship. Before 1950, World Vision, Compassion International, Catholic Relief Services, World Relief, Samaritan's Purse and Habitat for Humanity did not exist. But by the beginning of the twenty-first century these ministries of compassion for the global poor had become thoroughly mainstream in the North American church.

Now, in the first decades of the twenty-first century, Christians are coming to understand that the ministries that meet the needs of *alienation* and *deprivation* do not meet the needs of those suffering from *oppression*. These neighbors require a ministry of *justice*. Thus Christians in the twenty-first century are drawn into the mission described in Micah 6:8:

> He has told you, O man, what is good
>   and what does the Lord require of you?
> To act justly and to love mercy
>   and to walk humbly with your God.

Or as Jesus summarized: "justice, mercy and faithfulness" (Matthew 23:23).

What an extraordinary era in which to be alive! In this epoch God is mobilizing his people into perhaps the most robust and holistic witness of his love that the world has ever seen.

At International Justice Mission we see this movement most dramatically in what we have been calling "the Justice Generation"—the generation of younger Christians who find their hearts beating fast with their Maker's passion for justice, who show little tolerance for a gospel that does not embody Christ's call to serve the oppressed, and who are eager to discover how they can use what God has given them to bring a humble and courageous witness for God's justice into an aching world. I believe they will take what God has begun in the last decade and fashion a fundamental shift in the ministry of the global church to "seek justice, rescue the oppressed, defend the orphan, plead for the widow" (Isaiah 1:17 NRSV). And perhaps most gloriously, they will do so in a way that is quite new for the Western church—in relationships of mutual respect, in shared leadership and in common sacrifice *with* their brothers and sisters in the developing world, where the gravitational center of the Christian faith is increasingly shifting.

Finally, this emerging movement of Christian justice ministry will, I believe, begin to find its momentum just as the broader world is waking up to a fundamental flaw in a half century's worth of development assistance among the global poor—the neglect of justice. As a 2008 landmark report from the United Nations made clear in a stunning finding, *most poor people in the world live outside the protection of the law.* This is a statement of such startling implications that we must pause over it to fully absorb its meaning. Imagine if you and your family lived outside the protection of the law. Imagine living in a state of lawlessness in which there is no one to call on to protect you, your family or your property from being assaulted. Indeed, this is the brutal reality for most of the world's poor. In fact, "four billion people around the world are robbed of the chance to better their lives and climb out of poverty because they are excluded from the rule of law."[1] Or, as a global study conducted by the World Bank found, "Police and official justice systems side with the rich, persecute poor people and make poor people *more* insecure, fearful, and poorer."[2]

Over the last fifty years the affluent nations of the world have been pursuing poverty alleviation programs in countries—without first helping recipient nations to establish a basic platform of law and justice that will allow poor people to hold onto the benefits of these programs. We can give all manner of goods and services to the poor, but if we do not restrain the hands of the bullies from taking it all away, then poor people simply stay poor. This explains why hundreds of millions of poor people in the world are enslaved, imprisoned, beaten, raped and robbed with ferocious regularity—they simply do not get the protection of basic law enforcement.

This also explains why a whole generation is emerging to say enough is enough. As Bono, the rock star antipoverty activist, told a vast Christian audience in Washington, D.C., "fighting poverty is not a matter of charity; it's a matter of justice."[3] Indeed, in this next decade, International Justice Mission is seeking to lead Christians in an urgent movement to help empower poor people to build public justice systems in their communities that actually protect their families and neighbors from oppression and violence. IJM is seeking to leverage what it has learned from working thousands of cases among the poor to help targeted communities not only diagnose what is broken in the public justice system, but to serve with them in building structures of police, courts and social services that actually protect the poor from violence and abuse.

This is an ambitious goal that will require great miracles from God, but I have never been more energized with hope. Why? First, over this last decade I have seen the God of justice "do immeasurably more than all we ask or imagine" (Ephesians 3:2). Second, over the centuries, Christians were at the forefront of building the systems of justice that most of us now enjoy in the Western world. Third, Christians have never had such great resources and capacities to share this legacy of justice with the world as they do now. As I said more than ten years ago, "I believe that God has indescribable mysteries and miracles stored up for his people who seek justice in his name." Truly, after a decade of watching the God of justice at work through his people, like the apostle John, I simply want to declare "what we have heard, what we have seen with our eyes, what we have looked at and touched with our hands" (1 John 1:1 NASB). For in this good news about injustice, "we proclaim to you what we have seen and heard, so that you may have fellowship with us. And our fellowship is with the Father and with his Son, Jesus Christ. We write this to make our joy complete" (1 John 1:3-4).

Indeed, celebrations are about joy, and this tenth anniversary is no different. By his mercy we have been witnesses to God's great love, faithfulness and power in the world. And the day is his. May we each therefore eagerly join him in the banquet he is preparing in this next decade, and may we seek from him our own witness of courage in a hurting world.

PREFACE TO
THE FIRST EDITION

As the father of four small children I find myself thinking more and more about the core gift I would like to give them to take into the world. I don't actually know the degree to which this gift is mine to give, but if I had one essential provision to grant as they were going out our door, I think I know what it would be. More and more I pray that our children might leave our home as men and women of courage. As C. S. Lewis wrote:

> Courage is not simply *one* of the virtues, but the form of every virtue at the testing point, which means, at the point of highest reality. A chastity or honesty or mercy which yields to danger will be chaste or honest or merciful only on conditions. Pilate was merciful till it became risky.[1]

> Courage, however, is an odd gift because it's one we rarely think we'll want or need. It's like trying to get my preschoolers to put on their coats when there is no hint of winter's bitter cold inside our toasty home. Squirming and objecting, they doubt that it's as cold as all that outside, and more to the point, they're not sure they even want to be going out.

Similarly, as a North American Christian I am not all that eager to accept the gift of courage that my God extends to me. I'm not all that sure I want to go to the places where I'll need it—to the places where virtues become risky. Sometimes staying indoors feels risky enough.

But then Jesus gently lets me know that I'm not living with a domesticated God. His prodding sounds much like the appeal my wife and I give to our own children to get them out the door: "Mom and Dad are going outside. We'll help you with your coats if you want to come with us." Likewise, I hear Jesus calling, "I'm going outside to a world that needs me. I'll help you with the courage you'll need if you want to be with me."

This book is an attempt to articulate something of the courage and hope that God is yearning to bestow on those who want to follow Christ into a world that needs his love. But it is the courage to extend the love of Jesus to a particular category of persons: the men, women and children who are victimized by the abuse of power.

As Christians we have learned much about sharing the love of Christ with people all over the world who have never heard the gospel. We continue to see the salvation message preached in the far corners of the earth and to see indigenous Christian churches vigorously extending Christ's kingdom on every continent. We have learned how to feed the hungry, heal the sick and shelter the homeless.

But there is one thing we haven't learned to do, even though God's Word repeatedly calls us to the task. We haven't learned how to rescue the oppressed. For the child held in forced prostitution, for the prisoner illegally detained and tortured, for the widow robbed of her land, for the child sold into slavery, we have almost no vision of how God could use us to bring tangible rescue. We don't know how to get the twelve-year-old girl out of the brothel, how to have the prisoner set free, how to have the widow's land restored to her, or how to get the child slave released and the oppressors brought to justice.

It is perhaps more accurate to say that as people committed to the historic faith of Christianity, we have forgotten how to be such a witness of Christ's love, power and justice in the world. In generations past the great leaders of Christian revival in North America and Great Britain were consumed by a passion to declare the gospel and to manifest Christ's compassion and justice. But somewhere during the twentieth century some of us have simply stopped believing that God actually can use us to answer the prayers of children, women and families who suffer under the hand of abusive power or authority in their communities. We sit in the same paralysis of despair as those who don't even claim to know the Savior—and in some cases, we manifest even *less* hope.

In response this book has one simple message: it need not be this way. We can recover a witness of Christian courage in a world of injustice. We can rediscover our Maker's passions for the world and for justice—passions that may have grown unfamiliar to us. We can come to know the compassion of Jesus like never before as we go with him to look into the eyes of those who are in need of rescue. Moreover, we can be restored to the conviction that God is prepared to use *us* to "seek justice, rescue the oppressed, defend the orphan, plead for the widow" (Isaiah 1:17 NRSV).

Fundamentally, therefore, this book is offered as a testimonial, a reflection of what I have been learning about the world and about my Maker. And there has been much I've needed to learn. To be honest, few people could have grown up farther from the realities of injustice and oppression in our world than I did. I was raised in a wonderfully happy home. My loving family lived in an affluent suburb in a civil society—for which I am, frankly, enormously grateful. The realities of terror, oppression, abuse and injustice were kept far from my door. Not surprisingly, I came to understand God in ways that fit my experience. God seemed intensely interested in my life of personal piety and seemed most needed as a Savior from the only negative eventuality which I could not control—death. This is an oversimplification, of course, because I had the entire biblical revelation to draw on, but it serves to illustrate how relatively little I knew about a holy God who spent his days weeping beside children in brothels, prisoners in pain or orphans in trauma—a God whose core hatred of injustice was rivaled only by his hatred of idolatry.

I knew little about the needs of the world or how God regarded such suffering. I knew even less about what those needs had to do with me or how I could make a difference. But eventually I left home. I lived in places where there was no escaping the raw realities of a world in rebellion against its Maker—apartheid in South Africa, guerilla war in the Philippines, genocide in Rwanda, to name a few. In these contexts I met followers of Jesus Christ who knew God more deeply, knew the Bible more thoroughly and lived life more courageously than I ever had. They didn't judge me or dismiss me for my limitations; they simply loved me and shared what they had learned, frequently the hard way, about the God of hope and power and joy. In time I found that I had developed some skills as an investigator and a lawyer that could actually be used to "seek justice, rescue the oppressed, defend the orphan, plead for the widow." I discovered that God was more than prepared to use his people as his instruments of truth and justice. He was prepared to work miracles through our modest offerings of compassion and obedience.

My personal introduction to the abuse of power in our world began shortly after my graduation from Harvard University. I spent a year working with South African church leaders on the National Initiative for Reconciliation during the brutal state of emergency of 1985 to 1986. After returning to the United States and studying law at the University of Chicago, my exposure to the pain of oppression in the world was deepened through my work for the Lawyers Committee for Human Rights, investigating the atrocities of abusive soldiers and police in the Philippines. Eventually I took a job as a trial attorney in the civil rights division of the United States Department of Justice. There I served on the police-misconduct task force. While at the Department of Justice I was detailed to the United Nations in the fall of 1994 to serve as the director of the U.N. genocide investigation in Rwanda.

In the midst of these various overseas assignments I was struck by three simple but powerful facts. First, there were vast numbers of men, women and children in the world who were suffering. Second, within the communities where these abuses took place, Christian workers (missionaries, doctors, relief-and-development workers, and the like) knew a tremendous amount about these abuses yet felt helpless to do anything about them and had no idea where to turn for help. Finally, there were Christians who had the professional training, experience and resources to document these abuses and seek relief for victims—but there was no vehicle to bring their gifts and energy to bear on these needs.

In response to this need a number of Christian friends and colleagues came together to form International Justice Mission in 1994. This organization makes available a corps of Christian public-justice professionals (lawyers, criminal investigators, social workers, diplomats, government-relations experts and the like) to serve global Christian workers when they encounter cases of abuse or oppression in their communities. International Justice Mission documents the abuses and seeks relief for the victims, either directly or in partnership with indigenous advocacy groups or through other international human rights organizations. Through the grace of God, International Justice Mission has been able to bring effective advocacy and relief to hundreds of victims of abuse throughout the world—girls released from forced prostitution, children rescued from illegal bonded servitude, prisoners released from illegal detention and abusive police brought to account.

This then is the story of that journey, and my prayer will be answered if it conveys even a small measure of the hope and encouragement that the God of justice intends for his people. In expressing this prayer I hasten to add that this modest volume is not an exhaustive treatment of anything. It is not a thorough survey of injustice and human rights abuses in the world, for many of the most severe may not even be mentioned. Sadly, there is just too much material to work with. Neither is this a full theological treatment of the character of the God of justice, for, happily, there is too much biblical material to work with. My modest aspiration is to stimulate reflection not on sophisticated biblical arcana but on some of the most arrestingly blunt declarations of Scripture. Finally, I have not set out to write a complete manual on human-rights advocacy but merely to provide some concrete pictures of the practical difference Christians can make in rescuing the oppressed, and to offer starting principles for overcoming the forces of injustice.

This book is a simple introduction to three things: the injustice of our world, the character of our God, and the opportunity for God's people to make a difference. Part one opens with an overview of the reality of injustice, suggests how we can prepare spiritually to combat it and offers examples of how other Christians have tackled the task.

Since in the face of suffering we can easily be immobilized by despair, in part two, I deal with four affirmations that God makes about justice, which offer us hope to get beyond that despair. In looking at God's character we can see how he feels about injustice and those who suffer under it. Part three provides some answers to the difficult questions injustice raises for us as Christians and some real-world tools for understanding how injustice works, investigating the deceptions of oppressors, intervening for victims and doing what each of us can, given our talents and resources, to rescue the oppressed.

It should be noted that for reasons of security and personal sensitivity, pseudonyms have been used to obscure the identities of some of the individuals whose stories are shared in this book.

In preparing this work I have been profoundly assisted by the research and editorial support of my colleagues at International Justice Mission, particularly Jocelyn Penner, Leslie Grimes, Daryl Kreml, Kristin Romens, Lindsey Etheridge and Ryan Cobb. I am also grateful for the editorial assistance and encouragement of Gary Albert, Joan Albert and Ann Haugen Michael. While I was preparing the book, Sam Dimon, Art Gay, Clyde Taylor and Vera Shaw kindly and faithfully upheld me in prayer. I am very grateful for the personal encouragement of Dr. Luis Lugo and the financial support of the Pew Charitable Trusts. I have also been the beneficiary of much kindness and support from Hugh O. Maclellan Jr., Tom MacCallie and Daryl Heald. I and International Justice Mission staff would also like to express our thanks to the directors and staff of the Library of Congress and the library of the Virginia Theological Seminary. I am also very thankful for the encouragement and support of Dr. Steve Hayner, president of InterVarsity Christian Fellowship, and for the commitment and faith of InterVarsity Press in publishing this work.

As many will readily appreciate, I am deeply humbled by the kind encouragement and collaboration of the Reverend John Stott, and for the kindness extended by his assistant John Yates III.

My deepest gratitude goes to my wife, Jan. Words are too poor to express the measure of love and joy you have extended to me in your companionship throughout this project and the larger journey. My joy has been walking closely together in thought, in words, in heart, in laughter and in faith. You have been that sheltering tree of grace from which courage proceeds. You are abiding faith, hope and love.

Finally, whatever may be the strengths or weaknesses of this work, these words will be of little note and short remembrance in the scope of God's grace and work in our world. What will last is the Word of God and his work of love among us.

> But whatever was to my profit I now consider loss for the sake of Christ. What is more, I consider everything a loss compared to the surpassing greatness of knowing Christ Jesus my Lord, for whose sake I have lost all things. I consider them rubbish, that I may gain Christ and be found in him, not having a righteousness of my own that comes from the law, but that which is through faith in Christ—the righteousness that comes from God and is by faith. (Philippians 3:7-9)

ACKNOWLEDGMENTS

I would like to thank the many people whose response to God's call and commitment to justice has enabled International Justice Mission to create a different future for thousands of victims of violent oppression over the past decade. To those who have prayed for us, worked with us and provided the financial resources to make the work possible—thank you.

I would also like to thank the IJM staff who assisted me with this tenth anniversary edition: Pamela Livingston, Lori Poer, Larry Martin, Sharon Cohn Wu, Bethany Hoang, Sean Litton, Kathy Stout-Labauve, Christa Hayden, Holly Burkhalter, Susan Conway and my colleagues in the field, whose work inspires much of the hope in this volume.

And thank you to my friends at InterVarsity Press, Andy Le Peau in particular, for your partnership in sharing these stories.

Finally, I am most profoundly grateful to Jan, Solveig, Liv, Tad and Garrison. You have rescued me over and over again with joy and beauty and love, and you have made the existence of a good God undeniable to me.

PART ONE

TAKING UP
THE CHALLENGE

THE RAGE IN RWANDA

A SUBURBAN CHRISTIAN

CONFRONTS GENOCIDE

I remember looking up from my newspaper during my bus ride to work one morning in the fall of 1994 and finding everything oddly in place. The AT4 bus was proceeding apace at 8:17 a.m. in the carpool zone. I was comfortably settled in my usual seat one row from the center double doors. My good-natured but nameless neighbors were sitting where they ought and respectively sleeping, reading or talking too loud, according to schedule. The low morning sun was where it should be, creating the glare that always forced me to look up from my paper at that point in the route. In that moment, pausing and looking around at all that American commuter normalcy, something inside me wanted to say, "Excuse me, friends, but did you know that less than forty-eight hours ago I was standing in the middle of several thousand corpses in a muddy mass grave in a tiny African country called Rwanda?"

ASCENSION: COMING BACK FROM A HELL ON EARTH
The Scriptures do not tell us very much about Jesus' ascension, his

sudden transport from earth to heaven. But there have been moments
in my life when I wish they did. All we know is that he was standing
with his rather earthy friends on an earthen hill trying as ever to
explain something, when "he was taken up into heaven and he sat at
the right hand of God" (Mark 16:19). That is all there is to it: one
minute earth, the next minute heaven.

The very suddenness of it has always seemed to me something to
ponder. What was it like for Jesus, as a man, to be transported in an
instant from a horrifically fallen earth of darkness and death to a
heavenly country of light and life—to a city that "does not need the
sun or the moon to shine on it, for the glory of God gives it light"
(Revelation 21:23)? What sort of mental adjustment, if we may call it
that, was required to move so suddenly from the nightmarish world
of the cross—a world of betrayal and torture, of blood lust and wail-
ing women—to paradise? What was it like for the divine Man in
heaven to exchange in a moment the stench of death and his own
encrusted grave clothes for the very fragrance of life, a white robe, a
golden sash and a seat at the right hand of the throne of God—to be
home at last with his Father, where "there will be no more death or
mourning or crying or pain" (Revelation 21:4)?

These may be idle questions, but they have come to me with particular force as I have struggled with the unreality of my own ascension experiences—moments when I have been transported with
almost ethereal speed from a hell on earth to a heaven on earth. In
a matter of hours I have traveled from the slippery mud and corpses
of mass graves in Rwanda to my usual seat at the right hand of my
neighbor on our dependably boring and climate-controlled bus ride
to my office in Washington, D.C. I remember reclining on a comfortable living-room couch, among friends and family in California,
talking about soaring real estate values in Orange County when
only days before I had been exhuming the remains of a woman
raped and butchered by soldiers in the Philippines. Similarly, I recall watching from my train window as a low summer sun cast a
Norman Rockwell glow across Little League fields in Connecticut

when only days before I had been in a country where boys of a similar age but of a different color were being beaten like animals by the South African police.

I don't know whether Jesus experienced dreams while he was here on earth or whether he felt as if he had awakened from a particularly bad one when he found himself back in heaven after his ascension from the earth. But I have certainly felt that dreamlike separation from reality when I have returned from these hellish places around the world. In no time at all it begins to feel as if the nightmare I came from in Rwanda or the Philippines or South Africa has taken place not in another country but on another planet. Back home, it simply does not feel *real* anymore.

Thus my sudden urge to make that announcement about the Rwandan genocide to unsuspecting fellow bus commuters came not from a desire to shock them but from a desire to somehow affirm for myself the human reality and relevance of my own experience. Could it really be true, and could it really have anything to do with me, that in a period of about six weeks in the spring of 1994, nearly one million defenseless women and children were hacked to death by their neighbors in the towns and villages of Rwanda?

I remember very well what *I* was doing in the spring of 1994. I was trying to assemble cribs for twin girls who were coming into our home, ready or not. I was trying to match wits, and losing, with the class clown in my sixth-grade boys' Sunday-school class. I was seeking every advantage, and losing, in my effort to trade in our Honda Civic for a Taurus station wagon. I was prevailing in my arguments in a trial in federal court in Alabama, enjoying an occasional jog along the Potomac River in Washington, D.C., and denying that I had ever watched *Melrose Place* on TV.

Like most Americans in the spring of 1994, I was also starting to see horrible stories in the newspapers about some kind of "tribal warfare" in an African country I had never heard much about. Then I saw pictures on the evening news of bloated bodies floating down a river and heard commentators talking about genocide. Apparently thousands, maybe even millions, of Tutsis were being slaughtered by their Hutu compatriots in a genocidal hysteria sweeping across Rwanda. But like most of the great ugliness transmitted by TV across the world and into my living room, the terror in Rwanda just did not seem real. It seemed *true*, but not real—not to me. I did not dispute the accuracy of the reports, but they might as well have been pictures from Sojourner on Mars or reports about people who lived in ancient Rome or statistics about how many bazillion other solar systems are in the Milky Way—all true enough, but not real. Not real like my kids when they are sick, not real like my job when I am behind in my work, not real like my neighbors when one of them has been in a car accident, not even real like my Midwestern compatriots when they have been flooded out of their homes.

Meeting the Truth in Rwanda

But then in the fall of 1994 I went to Rwanda. Only forty-eight hours before taking my seat on the AT4 commuter bus, I had been in Kibuye, Rwanda, a beautiful town sprawling on the banks of Lake Kivu and clinging to the green highlands of eastern Rwanda—and a horrible town—where thousands of Tutsis (mostly women and children) were hacked and beaten to death by their Hutu neighbors over a period of several days. I was in Kibuye directing the U.N.'s genocide investigation in the country, on loan to the United Nations from the U.S. Department of Justice. My job was to march down a list of mass grave and massacre sites provided by U.N. military intelligence and deploy international investigative teams to gather preliminary evidence against the perpetrators. The evidence would eventually be turned over to the International Criminal Tribunal for Rwanda, which was just being established to bring the murderers to justice. There in Kibuye and in scores of other towns and villages across the country, the nightmare became real for me.

Kibuye was my last mass grave site before I was to head back home to America. One of my twin infant daughters had been stricken with meningitis, and while our worst fears had passed and she was on the mend, it was time for me to return to my family. For this final project in Kibuye I brought four other members of my U.N. investigative team: Luc, a jovial, bear-sized criminal lawyer from French Canada; Jim, a delightfully wry police officer from Northern Ireland; Thaddi, a Rwandan school teacher who served as interpreter; and Nehemiah, our U.N. military officer from Zimbabwe who mostly missed his family back home. We arrived in Kibuye after a jarring, five-hour, four-wheel-drive journey from our headquarters in Kigali.

Once we arrived, the most dangerous part of our assignment was over. Though low-level civil war still claimed the country, land mines peppered the fields and bandits roamed the land, the greatest danger was simply traveling on the roads. Narrow, mud-washed trails over sheer mountain cliffs wound their way over the eastern highlands and delivered us to the banks of Lake Kivu—one of the great, deep-blue lakes of Africa—separating Rwanda from Zaire (now the Democratic Republic of the Congo). Of course, the breathtaking beauty of the lake and its lush tropical shores were marred by human horror, for we knew that many corpses found their way to the placid waters during the genocide only a few months before.

Murder investigations generally begin where the bodies are, and as we arrived in Kibuye, I knew this meant that we would be heading for the biggest church in town—the Catholic cathedral and the adjoining Home St. Jeans, a complex of residential and educational buildings. The large, rough-hewn stone cathedral stood sturdy and squat on a peninsula over the lake. The stone and concrete interior had been scrubbed out, but as we stepped inside, we found the lingering, overpowering essence that could not be cleansed from the stones—the stifling, unnatural odor of a mass sepulcher. For within these walls and on this floor, hundreds of defenseless children, mothers, brothers and grandmothers had been hacked and clubbed to death in a murderous binge of torture and slaughter just months ago. Now the cathedral was empty, except for a lone, deranged man in rags, who had made the empty hall his home and was seen spending hours on his knees mumbling before the altar.

Gathering All the Facts

Our task in the coming days was to conduct an investigative site survey, locate survivors and other witnesses and begin to account for the bodies. The story that emerged was a familiar one. On April 6, 1994, the president of Rwanda was killed in a mysterious plane crash in Kigali, the capital city. Almost immediately extremist Hutu factions within the government and the military joined with extremist Hutu paramilitary groups across the country to incite a murderous hysteria against Tutsis and moderate Hutu. The quasi-ethnic divisions between Hutu and Tutsis in Rwanda had been highly politicized over the years, with each side viewing the struggle as a zero-sum game between governance and extinction. Claiming that Tutsis had killed their president and were now coming to slaughter all Hutu, these fanatical Hutu leaders used government military forces, citizen militia and local mobs to start hunting down and killing the Tutsis in their communities. In the days following the plane crash Tutsis in and around Kibuye began to hear of prominent members of their community being dragged from their homes and murdered. Disheveled Tutsi corpses began to appear in the streets.

By April 17 the violence and hysteria had reached a full boil in Kibuye. Seeking safety in numbers and following the orders of the provincial governor and the mayor, hundreds of Tutsi men, women and children huddled together at the cathedral and the Home St. Jeans complex. During times of ethnic conflict in years past, many Tutsi had found sanctuary within the sacred walls of churches across the country. So as the fever of violence escalated in Kibuye and across Rwanda, the churches became packed to the rafters with thousands of trembling women and children seeking refuge. For the hundreds huddled in the Kibuye cathedral, however, there would be no refuge, only a lure, a trap and a grave.

On that day in April the provincial governor and mayor, who had ordered all Tutsi to the cathedral (ostensibly for their safety), ordered that the complex be surrounded. Eventually a force assembled from members of the Gendarmerie Nationale (the national police), the local police from the commune, Interhamwe (the extremist Hutu militia group) and an armed mob of local civilians. The governor then unleashed this combined army upon the defenseless people.

Working largely with machetes, metal rods, spears and wooden clubs with nails partially embedded at the head, the mob cut the Tutsis—men, women and children—down by the hundreds and bludgeoned them to death.

In the days that followed, the Gendarmerie Nationale, Interhamwe and armed civilians hunted down and killed any survivors they could find. One survivor we interviewed, a young father of three children, said that he had seen his entire family murdered around him. He survived, but for three days he crawled among the dead on the cathedral floor, wounded and desperately thirsty. He said he nearly smothered a surviving child from another family who wanted to cry out when the murderers returned to beat more survivors to death.

When the orgy of murder had exhausted itself, the killers moved on to the Kibuye stadium where an even larger group of frightened Tutsis had gathered for protection. The brick-walled stadium sat between the town's main road and a steep hill made of the same red clay. By April 18 the police, Interhamwe militia and local mob had surrounded the stadium and were killing anyone trying to escape. Huddled by the thousands within the stadium walls and between the brick grandstand and the thick green grass in the oval, the Tutsi men, women and children cried out for rescue and for mercy, but found none. According to reports it was once again the provincial governor, Clement Kayishema, who raised his pistol to the air and fired off the signal to attack.

With a rush the blood-lusting mob waded into the sea of screaming and scrambling villagers. All day the mob hacked and blasted its way through its Tutsi neighbors—most deaths coming ultimately with a massive machete blow to the head. The exhausting task could not be completed in a single day, however, so with the police and militia sealing off the stadium during the night, the attackers took their evening rest, returning the next morning for another full day of mass murder. Thus by the end of the next day the stadium, like the cathedral, was silent with death and heaps of broken bodies.

BEYOND THE FACTS: ARTIFACTS AND SURVIVORS TELL THEIR STORIES

By the time I arrived in Kibuye to direct the U.N. military in digging up the two mass graves where all these broken bodies had eventually been flung, it was easy to think of them as exactly that: nameless, faceless, decaying and disconnecting body parts. I had a job to do—to turn over enough of the mass grave at the cathedral and the stadium to corroborate the testimony of our witnesses, and then to move on. It was a filthy, stinking job, but it had to be done. We were busy, and it simply did not pay to think very hard about any particular story represented by any particular set of the remains I was now rearranging for forensic photographs. It had not seemed worth thinking too much about months ago when I saw the pictures at home on TV of Tutsi bodies floating down a river somewhere in Africa. Now that those same anonymous corpses were at my feet, it still felt more comfortable to think of them as a tragic mass rather than as anything like the individual people that I knew and cared about back home.

But at Kibuye, as at every massacre site in Rwanda, a painful glimpse of the truth always came through. This was not an undifferentiated mass of lifeless clods on the inevitable dust heap of a fallen world. In truth each body, now dull and limp in the mud, was actually a unique bearer of the very image of God, a unique creation of the divine Maker, individually knit within a mother's womb by the Lord of the universe. For as difficult as it was to imagine, each crumpled mortal frame had indeed come from a mother, one single mother who somewhere in time had wept tears of joy and aspiration over her precious child—a child endowed with the mysterious spark of Adam and an immortal soul. We would never number all the mother's children in these mass graves, but their Father in heaven had numbered even the very hairs of their heads.

It made my job infinitely more difficult to look at the dead this way, but day after day, pieces of the truth would work their way into my heart. These mass graves might appear as vague, dark images of generalized evil in an unjust world, but in truth they were an intimate family portrait with a story for every face—each member of the human family having lived and died as one individual at a time.

These stories gradually emerged from the artifacts and survivors. Every massacre site had stories to tell from what was left behind. Tutsis had fled their homes from miles around to seek safety in these churches, stadiums and schools. Many brought with them their most cherished personal possessions, and it was these items that now testified to their humanity in a way that their lifeless forms could not. Of course, anything of value had long been stripped away, leaving only those things that people clutch in death but robbers do not steal—pictures from a wedding day, a French Bible with a loving inscription, a small calendar with pictures of faraway places.

And then there were the stacks of government-issued, mandatory identity cards. In sites where we had only skeletal remains, the identity cards said everything that needed saying. Each card featured a fading black-and-white photograph, a picture of just one person, with a face different from all the rest, looking tired, proud, embarrassed or caught off guard. And each bore a check in the box next to the word *Tutsi*. Despite the mind-numbing scale of the genocide, these little pale-green cards spoke the truth about injustice in the world. Just as with famine, despite appearances, people really do die one person at a time.

Yet it was still hard for me to connect myself to these people— these people who were no more, people I never knew, people who must be so different from me and mine. It certainly made my work more tolerable to view them this way.

In the end it wasn't the remaining artifacts but the survivors in Rwanda who took me across a mysterious bridge that allowed me to behold the same human heart, eyes and hands of these, my departed neighbors.

THE TRUTH OF INJUSTICE BECOMES PERSONAL AND REAL

Some time ago I stopped being surprised by the existence of survivors from such massacres. As I have learned, human beings are strangely easy, and strangely hard, to kill. And each survivor has a miraculous and horrible tale to tell.

I once took testimony from a woman in the Philippines who had been shot in the torso several times by a high-powered firearm at short range. She had the scars to show for it. This woman, called Rose, and seventeen other members of her little village in Northern Luzon had been rounded up by angry soldiers and gunned down in the middle of a rice paddy. She was pregnant at the time of the massacre, and she and the baby were in good health when I met them more than a year after the incident. She was, in fact, a charming young woman—engaging, funny, clever—who had a certain guarded melancholy, no doubt, but no despair. She was a hard-working, generous mother and neighbor. She cared for many, and many cared for her. The resilient spark in her eyes and the life in her smile made one wonder how brilliant that sparkle must have been before her nightmare with the Philippine Army.

Nevertheless, had one of the bullets taken even a slightly different course through her abdomen, I would have never known of Rose. I would have only known of eighteen, rather than seventeen, lifeless victims of an ugly, dirty war in the Philippines. Rose told the truth about a mass grave and about massive injustice in our world, and so did the survivors I met in Rwanda.

Two little girls in Kibuye, with shy smiles of perfect and brilliantly white teeth, showed us the thick, pink scars across the neck of one and across the head of the other. They were being interviewed by Luc and Thaddi in a dilapidated schoolroom when Jim and I joined them after a very long day at the mass grave near the stadium.

I had been picking through human garbage almost all day. I was exhausted, sunburned and dirty. Jim and I pulled up one of the frail, narrow school benches in the back of the room and watched the conversation between Luc, Thaddi and the little girls. They told stories about where they lived, the animals they liked, the families they used to have and the neighbors who were caring for them now. Through it all they were the picture of courage, sadness and sweetness. At the end of the interview they were dismissed and left the room tugging each other close with whispers. Luc finished his notes with Thaddi.

As Jim and I waited, I had too much time to think. I was pierced again with the true identity of the rubbish I had been forced to wallow in all day. These two little girls—they were the rubbish. Though "fearfully and wonderfully made" (like my own two little girls at home), the awfulness of evil, the remoteness of Rwanda and the lifelessness of death had conspired to very nearly rob these little ones of their human face. I found myself trying to blink back the wave of emotion and the tears in my eyes. I stared hard at the smooth concrete floor and started quietly whistling through my teeth.

After a moment, I heard my own idle tune: "Jesus loves me / This I know / For the Bible tells me so / Little ones to him belong / They are weak / But he is strong." In another moment, I heard Jim whistling a soft harmony behind me. Apparently he too had been to Sunday school. We sat waiting a bit longer for Luc to finish, walked back to the truck and rode silently home to our base camp. Jim and I never spoke of the moment to one another.

SEEKING JUSTICE: GOD'S COMPASSION, COMMANDMENT AND COMMISSION

These were tough moments for me, but there was no longer any question about what this horrible injustice in Rwanda had to do with me, a suburban American lawyer who rode a bus to work during the week and taught sixth-grade Sunday school on the weekend. It had everything to do with me because of what my God loves and what my God hates. To quote another Sunday school chorus: "Jesus loves the little children / *All* the children of the world / Red and yellow, black and white / They are precious in his sight." Rwanda might seem far away, and these Rwandan children might seem different from my own, but I do not know anything about my God or the truth of my own child-

ish choruses if I do not understand that, truly, "red and yellow, black
and white, they are precious in his sight."

Moreover, this has everything to do with me because God hates
injustice.

> The LORD examines the righteous,
>   but the wicked and those who love violence
>   his soul hates. . . .
> For the LORD is righteous,
>   he loves justice. (Psalm 11:5, 7)

The Bible says that when officials are acting like "wolves tearing
the prey, shedding blood, destroying lives to get dishonest gain," the
Lord looks for someone to "stand in the breach," to "intervene" and
to "seek justice" (Ezekiel 22:27, 30; Isaiah 59:15-16; 1:17 NRSV). By the
time I arrived in Kibuye, I was much too late to stop the killing. I
couldn't bring the dead back to life or back to their families. But it
matters to God whether the evildoers are brought to justice:

> [The wicked man] lies in wait near the villages;
>   from ambush he murders the innocent,
>   watching in secret for his victims.
> He lies in wait like a lion in cover;
>   he lies in wait to catch the helpless;
>   he catches the helpless and drags them off in his net.
> His victims are crushed, they collapse;
>   they fall under his strength.
> He says to himself, "God has forgotten;
>   he covers his face and never sees."
> Arise, LORD! Lift up your hand, O God.
>   Do not forget the helpless.
> Why does the wicked man revile God?
>   Why does he say to himself,
>   "He won't call me to account"?
> But you, O God, do see trouble and grief;
>   you consider it to take it in hand.

> The victim commits himself to you;
>> you are the helper of the fatherless.
> Break the arm of the wicked and evil man;
>> call him to account for his wickedness
>> that would not be found out. (Psalm 10:8-15)

It matters to me, therefore, that the leaders of the Kibuye massacre (the governor, the mayor and their accomplices) have been captured and indicted by the International Criminal Tribunal for Rwanda. As I sat down to write *Good News About Injustice* in 1998, they were being "called to account." The prosecution had presented closing arguments and recommended four terms of life imprisonment on counts of genocide and crimes against humanity, and a minimum of forty additional years on violations of the Geneva Convention. This was partly through the testimony of survivors and witnesses that we interviewed inside that little schoolroom—including those two little orphans with shy smiles of perfect teeth. Over the next few years the Trial Chamber of the International Criminal Tribunal Courts found these men guilty of aiding and abetting genocide, committing genocide and conspiring to commit genocide. They were each sentenced to ten to twenty-five years in prison.

Of course, convicting the war criminals of Kibuye ultimately cannot bring true justice and healing to Rwanda or to those little girls. Nor can it or any other human mechanism promise ultimate peace and salvation for the human race. But by calling these men to account we can hope that the next generation of wicked "princes" will think twice about perpetrating such abuses, and the dead will not be mocked by impunity for their murderers.

In any case, seeking justice is a straightforward command of God for his people and part of Christ's prayer that his Father's will be done "on earth as it is in heaven" (Matthew 6:10). At least for me as a Christian, it is part of my testimony about the character of the God I love:

> You hear O LORD, the desire of the afflicted;
>> you encourage them, and you listen to their cry,

defending the fatherless and the oppressed,
> in order that man, who is of the earth, may terrify no more.
>> (Psalm 10:17-18)

The great miracle and mystery of God is that he calls me and you to be a part of what he is doing in history. He could, of course, with no help from us proclaim the gospel of Jesus Christ with lifeless stones, feed the entire world with five loaves and two fish, heal the sick with the hem of his garment, and release all the oppressed with his angels. Instead God has chosen us—missionaries, agricultural engineers, doctors, lawyers, lawmakers, diplomats, and all those who support, encourage and pray for them—to be his hands in doing those things in the world that are important to him.

When Christ ascended into heaven, he left behind only two things for the fulfillment of all his aspirations for the world: his Spirit and his followers. With the Holy Spirit we have been commissioned to demonstrate Christ's love for all the world: to disciple the nations, to feed the hungry, to clothe the naked, to heal the broken and even to rescue the oppressed. When we sing that all children are "precious in his sight," we must not forget that he, of whom we sing, has declared himself to be the God of justice. Scripture describes the one who follows God:

He will deliver the needy who cry out,
> the afflicted who have no one to help.
He will take pity on the weak and the needy
> and save the needy from death.
He will rescue them from oppression and violence,
> for *precious is their blood in his sight.* (Psalm 72:12-14,
>> emphasis added)

The Scriptures promise that "a scepter of justice will be the scepter of [God's] kingdom" (Psalm 45:6). And while the kingdom of God will be complete only in the coming of Christ, today our great joy and privilege is to work as colaborers with the Creator in extending his kingdom over one more life, one more family, one more neighborhood, one more community. The people of God will find in Christ the compassion and courage to engage the call to justice, for we know God *promises* that we who do not "become weary in doing good . . . will reap a harvest if we do not give up" (Galatians 6:9).

WHEN WE SEE INJUSTICE, WE HAVE A CHOICE

Many who lack faith will shrink away from the distant, dark world of injustice. Still others will water down the Word and imagine that they can love God without loving their brother, or wanting to "justify" themselves, they will invent elaborate quibbles with Jesus about who is and is not their neighbor (Luke 10:25-37; 1 John 3:10, 16-18). To these the Lord says:

> When you stretch out your hands,
>   I will hide my eyes from you;
> even though you make many prayers,
>   I will not listen. . . .
>   learn to do good;
> seek justice,
>   rescue the oppressed,
> defend the orphan,
>   plead for the widow. (Isaiah 1:15, 17 NRSV)

Others, by contrast, recognizing the voice of their good Shepherd will respond with joy: "Here am I. Send me!" (Isaiah 6:8). They will embrace the orphans and widows of the world, as their Savior did. With the hurting, the oppressed and the abused in mind, these people will come to the Master with their meager offering, their widow's mite, their inadequate loaves and fishes, and simply say, "Jesus, can you do anything with these?" And while the men "close" to Jesus will scoff, "How far will they go among so many?" Jesus himself will say, "Bring them here to me" (John 6:9; Matthew 14:18).

To be witnesses to the love of Christ in such a large, brutally unjust world seems overwhelming and beyond our calling. Even so, Jesus speaks to us. When he departed this earth for heaven—so suddenly, so mysteriously—he left much unexplained. But he wanted us to know one thing: we will receive from him power, the power to be his witnesses in word and deed "to the ends of the earth" (Acts 1:8-9).

For the little Filipino girl abducted into prostitution, for the Pakistani boy chained to a weaving loom, for the Latin American widow pushed off her land and even for the African father rotting in his prison cell without a charge or a trial, we share Christ's saving love on the cross and the servant love of our hands. As it was in days of old, "it will be a sign and witness to the LORD Almighty in the land of Egypt. When they cry out to the LORD because of their oppressors, he will send them a savior and defender, and he will rescue them" (Isaiah 19:20).

"Here am I, Lord. Send me!"

PREPARING THE MIND AND
SPIRIT THROUGH SCRIPTURE

Anyone who has spent time with infants knows what amazing machines of tireless learning and curiosity they are. We can also see that during an early stage of development, an infant cannot maintain interest in anything that is not immediately before its eyes. When a brightly colored ball or rattle is held up before babies, their attention is riveted on it. Their eyes seize on the new item with urgent curiosity. They display an almost compulsive urge to touch it, feel it, embrace it. But move the toy out of sight and infants lose all interest. They do not look for it. They do not try to bring back the hand that took the toy away. They do not express any disappointment that the toy is no longer there to explore. As far as child psychologists are able to discern, to babies the toy ceases to exist the very moment it is removed from sight. They have not yet developed the mental capacity for *object permanence*, that is, the understanding that objects exist even when they are out of sight. It is truly a case of out of sight, out of mind.

I must confess that this is very much the way my mind often works when it comes to maintaining an interest in the reality of injustice in our world. I read about innocent people being slaughtered in the Congo on page A1 of the *Washington Post,* and I am appalled. But my mind moves on to other things with amazing speed and thoroughness when I read on page D15 that the movie my wife and I were hoping to see actually starts a half hour earlier than we thought. When I read about the way abandoned orphan girls in China are tied to their bed rails and left to starve and die in state-run orphanages, I am very nearly moved to tears. But a year later when a conversation with a friend reminds me of the article, I realize that I have not shed a tear, uttered a prayer or even given it thought since the day I put down that newspaper article. I can move from torture on the evening news to touchdowns on Monday Night Football with almost the same mental and emotional ease as my channel changer.

Of course, much of this is perfectly natural and probably healthy. I do not aspire to be someone with a psychotic fixation on evil and human suffering. It is a poorly lived life that cannot experience joy, peace, laughter and beauty despite all the oppression and injustice that mars the goodness of God's creation. If the evening news or the morning paper keeps me from taking my wife to a movie, laughing at my daughter's stories or enjoying the exhilaration of a bike ride on a crisp fall day, then something is surely out of balance.

But we *can* grow into a more mature way of engaging the reality of injustice in our world if we take just two steps: (1) We can develop a compassion for the people suffering injustice by looking through the eyes of missionaries and other Christian workers who see this suffering firsthand, and (2) we can prepare ourselves to help people by looking at them through God's eyes, that is, through his Word.

THE FIRST STEP: CULTIVATING A COMPASSIONATE AWARENESS

Perhaps a next step in our development as children of God is a capacity for *compassion permanence*—a courageous and generous capacity to remember the needs of an unjust world even when they are out of our immediate sight. Not content with the infant's out-of-sight, out-of-mind approach, God calls us to a grown-up capacity to engage a world of oppression with our heart and mind, even though (thankfully) it is not always before our eyes.

Christians, of course, are meant to be particularly gifted in sustaining a commitment to what is true and important though unseen. The very essence of faith, we are told, is "the conviction of things unseen" (Hebrews 11:1 NRSV). Therefore, we who are only rarely exposed first- or secondhand to the truth about those who suffer injustice in our world are taught in Scripture to "remember" what we know, even after it leaves our sight or experience. "Remember those in prison as if you were their fellow prisoners, and those who are mistreated as if you yourselves were suffering" (Hebrews 13:3). We are to recall the plight of the poor and the imprisoned (Galatians 2:10; Colossians 4:18). Precisely because it is not our first and natural inclination, we are called to a conscious effort of reserving a space in our thought life for those who suffer abuse and oppression in our world.

Admittedly, this calling strikes me as burdensome. On any given day I am so busy trying to order the stress and vulnerability out of my own life that the notion of remembering a child prostitute in India, a torture victim in Indonesia or a child laborer in Honduras seems beyond the core of my Christian calling. But what is the core of my Christian calling? Every Christian who knows his or her Bible has a ready answer: to love God and to love our neighbor as ourselves (Matthew 22:37-40). Christ taught us that to love our neighbor was to treat people the way we would like to be treated (Luke 6:31). Accordingly, the call to remember the oppressed is couched in the logic of love: "Remember . . . those who are mistreated *as if you yourselves were suffering.*" The Scriptures are confident that if we imagine we are the child prostitute, the torture victim, the child laborer, we would not want to be forgotten. Surely it is God's job to remember *all* the victims of injustice in our world, but might there not be one child, one prisoner, one widow, one refugee that I can remember?

Seeing and listening to what the body of Christ sees and hears. For Christians living in a relatively affluent and orderly civil society, this act of remembering the injustice and abuse in the world is not an easy one. But it is not a new challenge either. In the third century St. Cyprian wrote to his friend in North Africa about the trouble he was having remembering the true nature of the world into which Christ had cast his disciples:

> This seems a cheerful world when I view it from this fair garden under the shadow of these vines. But if I climbed some great mountain and looked out over the wide lands, you know very well what I would see. Brigands on the high road, pirates on the seas, in the amphitheaters men murdered to please the applauding crowds, under all roofs misery and selfishness. It is really a bad world, Donatus, an incredibly bad world.

To be honest, as an American suburban professional I pass most of my days with my family in the gentle shade of a very fair garden. We have our problems and stresses, but on most days, if we are not indulging our own self-pity or covetousness, the world we see seems cheerful indeed. I say that not as one who is unfamiliar with the injustice and oppression that persists in American communities. In fact, after a career as a trial attorney in the civil rights division of the U.S. Department of Justice, I imagine I have seen more than most—especially after my tour on the police-misconduct task force. One case I encountered in New Orleans, where two police officers raped a teenage runaway and dropped her back out on the streets, rivaled the brutality I have seen in almost any country. Even so, this girl did have a place to turn for justice, and those two police officers are now behind bars. Throughout the world, however, such incidents are repeated with impunity hundreds of times a day. Relative to what lies out in the world, ours is among the shadiest and fairest of gardens.

So to see the hurting world as God sees it, we need to go with St. Cyprian and look out over the wide lands of this incredibly bad world. And who better to help us do that than the countless Christian missionaries and service workers that we send out around the globe?

In 1996, one year before IJM became operational, several colleagues and I asked nearly seventy Christian ministries serving globally in missions and relief and development to be the church's eyes and ears in the world. These ministries represented tens of thousands of Christian workers in more than a hundred countries. When asked in our survey, every single ministry indicated that they had workers serving in communities where people suffered injustice and abuse in circumstances where local authorities could not be relied on for relief. These seventy ministries named the following categories of injustices as the most widely observed:

- abusive child labor
- abusive police or military
- child pornography
- child prostitution
- corrupt seizure or extortion of land
- detention or disappearance without charge or trial
- extortion or withholding of wages
- forced prostitution
- forced migration
- genocide
- murder of street children
- organized political intimidation
- organized racial violence
- public justice corruption
- state, rebel or paramilitary terrorism
- state-supported discrimination or abuse of ethnic minorities
- state-sponsored religious persecution
- state-sponsored torture

Of course these are just words on a list. It took the stories from those Christian workers to give them meaning.

Child prostitution. One ministry that works with street children in Manila told me about the day they noticed some of the little girls with whom they had been working were disappearing from their ministry.

These were orphans and runaways between the ages of eleven and thirteen. They had been living on the streets until these Christians brought them into their program and started to show them something of the love of Christ. Quite suddenly, however, these girls stopped showing up and could not be found in their usual hangouts on the streets. After asking around, the missionaries heard that the girls had been abducted into a brothel. There they would be raped several times a day for the greed of others. Worse yet, the missionaries were informed that the brothel was being run by the local police.

As it turns out, their story provided us with just a glimpse of this "incredibly bad world." The vastness of the injustice that international Christian workers encounter is truly staggering. Each year, for example, more than a million children around the world are forced into prostitution—a million *new* children each year.[1] It is nearly impossible to get our minds wrapped around the human magnitude of these numbers.

I have been gaining a more concrete vision of the way this must appear to our all-knowing God. In 1998 I was able to look physically on a gathering of a *million* men on the mall in Washington, D.C., at the solemn assembly convened by Promise Keepers. In the midst of that seemingly endless crush of humanity, I felt a deep sadness come over me. I realized that over the coming year the same number of children would be packed into the world's darkest brothels.

Slavery and abusive child labor. Prostitution is just one of the abuses that confront vulnerable children of our world. In our survey, every third mission agency reported that they were also serving in communities that allowed abusive child labor or slavery. Perhaps the story of just one little boy will help us understand what Christians working throughout the world know.

When he was only five years old, Kumar suffered great loss: his father died suddenly and his mother abandoned him after the death. Orphaned and alone, Kumar went to live with his uncle, who did his best to provide him with some stability and security. But two years after his father's death, Kumar's tragedies were compounded when a corrupt brick-kiln owner used a small debt incurred by a relative to illegally conscript seven-year-old Kumar into slavery at his kiln.

The brick kiln was a massive operation that churned out hundreds of hard clay bricks every day. Slaves—children, women and men—gathered water, sifted sand, molded bricks and hauled them in and out of the sun for the owner's profit. As other children his age were just beginning school, Kumar was initiated to a life of slavery.

Kumar struggled alongside adults at the kiln, bewildered and scared by what he saw. All day, seven days a week, he carried heavy clay bricks back and forth in the kiln as they dried. Every moment was occupied. He woke early each morning to begin laboring at 6:30 and continued until the evening hours, his hands raw and his small body exhausted from the strain of the brickwork.

Kumar's owner hurled abusive threats at him and the other slaves when he felt they were not working hard enough. "They tortured me so much," he remembers. "We worked hard and suffered terribly." Even when Kumar was sick, his owner beat him and dragged him to the kiln.

Though he was only a child, Kumar knew that his situation was wrong. "I wanted to study. I wanted my parents. I wanted to play. At times I would think of all those things," he remembers.

Kumar was trapped. When another slave at the kiln had attempted to flee, the owner tracked him down and brought him back to the facility, publicly beating him as a warning to the others. Kumar knew exactly what awaited him if he attempted to run away. There was no escape: "The owner will not let us go. I did not think about freedom."

As inconceivable as it may seem, Kumar's story is repeated in India several million times over as destitute children, women and men are trapped into indefinite servitude by the lies and threats of those who profit on the backs of slaves. Just as it says in the ancient Scriptures, so it is today: "the infant of the poor is seized for a debt" (Job 24:9). And all of this goes on despite the fact that such practices are explicitly illegal in the country and have been for decades.

Evil at work the world over. Indeed, it is not difficult to "look out over the wide lands" just beyond each fair garden and see what an "incredibly bad world" it is. Consider this brief tour around the globe.

Sexual and domestic violence. Communities in the West certainly have tremendous, silent struggles against persistent gender violence, but very few Westerners (male or female) have any idea what the reality is like for common poor women and girls in the developing world. When they are beaten or sexually assaulted, the odds of their abuser being brought to justice are literally about zero. They are very likely to know someone else who has suffered such an assault and very unlikely to have even heard of someone who was brought to justice for such an assault. As Amnesty International has affirmed after years of global experience with gender violence:

> Most acts of violence against women are never investigated. The perpetrators are not prosecuted. They commit their crimes with impunity. This contributes to a climate where violence against women is seen as normal, rather than criminal, and where women do not seek justice because they know they will not gain it.[2]

Abusive police. A Christian ministry leader told me about a hollow-eyed woman in Indonesia he had met. Looking at her, he guessed she was in her fifties. In fact, she was barely thirty years old. For the last several years her husband had been languishing in a filthy Indonesian jail. His survival depended on her visits and extra provisions, but in order to exercise her visitation rights, she was forced to prostitute herself to six different prison guards. She is getting old very quickly.

It is no exaggeration to say that the most pervasive criminal presence in the lives of the global poor is probably their own police. Regarding the people in the developing world who are *supposed to enforce* the protection of national law, the massive World Bank study on the lives of the global poor concluded: "At best, the police are reported as largely inactive in their policing roles; at worst, they actively harass, oppress and brutalize."[3]

Detention or disappearance without charge or trial. Illegal detention is a massive source of suffering for the global poor, and it springs from naked failure to enforce national laws designed to protect vulnerable people. *New York Times* reporter Michael Wines recently found that "two-thirds of Uganda's 18,000 prison inmates have not been tried. The same is true of Mozambique's prisoners, and four fifths of Cameroon's. Even in South Africa, Africa's most advanced nation, inmates in Johannesburg Prison have waited seven years to see a judge." In Malawi, poor people will rot in prison for months and years "for lack of bail that can total less than $10 or $20."[4] And in many countries, governments use detention or disappearance as a political weapon against perceived enemies.

Illegal property seizure. For millions of poor people, their greatest and most hopeful source of wealth and well-being comes from the little plot of land they have acquired for housing and cultivation. With a patch of land, they can provide a shelter for their family, grow a bit of food and even operate a small enterprise. Take away their land and their means of survival is stolen. And yet, for millions of poor people, that is exactly what happens. Their land is simply stolen from them by more powerful forces in the community, by corrupt authorities, wealthier families, greedy in-laws or grasping corporations.

Once again, there are laws in all of these countries prohibiting the theft of land and property, but without effective enforcement of these laws, there is no law at all. In fact, the struggle for land in the developing world has come to be governed by the medieval equation of *might makes right.* Again, most countries have made tremendous strides over the last generation in adopting laws that embody international standards protecting the rights of property ownership for traditionally weaker citizens, namely, women, ethnic minorities, tribal groups and informal settlers. Without effective enforcement systems, however, such laws can feel like another cruel joke on the poor.

State-sponsored abuse and torture. Around the world, citizens suffer directly at the hands of their own governments—not just through failure to enforce laws on the books designed for their protection, but through direct persecution and aggression. News reports continue to tell of state-sponsored abuse carried out from on high by the government of Burma, for example. Human rights groups and Burmese dissidents have criticized the government for imprisonment and torture of activists as well as members of several minority groups. In 2008, news media around the world were awash with the images of abuse in Burma's streets during pro-democracy protests. But these protests—and the bloodshed that accompanied them—were only a small window into one of the many countries where impunity reigns, and citizens can be tortured and abused by the government structures that should exist for their own protection.

No doubt about it, as it was in the third century so it is at the beginning of the twenty-first: this is "an incredibly bad world."

But honestly, what are we supposed to do with this information?

Don't despair, take heart! In a matter of seconds we can go from knowing next to nothing about children in India to knowing that fifteen million of them are enslaved in short, brutal, dead-end lives of slavery.[5] Now what? In our hearts we feel like deer frozen by headlights. The very information that should move us is so overwhelming that it actually paralyzes. It is like a big meal that is supposed to provide fuel for our body but actually makes us feel like lying down and taking a nap. Instead of energizing us for action, the overwhelming injustice in our world actually makes us feel numb. We sense our hearts melting and our feet sinking into concrete.

This is when we need to listen to the voice of Jesus, who encouraged the paralytic to "take heart" (Matthew 9:22). When their spirits are crippled by the sheer weight of the world's injustice, Jesus tells his disciples, "Take heart! I have overcome the world" (John 16:33). He makes this declaration, however, not that we might sit cheerfully in our paralysis but that we might actually get up and walk. Even to the lame, Jesus begins with a straightforward question: "Do you want to get well?" (John 5:6). Likewise, Jesus calls us to a moment of honest reflection. Do we really want to move to a new place? Do we really want to stand before a needy world, free of all hindrances of the heart? Do we really want to see the world with the heart of Jesus and the courage of his Spirit?

Of course we do. But we often do not know how to go from awareness to action.

THE SECOND STEP: PREPARING OUR MIND FOR ACTION

As one who wept over his own faintness of heart, the apostle Peter urges us to begin by preparing our minds for action (1 Peter 1:13; see Matthew 26:69-75). Such preparation comes from a return to biblical truth. In particular we need to see what the Bible says about the world's true nature and its real needs.

The Bible declares that the world is fallen, sinful. Often I am ill-prepared for action in a dark world of injustice because I have gotten used to a little lie: the idea that the fair garden that I have worked so hard to carve out for myself and my family is normal. I have gradually adjusted to the idea that "the world" into which Christ has sent his disciples is actually a reasonably pleasant backyard patio. Certainly it is no Garden of Eden—there are unruly shrubs, unpleasant neighbors, rainy days, tearful nights and even vandals. But in my garden the Fall into sin is being managed. Gradually in my mind "the world" referred to in the Bible is defined more and more by the boundary hedges I share with my neighbors. Accordingly, I hone my Christian witness for engagement in this domesticated garden. I come to see the full armor of God as battle dress for fighting weeds, backyard pests and trespassers.

Having strayed in my mind so far from the truth of Scripture, I am caught totally off guard when the true nature of "the world" passes before my eyes. When confronted with the massive, violent oppression in our world, I feel that something has gone wrong and that things are out of control. I feel like I've made a wrong turn and I'm out of place. Even in moments when I am feeling most earnest about my faith and convinced of God's power and presence in my life and in the world, when I am forced to consider the millions of men, women and children who suffer the great brutalities of injustice in this world, I feel disoriented. I may have assembled something of a Christian worldview, but when the evening news shows the weak of the world

being beaten up so badly on such a massive scale, I feel vaguely like
I'm not where I'm supposed to be.

"Oh, but you are!" says Jesus. And this is the point. Preparing
our mind for action means coming to grips with the true nature of
the world into which Christ has cast us, his disciples. It means
coming to grips with how the Fall is playing itself out around the
world in the present day. When humanity rejected its Maker—the
very God of love, mercy, justice, goodness and compassion—it set
on the throne the human will to power. The outcome in the twentieth century could be described in various ways, but I would just call
it an open-mouthed grave: an entire generation of European youth
composting the World War I battlefields of Verdun and the Somme,
Hitler's six million Jews, Stalin's twenty million Soviet citizens,
Mao's tens of millions of political enemies and peasant famine victims, Pol Pot's two million Cambodians, the Interhamwe's million
Tutsi Rwandans, and the millions of lives wasted away during apartheid's forty-year reign.

We can easily forget that the same spirit of darkness rules our
present age. In the affluent West it manifests itself in a spiritual bar-
renness that made non-Western Christians like Mother Teresa and
Aleksandr Solzhenitsyn gasp and grieve. For these Eastern Christians, Western brokenness and deathlike alienation from the sacred
evokes a guttural reaction not unlike that experienced by Americans
and Europeans at the sight of starving children. Outside the affluent
West, however, in the Two-Thirds World where most of the children
God created actually live, the Fall is being played out in ways more
familiar to the biblical writers: it is manifest in a world of brutal injustice. As the apostle Paul wrote about the fallen world, quoting the
prophet Isaiah and King David:

> Their feet are swift to shed blood;
>   ruin and misery mark their ways,
> and the way of peace they do not know.
>   There is no fear of God before their eyes. (Romans 3:15-18)

Isaiah finished the same thought this way:

> The way of peace they do not know;
>> there is no justice in their paths. . . .
>> no one who walks in them will know peace.
> So justice is far from us,
>> and righteousness does not reach us.
> We look for light, but all is darkness. (Isaiah 59:8-9)

The Bible declares the world's need for salvation and justice. Biblical Christians understand that Christ has called us to be his witnesses to the uttermost parts of a very dark world—a dark world of injustice. Preparing our minds for action in the world means coming to grips with the notion that the world we are sent into as salt and light is a world that needs salt and light precisely because, among other things, it is full of the corruption and darkness of injustice. All those old Scriptures about "the world," which always seemed rather melodramatic when I heard them in my suburban church as a kid, turned out to be much more worthy of my attention than I ever knew.

UNCOMMON COURAGE FOR COMMON CHRISTIANS: THE GIFT OF GOD'S WORD

Much of my shock, disorientation and paralysis in the face of an unjust world simply come from my failure to truly hide God's Word in my heart (Psalm 119:11). God intends that I face the world with courage, joy and a steady eye because of the truth of his Word. Through his Word God's people are given every advantage for living in the world, because despite deceitful appearances, the Bible tells the truth about the nature of the world and the nature of the God we serve.

These may not be our favorite passages of Scripture, and they may never get featured on our calendar of daily inspiration, but truth be told, the Bible is not coy about the kind of world into which Christ has sent his disciples.

> Men move boundary stones;
>> they pasture flocks they have stolen.

They drive away the orphan's donkey
   and take the widow's ox in pledge.
They thrust the needy from the path
   and force all the poor of the land into hiding. . . .
The fatherless child is snatched from the breast;
   the infant of the poor is seized for a debt.
Lacking clothes, they go about naked;
    they carry the sheaves, but still go hungry.
      (Job 24:2-4, 9-10)

The wicked draw the sword
   and bend the bow
to bring down the poor and needy. (Psalm 37:14)

It is you [the elders and princes] who have ruined my
     vineyard;
   the plunder from the poor is in your houses. (Isaiah 3:14)

Women have been ravished in Zion,
   and virgins in the towns of Judah.
Princes have been hung up by their hands;
   elders are shown no respect.
Young men toil at the millstones;
   boys stagger under loads of wood. (Lamentations 5:11-13)

The people of the land practice extortion and commit robbery;
they oppress the poor and needy and mistreat the alien, denying them justice. (Ezekiel 22:29)

They cast lots for my people
   and traded boys for prostitutes;
they sold girls for wine
   that they might drink. (Joel 3:3)

He [Ammon] ripped open the pregnant women of Gilead
   in order to extend his borders. (Amos 1:13)

Bible-believing Christians should be the last people to get caught off guard by injustice in the world. For even as we celebrate the coming of Christ into the world, in Scripture we are powerfully reminded of the kind of world into which he has come. We seldom speak of it at Christmastime (although medieval Christians clearly did), but even the birth of Jesus was accompanied by one of the most brutal acts of injustice in history. As we may recall, King Herod felt threatened by the prospect of a new king of the Jews and "gave orders to kill all the boys in Bethlehem and its vicinity who were two years old and under" (Matthew 2:16). The early church numbered the victims in the thousands. In his Gospel the apostle Matthew hides nothing from our eyes. He treats us like grown-ups. He looks us straight in the eye and lets us know that ours is a world in which even a baby "away in a manger" is not safe from the brutal abuse of power.

The Bible could not be plainer: "If you see the poor oppressed in a district, and justice and rights denied, do not be surprised at such things" (Ecclesiastes 5:8). Thus the Word of God leads us in preparing our minds for action. Through his Word and his Spirit, God speaks the word of truth that steadies our hearts for service in a difficult world. "Stand firm then, with the belt of truth buckled around your waist . . . and with your feet fitted with the readiness that comes from the gospel of peace" (Ephesians 6:14-15). We need not feel overwhelmed or out of place in such a dark world of injustice. This is precisely the world into which Jesus intended his followers to go. "You are the light of the world. . . . Let your light shine before men, that they may see your good deeds and praise your Father in heaven" (Matthew 5:14, 16). Moreover, as we serve him in the world, Jesus assures us, "All authority in heaven and on earth has been given to me. . . . And surely I am with you always, to the very end of the age" (Matthew 28:18, 20).

Even so, as we take our first steps out of our familiar boat of safety and into the seas of a troubled and needy world, we can hear the words of our Master beckoning us, "Take courage! It is I. Don't be afraid" (Matthew 14:27).

CHAMPIONS OF JUSTICE

THREE COURAGEOUS CHRISTIANS

In the *Screwtape Letters*, an ingenious reflection on the forces that drain the lifeblood from Christian faith, C. S. Lewis makes a startling statement. He writes that "despair is a greater sin than any of the sins that provoke it."[1] And surely for Christians looking at our evil world of injustice and oppression, despair can always be found lurking at the door of our hearts, waiting to hobble us the moment we begin to take our first steps forward. After all, what can *we* do? How can *we* make a difference in a world of such massive and brutal injustice?

STRONGHOLDS OF INJUSTICE

Sister K., Brother E. and Sister J. know about the temptations of despair. In Sister K.'s country there is a booming business in forced prostitution. The local police protect it and even hunt down girls who try to run away, often returning them to the stockades where they are held. Sister K. is personally aware of almost sixty brothels where she has found hundreds of young girls kept in subjection by "whip, fist, boot and bulldog"—some girls only thirteen and fourteen years old.

A state-appointed investigator assigned to look into the issue visited a single brothel and concluded that there was "no necessity for state interference in the matter." But Sister K. knows differently, and the brutal reality is beyond comprehension. She learned that one of the women held in prostitution was actually murdered by being soaked in oil and burned alive. The coroner's report of her death even named the perpetrator. It read: "Burned to death by W. H. Griffin." But the man was never charged with a crime. Local politicians prevent any legal action from being taken against the forced prostitution rings because they owe their position and influence to the wealthy business interests behind the brothels.

In the face of such injustice what can Sister K. do?

In Brother E.'s country abusive child labor is a plague on the land. Where he lives, about two million children between the ages of ten and fifteen years work in textile mills, tobacco-processing plants, mines and other factories. Children work twelve hours a day, six days a week, sometimes on dangerous night shifts. Some must endure working eighty-two hours per week in a factory during peak weeks of the year. Many of the girls work in silk mills just as the boys work as "breakers" in the coal mines. Every day the breaker boys breathe in the heavy soot that covers them as they pick the debris out of the coal by hand. According to one person, the children of the breakers and the mills are "stooped and skinny, often missing thumbs and fingers and always giving the impression of being older than they were. Only when they were maimed so seriously that they can no longer work did such children attend school." As a prominent national lawyer commented, "You sell your boys to be slaves of the breakers and your girls to be slaves in the mills."

In the face of such oppression what can Brother E. do?

In Sister J.'s country summary execution by mobs is a way of life. The majority ethnic group maintains its dominance over the minority ethnic group through the intimidation of extrajudicial murder. Every year fifty, sixty or a hundred people are burned alive or hanged after being accused of committing some offense against the majority ethnic group. These brutal events are gruesome public affairs, often performed in the presence of local officials on the basis of a simple denunciation by a member of the majority group. Without any opportunity to defend themselves, the accused are hustled off to a terrifying death. Local law-enforcement officials simply refuse to intervene and occasionally carry out the executions themselves.

In the face of such brutal human rights violations what can Sister J. do?

Sister K., Brother E. and Sister J. are very real people. The circumstances described are documented beyond any dispute. They are, in fact, part of history. Kate, Edgar and Jessie are actually devout Christians of another era, and the country in which they encountered such staggering injustice is the United States of America. But today, although Americans have certainly not purged injustice from their society, these conditions no longer exist, in large part because of the courageous obedience of Christians to the call of God. In the face of brutal injustice and oppression that rivals anything anywhere on our globe today, courageous Christians refused to despair. Thankfully, America has never been the same.

KATE BUSHNELL: ABOLISHING FORCED PROSTITUTION
A hundred years ago Dr. Kate Bushnell served as a national evangelist for the Women's Christian Temperance Union (WCTU) in the United States. A devout Christian, Dr. Kate Bushnell was heartbroken by the plight of girls victimized by forced prostitution in America. Hard as it may be to imagine today, the dens of forced prostitution described earlier were rampant in the logging camps and mining communities of northern Wisconsin and Michigan in the 1880s. Dr. Bushnell encountered the murder of the woman who was burned alive with impunity in Ashland, Wisconsin.

While in some cases police responded to the pleas of women who were seeking to escape their bondage, other times they didn't listen and even returned runaways to their brothels. The existence of these dens and dance halls of rape was largely supported by the local community. The owners and patrons of such establishments exercised enough political power to prevent legal action against the brothels. Local doctors supported their existence because their frequent examination of the women provided a source of additional income. And local businessmen found that brothels provided a boost to the local economy.

Dr. Bushnell looked in vain for someone to properly investigate these conditions. Finding no one willing to take the risks, she did it herself. Facing tremendous personal danger, she infiltrated scores of brothels and interviewed hundreds of women held in bondage. "She would search for reliable witnesses having personal knowledge of an involvement in the case under investigation. She insisted on talking to inmates, viewing the situation herself. One side of the story, from one witness, was not enough. . . . Having penetrated the brothel by one excuse or another, she was able by various pretexts to obtain proof of the conditions that existed there."[2]

Dr. Bushnell reported her findings at a Chicago convention of the WCTU. The state of Wisconsin vehemently denied her findings, and the state inspector even attempted to discredit her by accusing Dr. Bushnell herself of "unchastity." When she appeared before the Wisconsin state legislature, she had to be escorted by police because of threats of violence against her. Standing before the hostile assembly, she initially felt overwhelmed as the only woman in the room. But

> being a woman of prayer, she lifted her heart to God, "whereupon the door opened quietly, and about fifty ladies of the highest social position at the State Capitol filed in, and stood all about me. There were no seats for them; they stood all the time I talked—and I had plenty of courage as I realized how good God was to send them."[3]

Despite the attacks on Dr. Bushnell and her study, "the whole country was agitated on the white slave question by the disclosures" she had made.[4] Her findings were substantiated by subsequent studies conducted by both public officials and private researchers. The result of her work was the passage of a bill in the Wisconsin legislature that finally dealt seriously with the scourge of forced prostitution. The bill was appropriately labeled "the Kate Bushnell Bill." Later Dr. Bushnell took her Christian witness to India and China, where she and other Christians challenged the complicity of British colonial officials in the rampant trafficking of women and girls in forced prostitution.

Edgar Murphy: Transforming the Destiny of Child Laborers

Today we look with horror and despair at reports of the millions of children who toil under abusive labor conditions around the world. And yet at the turn of the century similar conditions were not uncommon in North America. Edgar Gardner Murphy, a minister of the gospel from Alabama, was certainly familiar with them. Murphy was particularly burdened by the oppression suffered by the tens of thousands of children under age fourteen who toiled in the textile mills of his native American South. I found myself thinking of my sister's own six-year-old daughter as I encountered the comments of an observer from 1902 who described the fate of just one of these children.

> Mattie . . . is six years old. She is a spinner. Inside a cotton mill for 12 hours a day she stands in a 4-foot passage-way between the spinning frames where the cotton is spun from coarser into fine threads. . . . From daylight to dark she is in the midst of the ceaseless throb and racket of machinery. When I first met her it was Christmas Eve. The eve of the children's festival when the whole of Christendom celebrates the birth of the Child whose coming was to bring freedom to children. She was crying, and when I asked the reason, she said between her sobs, that she wanted a doll that would open and shut its eyes. "When would you play with it?" I asked the little toiler, whose weary eyelids were ready to close over her tired eyes directly after the long day's work was over. "I should have time aplenty on Sunday," replied the little slave whose daily wage of ten cents helped to swell the family income.[5]

As a disciple of Jesus Christ, Rev. Murphy chose not to surrender to despair in the face of such a tragedy. In 1901 in response to his expanding knowledge of the atrocities of child labor in the mills, Murphy founded the Alabama Child Labor Committee. He began to write to inform the public of the horrors he witnessed. He authored nine pamphlets on the subject and distributed twenty-eight thousand copies throughout the United States, often at his own personal expense. His writing effort has been called "the first body of printed material of any considerable extent or value" in favor of legislation restricting child labor in the American South.[6]

Rev. Murphy believed that children belonged in "God's outdoors, in the home, or in the schoolroom." On one occasion Rev. Murphy examined a seven-year-old's hand that had had three fingers torn from it during dangerous mill work. When the mill owner explained that the child had been careless, Rev. Murphy replied, "Hasn't a child seven years of age got a right to be careless?"[7]

In 1904 Murphy joined with other advocates of reform to found the National Child Labor Committee (NCLC). The NCLC came to be regarded as the most effective voice in bringing about the abolition of child labor in America, and Rev. Murphy is referred to by contemporaries and historians alike as its father and founder. Perhaps Murphy's greatest personal victory came, however, when his home state of Alabama finally issued legislative restrictions on child labor in 1907. Even more substantial was the fact that he had "pricked the conscience of the country alive to the existence of child labor as a shame and a curse to America."[8] One man's faithful devotion to his Master's call to care for "the least of these" helped transform the destiny of millions of American children.

ENOUGH IS ENOUGH: CHURCH WOMEN AND LYNCHING

In recent years summary executions by vigilante groups and "disappearances" by secret death squads have been among the uglier human rights violations that have struck terror in the hearts of millions of people living in communities of social and political conflict around the world. Such state-sanctioned horror may seem distant, but there was a time not long ago, within the memory of many living

Americans, when millions of their compatriots lived under such a threat.

In the first two decades of the twentieth century, thousands of African American citizens were publicly lynched—including almost a hundred women. In four years, from 1918 to 1921, twenty-eight African Americans were burned at the stake by mob action.[9] As late as the 1940s, lynching was still a common method of social control and intimidation in the Southern states. But again it was the courageous faith of devout Christian women who helped end this scourge.

In the segregated South the practice of lynching was largely defended as a means to protect the honor of white women. It was often perpetrated against African American men who were accused of raping a white woman or of simply addressing a white woman in a socially inappropriate fashion. Jessie Daniel Ames, a Southern white woman, believed that the most effective voice against lynching could come from those it was intended to benefit. In 1930, with only twelve compatriots, she created the Association of Southern Women for the Prevention of Lynching (ASWPL). These twelve women simply "went home and began to work and to talk and to retell the facts as they learned them."[10]

Ames and the other charter members were all officers in various Protestant denominations. Apart from the brutal injustice of the practice, they were deeply concerned that the lynching of African Americans by white "Christians" tended to "discredit Christianity, and impede the work of missionaries among non-white peoples." As Ames later stated, "That was one of the strongest appeals we could make."[11]

Although Ames was its only salaried worker, the ASWPL had councils in all eleven former Confederate states and more than forty thousand active members. The key to her success seemed to be her reliance on volunteers and a preexisting network of religious and secular women's organizations, which provided cohesiveness for the ASWPL. By the early 1940s, 109 women's associations, representing four million women, supported the ASWPL's work. Not only did the women's organizations of the southern Protestant churches endorse

ASWPL, but they also included antilynching literature in their respective educational materials.

Through literature, speeches and word of mouth within its vast network, ASWPL undermined the chivalric notions that fueled lynching and revealed the truth of the barbaric practice. They circulated petitions to show elected officials that there was widespread support for antilynching laws. They persuaded law-enforcement officials to sign a pledge expressing opposition to lynching. By 1941, 1,355 police officers had signed the pledge. Also in that year police officers in forty documented cases had successfully opposed lynch mobs. Furthermore, ASWPL exposed by name officers who failed to uphold the law. In some instances ASWPL women physically confronted the mobs. ASWPL members were credited with "preventing the lynching of scores of blacks, because of their timely phone calls to a sheriff or visits to a local jail."[12]

While Southern senators blocked federal antilynching legislation and thwarted any nationwide remedy, the ASWPL was able to fundamentally change the cultural mores and beliefs that undergirded the practice. And the impact was dramatic. As the distinguished Yale historian Dr. C. Vann Woodward has observed, "Efforts of civil rights groups to secure passage of federal anti-lynching laws failed repeatedly, but effective work by white and Negro groups, *many of them Southern church organizations*, virtually eliminated lynching for a time. The NAACP conceded the 'virtual disappearance of this form of oppression' in the early 1950s."[13] Of course the women of the ASWPL were not perfect and manifested many of the narrow attitudes common to many Southern white women of the day. Nevertheless, as one historian has commented on the era, "From its inception, the anti-lynching campaign was rooted firmly in a tradition of evangelical reform."[14]

ORDINARY PEOPLE, EXTRAORDINARY FAITH
To me these stories are part of the great encouragement of a Christian heritage. Sometimes when I am utterly overwhelmed by the injustice in our world, recalling or reading about the faithful heroes of the past

allows me to find my courage. When I raise my eyes, even for a moment, to the history of God's courage expressed in his people, I find hope and steadiness of heart.

Without the encouragement of stories like these, I can easily get buried in the intimidations of today. I can easily lose all perspective and hope. It makes me think of days as a small boy playing at the ocean and experiencing the terrific intimidation and disorientation of the waves as I waded farther and farther from the beach and other people. I vividly remember one occasion when, having been lulled to inattention by the temporary calm, a swelling wave blind-sided me without warning. It picked me up and rolled me over and over underwater. With something close to terror, I kicked and flailed my arms trying to swim to safety. Then just as wild panic began to grip my heart, my head was shoved above the surface just long enough to steal a glance down the shore line. There, very near me, were my two brothers, standing sturdily—in the same three feet of water in which I was flailing. Letting my feet float down, I quickly found the hard, sandy bottom and stood up—embarrassed a bit but greatly relieved.

Alone in the waves, I had lost perspective. Things were not as they appeared. The water felt infinitely deeper than it was. I had no idea of the sturdy ground that was actually well within reach. I felt helpless, lost and overwhelmed. And as long as I felt that way, I possessed neither the power nor the presence of mind to stand amid the waves.

Likewise, when I see the great forces of injustice that crash upon our world, I find myself going from moments of easy obliviousness to moments of total disorientation and despair. But it is in these moments that I need to look down the shoreline of history and see my brothers and sisters of the faith—Dr. Bushnell, Rev. Murphy, the Christian women of the ASWPL and so many others—standing amid the crashing waves. The injustice and oppression in the world is powerful, relentless and pervasive, but as these three faithful witnesses attest, we are neither without a foothold to withstand its blows nor powerless to rescue those pulled under by its force.

There is a testimony of great hope in seeing how God has used ordinary people—from all nations—extraordinary in their Christian faith, to bring rescue to those who were hurting.

WHAT CAN WE LEARN FROM FAITHFUL CHRISTIANS?

These champions of justice teach us a couple of truths which at times we may question: bringing about justice can be within our reach, and it is also an integral part of our faith.

First, we learn that *we can change things.* Our despair, cynicism and laziness may insist to us that nothing ever really changes and that we can never make a difference. But on high we see a great cloud of witnesses stand to their feet with a different testimony. Rank upon rank of vulnerable and voiceless girls tell us that for them Dr. Bushnell's faithfulness to God made a difference. Legions of children, each with a name, stand to bless Rev. Murphy for his obedience to Christ. Likewise, in honor of the faithful Christians who took a stand, countless African American families can testify to the difference it makes to live in an American South without lynching. Still more give thanks to God for Dr. Martin Luther King Jr. for the opportunity to live in a South without apartheid. Like the blind man healed by Jesus, these witnesses show little interest in quibbling over historical or theological complexities. They only offer simple stories about the difference faith can make: "One thing I do know. I was blind but now I see" (John 9:25).

We are not caught up in a Pollyanna-like dream of bringing heaven to earth and abolishing injustice. On the contrary, we know that an ocean of oppression will pound humanity until he whom "even the wind and waves obey" shall command the storm to cease (Matthew 8:27). Moreover, we know that there are waves of injustice in this world against which even the most faithful will not be saved. But still we do not despair. As Dr. Martin Luther King Jr. said, "The arc of the moral universe is long, but it bends toward justice."[15] Calling us to "action in hope," the great missiologist David Bosch declares that "like its Lord, the church-in-mission must take sides, *for* life and against death, *for* justice and against oppression."[16]

Precisely the vision of God's triumph makes it impossible to look for sanctuary in quietism, neutrality, or withdrawal from the field of action. We may never overrate our own capabilities; and yet, we may have confidence about the direction into which history moves, for we are not, like Sartre, peering into the abyss of nothingness, nauseated by the emptiness of our freedom, leaping into a future which only confirms the meaninglessness of the present moment.[17]

In the words of the apostle Paul, "Let us not become weary in doing good, for at the proper time we will reap a harvest if we do not give up" (Galatians 6:9). This is not a vague affirmation about the happy ending of history, the evolving goodness of man, the triumph of the scientific mind or the promise of a civilized world. It is a bedrock conviction about the nature of God and what it means to serve him in faithfulness. As he gives us eyes to see those in need, we will simply respond in love. As Bosch declares:

> We hope because of what we have already experienced. Christian hope is both possession and yearning, repose and activity, arrival and being on the way. Since God's victory is certain, believers can work both patiently and enthusiastically, blending careful planning with urgent obedience, motivated by the patient impatience of the Christian hope.[18]

Second, we learn from Dr. Bushnell, Rev. Murphy and the Christian ladies of the ASWPL that *the biblical mandate to seek justice and rescue the oppressed is an integral and magnificent theme of the Christian heritage* (Isaiah 1:17). They may be unfamiliar to us now, but many of the greatest heroes of biblical Christianity in history were fully engaged in the work of seeking justice.

It would never have occurred to the great Christian leaders of the nineteenth century who battled so bravely to abolish slavery—William Wilberforce, Charles Finney, William Lloyd Garrison, Edward Beecher, Elijah Lovejoy, Theodore Dwight Weld—that Jesus could be honored by a life of Christian devotion that did not include a response of Christian love to those who are oppressed. For some it was precisely their conversion to Christ that moved them to take up the slavery cause. For John Gregg Fee, the evangelical founder of Berea College in Kentucky, it was while on his knees in anguished prayer that he confronted the costs of discipleship. "I saw that to embrace the principle of abolition and wear the name was to cut myself off from relatives and former friends." But he prayed, "Lord, if needs be, make me an Abolitionist." Later he said that he rose from prayer that day "with the consciousness that I had died to the world and accepted Christ in all the fullness of his character as I then understood him."[19]

In fact, historians have long recognized that the great achievements in humanitarian reform and social justice in the West during the nineteenth century—the abolition of slavery, prison reform, the establishment of hospitals and schools for the poor, women's rights, opposition to forced prostitution, the fight against child labor—were largely built on the faithful zeal of Christians. As American historian Sydney Ahlstrom of Yale University explained about that great humanitarian movement, "If the collective conscience of evangelical America is left out, the movement as a whole is incomprehensible." It was built, he said, on "the Puritan's basic confidence that the world could be constrained and reformed in accordance with God's revealed will," and fueled by the revivalists' "demand for holiness, [and their] calling for socially relevant Christian commitment as the proper sequel to conversion."[20]

RECOVERING OUR MINISTRY OF JUSTICE

In a detour away from biblical faith, many Christians in the twentieth century neglected this heritage of service to a hurting world. As Bosch observes:

> It was a stupendous victory of the evil one to have made us believe that structures and conditions in this world will not or need not really change, to have considered political and societal powers and other vested interests inviolable, to have acquiesced in conditions of injustice and oppression, to have tempered our expectation to the point of compromise, to have given up the hope for a wholesale transformation of the status quo, to have

been blind to our own responsibility for and involvement in a world en route to its fulfillment.[21]

But Christ has not neglected us, and now he calls us to recover the ministry of justice that once was ours. As the great evangelical theologian Carl F. H. Henry has said of evangelicals of the eighteenth and nineteenth centuries, their

> evangelical movement was spiritually and morally vital because it strove for justice and also invited humanity to regeneration, forgiveness, and power for righteousness. If the church preaches only divine forgiveness and does not affirm justice, she implies that God treats immorality and sin lightly. If the church proclaims only justice, we shall all die in unforgiven sin and without the spirit's empowerment for righteousness. We should be equally troubled that we lag in championing justice and in fulfilling our evangelistic mandate.[22]

As we peer down the halls of Christian history, we give thanks for those great champions of justice and evangelism who give us hope. For God intends that we remember his ancient work in equipping his people "to act justly and to love mercy and to walk humbly" (Micah 6:8). As the psalmist urges us:

> Look to the LORD and his strength;
> seek his face always.
> Remember the wonders he has done,
> his miracles, and the judgments he pronounced.
> (Psalm 105:4-5)

And even as we remember, we lift our eyes to the horizon and ask, What great work of justice might God perform through us, in our time, to the glory of Christ? How might God renew through us the witness for biblical justice in the world? What child in India, what girl held in prostitution in Manila, what innocent man rotting in a Kenyan jail might yet stand and testify that the hand of a faithful God touched them and loved them through the obedience of Christians who refused to despair?

PART TWO

HOPE AMID
DESPAIR

God's Four Affirmations
About Justice

HOPE IN THE GOD
OF JUSTICE

The battle for justice in the world is not fought where we think it is. The struggle against injustice is not fought on the battlefield of power or truth or even righteousness. There are pitched battles waged on these ramparts, but the war is ultimately won or lost on a more forward front. In the end the battle against oppression stands or falls on the battlefield of hope.

No one knows this better than the oppressors. They know that they never have enough power, lies or loyalty to withstand the onslaught of even a fraction of the power, truth and courage that humanity could at any minute amass against them. Therefore they rely on, utterly depend on, the inaction of despair. They know full well that their preeminence depends on most people in their community, their nation and their world doing nothing. This is the essence of Edmund Burke's conviction about human history: "All that is necessary for the triumph of evil is for good men to do nothing."

The oppressor knows that the primary reason we do nothing is because we have lost any hope of making a difference. It is not that we lack power, compassion, courage or knowledge. Rather, we lack a sense of hope that allows us to take what we have into the fray. By sheer inertia, therefore, we lend our own weight to the downward cycle of despair. Our lack of hope keeps us from the front lines of engagement. And our absence only makes the oppressor look stronger, compounding our own despair and that of those who might otherwise be prepared to fight.

But as faithful Christians through the ages have demonstrated, we don't have to be this way. We have access to a hope that changes everything. Great people of the faith—William Wilberforce and Dr. Martin Luther King Jr.—and lesser-known giants like Dr. Bushnell and Rev. Murphy changed their communities, their nation and their world because they found the hope to seek justice.

MY HOPE IS IN GOD

Where did they find such hope? Where can we find such hope today? Where can we find a hope solid enough for action when we are surrounded by injustice? I don't know where others find their hope, but I have found mine where Wilberforce, King, Bushnell, Murphy and the ancient psalmist found theirs: I have put my hope in the Word of God (Psalm 119:147).

As one who has with his own hands sorted through the remains of thousands of slaughtered Tutsi corpses, as one who has heard with his own ears the screams of boys being beaten like dogs by South African police, as one who has looked with his own eyes into the dull, blank stares of Asian girls abused in brutal ways, I hope in the Word of God. For in the Scriptures and in the life of Jesus Christ, I have come to know God—my Maker, the Creator of heaven and earth, the sovereign Lord of the nations. It is through his Word that God reveals his character, and it is God's character, and God's character alone, that gives me hope to seek justice amid the brutality I witness.

This hope is not cheap, nor is it easy. In a genuinely fallen world Jesus offers us neither cheap grace nor cheap hope. But it is a hope honest enough to contend with the ugly oppression of our world, and it has power to prevail against the worst that hell can bring to earth.

Make no mistake: nothing challenges one's faith and hope in God like the rank evil of naked injustice. And nothing short of the authoritative, divine Word of God will withstand its withering scorn. Every Christian worldview, Western ideology and personal conviction ultimately will be obliterated by the painful questions posed by harsh oppression—unless bolted soundly and solely to the Word of God. As Katherine Bushnell, the courageous champion against the brutalities of forced prostitution, once wrote: "We are mistaken if we think that we can get along with slovenly and incomplete knowledge of the Bible. No amount of spiritual experience, or even the Spirit's help and instruction, will take the place of the *study* God requires us to put upon His Word."[1]

Do we know the Word of God like that? What do we know about the nature of the God who rules the earth and holds our eternal destiny? What do we know about how he feels about injustice, about the downtrodden and about us Christians? Scripture offers answers for these and other questions, but they are rarely easy in their deepest applications, nor are they without mystery or even sorrow this side of heaven. But God has given us the words of hope. This is no small gift; for it is hope, more than anything else, that we need.

FOUR TRUTHS ABOUT GOD'S CHARACTER

Amid a world of injustice, oppression and abuse, we can know some simple truths about God if we study his Word. No matter what the circumstances, we can depend on what he has revealed about himself. In regard to injustice our heavenly Father bids us to trust in four solid truths about his character.

- God loves justice and, conversely, hates injustice.
- God has compassion for those who suffer injustice—everywhere around the world, without distinction or favor.
- God judges and condemns those who perpetrate injustice.
- God seeks active rescue for the victims of injustice.

These four truths are deceptively easy to state, but in a world like ours they often seem hard to believe and even harder to live by. Jesus, however, desperately wanted us to know that the truth will make us free and equip us to stand firm amid evil.

In this chapter we will see what the Scriptures say about the first of these truths—that God is a God of justice. Chapters five, six and seven show how the remaining three truths offer us hope and empower us to act against injustice.

JUSTICE: THE RIGHT EXERCISE OF POWER

The centerpiece of our hope is the revelation from the Almighty that he is a God of justice. As the prophet Isaiah declared, "The Lord is a God of justice. / Blessed are all who wait for him!" (Isaiah 30:18). Justice is fundamental to the holiness of God. "For I, the Lord, love justice," declares our Maker (Isaiah 61:8).

But what does this mean? What does God mean when he says he is a God of justice? What is "justice" anyway?

Before we seek some useful answers to these questions, one caution might be helpful. It would be ironic if in our pursuit of hope we immediately lost our way in the quagmire of semantics. In my over-educated experience few questions have generated more heat and less light than the inquiry into the "true" meaning of justice. If by our inquiry into the meaning of justice we are looking for the definition of a magic word, we will be most disappointed.

I remember as a boy of nine or ten being detained for some minor indiscretion during recess in my school library. There I discovered the wonderfully obese Oxford English Dictionary. I had looked up all the slang words I could think of when I began to discover where the writers seemed to be cheating. I found words like life, which they said meant "being," but when I looked up being, they just said it meant "life." I thought, How unhelpful.

What I had discovered, of course, is that although a dictionary is supposed to tell us the meaning of words, every word is defined only by other words. Life is a word, but a dictionary can tell us next to nothing about the "meaning of life." Likewise, a meaningful understanding of "justice" or of a "just God" does not emerge from a neat, all-purpose definition of the word *justice.*

Some of us grow so frustrated by the fact that something as important and wonderful as justice cannot be reduced to a handy word formula that we begin to give up on justice—believing that something so vague cannot be so important or wonderful after all, even concluding that it probably doesn't actually exist. Similarly, some people find the meaning of life so elusive that they also give up on its pursuit. But we call this suicide. We should not be likewise tempted into despair about the pursuit of justice because of the limits of our vocabulary.

Having said that, what does it mean to say that ours is a God of justice? Is there anything that we can usefully understand about justice in the Bible? I believe there is. Fundamentally, justice has to do with the exercise of power. To say that God is a God of justice is to say that he cares about the right exercise of power or authority. God is the ultimate power and authority in the universe, so justice occurs when power and authority is exercised in conformity with his standards. In fact, in the Old Testament the Hebrew words for justice and righteousness are almost interchangeable, both indicating a conformity to God's standards of holiness or moral excellence. Ultimately, the sovereign God of the universe will establish justice over all peoples and spirits because at that time all power and authority in the cosmos will be exercised in accordance with his standards of moral purity.

So justice occurs on earth when power and authority between people is exercised in conformity with God's standards of moral excellence. There is always a distribution of power among people in every human society—some have more, some have less. All kinds of power is distributed: political, economic, social, moral, religious, cultural, familial, coercive, financial, intellectual and so on. To say that God is a God of justice is one way of saying that he is concerned about whether those who have power or authority over others are exercising it in accordance with his standards. When power is exercised in a way that violates those standards we call it *injustice.*

Injustice: The Abuse of Power

When does the use of power violate God's standards of moral excellence? What is injustice? Here again, no one-size-fits-all definition is available to us, but the biblical text does seem to provide a rather consistent, thematic definition. *Injustice occurs when power is misused to take from others what God has given them, namely, their life, dignity, liberty or the fruits of their love and labor.*

Typically the Bible defines its core concepts not so much with elaborate definitions but with stories: love (the good Samaritan), faith (Abraham's offering of Isaac), grace (the prodigal son). One of the best examples of the Bible's simple definition of injustice comes from the only teaching parable of the Old Testament—the prophet Nathan's story of the rich man who uses his power to steal the poor man's only lamb. Nathan told this story to describe to David the grave injustice he had committed in using his kingly power to take Uriah's wife and then to arrange Uriah's death.

Fundamentally, injustice is about the abuse of power. As it says in Ecclesiastes:

> Again I looked and saw all the oppression that was taking
>   place under the sun:
>
> I saw the tears of the oppressed—
>   and they have no comforter;
>   power was on the side of their oppressors. (Ecclesiastes 4:1)

Injustice is the strong using force and deceit to take from the weak.

When I worked for the police-misconduct task force of the U.S. Department of Justice, my job was to confront injustice committed by police officers—officers who abused their power to take what was not theirs from vulnerable citizens. One case dealt with a young teenage girl who had run away from her abusive home in the country to seek refuge on the streets of a big city in the South. One evening the young girl had gotten herself in a difficult situation on the street, and a police car pulled up to lend her a hand. She was nervous about getting in trouble for being a runaway, but being homeless she accepted the offer of the two policemen to put her up in a motel for the night. With a mixture of fear and hope that she might find safety with these two officers, she slid her small frame into the back of the squad car. When they arrived at the motel, one of the officers retrieved a room key, walked her to the door and escorted her in. But instead of leaving, the officer forced her onto the bed and raped her. After a while the other officer entered the room, and for a moment the girl thought that she had found a rescue. Instead, she found another rapist. When the two policemen finished, they put her back in the car and dumped her on the street.

This is injustice: the strong preying on the weak. These officers used the authority of their position to obtain her young trust. Then they used violence to rob her of what God had given her—her dignity as a child made in the image of God, the inviolability of her body as a temple of the Holy Spirit and her freedom to be known only by the soul mate chosen by her heart.

Such injustice is the plague of our earth. It occurs every day around the world. Immoral soldiers take people's dignity, freedom, health and well-being through beatings, torture and incarceration. Corrupt authorities and moneylenders rob children of their childhood, health, innocence and joy through abusive servitude. Wealthy landowners rob widows of their land, livelihood and dignity. Brutal bigots in positions of power take away the loved ones, the livelihood and even the very lives of those who are of a different race, religion, gender or culture.

As I wrote *Good News About Injustice* ten years ago, I read in the newspaper that more than sixty men, women and children of low-caste peasant families in India were murdered in their sleep by the private army of local high-caste landowners to enforce acknowledgement of their supremacy. And not much has changed. A 2007 report by Human Rights Watch details the depths of injustice still endured by members of India's lowest castes: women are raped and their perpetrators face no recourse; in some provinces, acquittal rates for accused perpetrators of racial violence are as high as 97 percent; police systematically fail to protect low-caste citizens from looters, arsonists and violent thugs who sexually assault and torture them.[2] The strong continue to abuse the weak.

The oppressors who commit these acts do not believe in God or in his need for justice. They think that no one cares and no one will interfere with their plans.

> In arrogance the wicked persecute the poor. . . .
> For the wicked boast of the desires of their heart,
>   those greedy for gain curse and renounce the LORD.
> In the pride their countenance the wicked say, "God will not
>   seek it out." . . .
> Their eyes stealthily watch for the helpless;
>   they lurk in secret like a lion in his covert;
> they lurk that they may seize the poor;
>   they seize the poor and drag them off in their net.
> They stoop, they crouch,
>   and the helpless fall by their might.
> They think in their heart, "God has forgotten,
>   he has hidden his face, he will never see it."
>   (Psalm 10:2-4, 8-11 NRSV)

How Does God Regard Such Suffering?

The Word of God tells us God has not forgotten injustice or the suffering of the victims. The psalmist asks:

> Why does the wicked man revile God?
>   Why does he say to himself,
>   "He won't call me to account"?
> But you, O God, do see trouble and grief;
>   you consider it to take it in hand.
> The victim commits himself to you;
>   you are the helper of the fatherless. (Psalm 10:13-14)

The oppressors could not be further from the truth: God does care. All of the biblical teaching about the God of justice can be summed up in a simple affirmation: God hates injustice and wants it to stop.

This truth is fundamental to the nature of our God, and the Bible makes clear that those who do not understand this aspect of God's holiness simply do not know God. "For I, the LORD love justice; / I hate robbery and iniquity" (Isaiah 61:8). God's interest in the abuse of power is not mild. Nor is he at all resigned to injustice in a fallen world. The use of power by the strong to abuse the weak strikes at the very core of his holy heart.

While we may have grown numb or oblivious to much of the brutal abuse in our world, God maintains a fresh, holy hatred of injustice. "God is a righteous judge, / a God who expresses his wrath every day" (Psalm 7:11). And

> The LORD examines the righteous,
> but the wicked and those who love violence
> his soul hates.
> On the wicked he will rain
> fiery coals and burning sulfur;
> a scorching wind will be their lot.
> For the LORD is righteous,
> he loves justice. (Psalm 11:5-7)

If we want to know God, to really understand him, we must come to understand his passion for justice and his gut-level indignation at the abuse of power.

This is what the LORD says:

> "Let not the wise man boast of his wisdom
> or the strong man boast of his strength
> or the rich man boast of his riches,
> but let him who boasts boast about this:
> that he understands and knows me,
> that I am the LORD who exercises kindness,
> justice and righteousness on earth,
> for in these I delight." (Jeremiah 9:23-24)

Just how well do we know our God? Our passion for justice and the defense of the weak will reflect it.

> "Did not your father . . .
> do justice and righteousness?
> Then it was well with him.
> He pled the cause of the afflicted and needy;
> Then it was well.
> Is not that what it means to know Me?"
> Declares the Lord. (Jeremiah 22:15-16 NASB)

Jesus certainly understood the character of his heavenly Father. Jesus saved his harshest words for the Pharisees who claimed great knowledge of God but neglected "the more important matters" of God's law: "justice, mercy and faithfulness" (Matthew 23:23). In the words of Solomon, "The evil do not understand justice, / but those who seek the Lord understand it completely" (Proverbs 28:5 NRSV).

I have never heard the point made more clearly than when I heard Joseph Stowell, former president of Moody Bible Institute, speak to the leaders of various Christian mission agencies. He began by describing how terrible it would be to grow up with a father who never told us what pleased him and what he expected of us. As much as we might love him, we could never have the joy of making him happy if he never told us what he liked and disliked, and therefore what he would like from us. Stowell went on to say how wonderful it was that our heavenly Father wasn't like that and what a blessing it is that he tells us precisely what makes him happy and what he expects from us. Stowell then directed our attention to the prophet Micah who set forth these requirements with crystal clarity:

> He has told you, O mortal, what is good;
> and what does the Lord require of you
> but to do justice, and to love kindness,
> and to walk humbly with your God? (Micah 6:8 NRSV)

Here we have set forth the heart of God, and the short list begins with justice.

CLAIMING THE HOPE: DESIRING AND DOING JUSTICE

Our God loves justice. This is the great hope that allows Christians to be a mighty force for justice in a tired, despairing world. For many of us, however, this hope in the character of a just God often lies forgotten and fallow in the neglected corners of our hearts. Unwittingly we become the hoarders of hidden hope.

We are like the widow in California I heard about who after her husband's death allowed her family to slide into financial ruin simply because she refused to believe what her lawyers told her about the fortune her husband had secreted away in a local bank. Over time the unemployed widow couldn't pay her bills, got evicted from her home and wandered about the county with her children—homeless, ill-fed and ill-clothed. They were destitute, all because she simply refused to believe in her inheritance. And there it sat, hundreds of thousands of dollars. The money was truly hers, but it could do her no good until she claimed it.

Likewise, our great inheritance of hope from a God of justice does us and the world no good unless we claim it. When we truly believe the testimony of the Scriptures and of Jesus Christ that our heavenly Father is a God of justice, we are equipped to be light in a dark world. The hope is truly ours; we just have to claim it. We have a great witness for a weary world, if we are simply willing to believe.

Blessed is he whose help is the God of Jacob,
    whose hope is in the LORD his God,
the Maker of heaven and earth,
    the sea, and everything in them—
    the LORD, who remains faithful forever.
He upholds the cause of the oppressed
    and gives food to the hungry.
The LORD sets prisoners free,
    the LORD gives sight to the blind,

the LORD lifts up those who are bowed down,
   the LORD loves the righteous.
The LORD watches over the alien
   and sustains the fatherless and the widow,
   but he frustrates the ways of the wicked.

The LORD reigns forever,
   your God, O Zion, for all generations.

Praise the LORD. (Psalm 146:5-10)

HOPE IN THE GOD
OF COMPASSION

The second fundamental truth that God wants us to count on in a world of injustice is that God has compassion for those who suffer injustice. Again this truth is infinitely easier to state than it is to believe—especially during the long stretches of silence when we picture the cries of the oppressed arcing out from the earth only to be lost in a dark, endless void that neither hears nor speaks.

We who know God, however, trust that he hears and cares, for he is a God of compassion. The cries of those who suffer injustice move him. We have hope because we know we serve such a God. "Our God is full of compassion," says the psalmist (Psalm 116:5). He is "the Father of compassion," says the apostle Paul (2 Corinthians 1:3).

The word *compassion* comes from two Latin words: *passio,* meaning "to suffer," and *cum,* meaning "with." To say that God has compassion for the victims of injustice is to say that he actually "suffers with" them.[1] At the root of God's compassion is the fact that he sees, witnesses, directly observes the suffering of the abused.

GOD'S PRESENCE AMID THE SUFFERING
When it comes to the brutality of injustice in our fallen world, there is no place for an all-knowing God to hide—a God who "has compas-

sion on all he has made" (Psalm 145:9). When the Israelites were oppressed in Egypt, God told Moses, "I have indeed seen the misery of my people in Egypt. I have heard them crying out because of their slave drivers, and I am concerned about their suffering" (Exodus 3:7). Today when the taskmaster beats the seven-year-old slave in Pakistan for not making his quota of bricks, God sees and hears. When the two police officers rape the runaway girl, he witnesses it. When mobs mercilessly hack to death thousands of Tutsi women and children, God suffers with them.

Over and over in the Scriptures God lets us know that he sees and hears the suffering of the oppressed. When the strong abuse their power to take from those who are weaker, the sovereign God of the universe is watching and suffering.

> If you take your neighbor's cloak as a pledge, return it to him by sunset, because his cloak is the only covering he has for his body. What else will he sleep in? When he cries out to me, I will hear, for I am compassionate. (Exodus 22:26-27)

> The LORD is a refuge for the oppressed. . . .
>   he does not ignore the cry of the afflicted. (Psalm 9:9, 12)

> "Because of the oppression of the weak
>   and the groaning of the needy,
> I will now arise," says the LORD.
>   "I will protect them from those who malign them."
>   (Psalm 12:5)

> To deprive a man of justice—
>   would not the Lord see such things? (Lamentations 3:36)

> Look! The wages you failed to pay the workmen who mowed your fields are crying out against you. The cries of the harvesters have reached the ears of the Lord Almighty. (James 5:4)

WHY GOD PASSIONATELY HATES INJUSTICE

Coming to understand God's compassion for the oppressed and the way he suffers with them has completely transformed my understanding of God. His real presence amid the horrendous injustice of our earth has finally allowed me to understand why God *hates* injustice so much. I have had to imagine what it would be like if I, like my God, had to watch, hear and witness every brutal act of injustice on the earth, every day.

In Rwanda, where I had to bear the burden of digging through the twisted, reeking remains of horrific mass graves, I tried to imagine, for just a minute, what it must have been like for God to be present at each of the massacre sites as thousands of Tutsi women and children were murdered. Frankly, the idea was impossible to bear. But the thought led me to imagine what it must be like for God to be present, this year, at the rape of all the world's child prostitutes, at the beatings of all the world's prisoners of conscience, at the moment the last breath of hope expires from the breast of each of the millions of small children languishing in slavery. As I would approach my God in prayer, I could hear his gentle voice saying to me, "Son, do you have any idea where your Father has been lately?"

I remember coming home from the killing fields of Rwanda and feeling a bit wounded by friends who seemed to have no interest in trying to understand where I had been and what I had seen. I doubt that I ever mentioned this to any of them. But I felt something of the shallowness of some of my friendships when, coming back fresh from an eyewitness experience of one of the most appalling events in human history, they did not express even ten minutes of curiosity about what I had seen. Given how unpleasant it all was, I really didn't blame them for their lack of inquiry. In fact, most of the time I didn't like talking about it very much.

But those closest relatives and friends who really wanted to know me wouldn't let me get away with keeping the experience to myself. They wanted to understand where I had been, what I had seen and how I had been touched. They knew that they could never understand the deepest part of me if they didn't have some understanding of the hard things I had seen.

Likewise if we really want to know God, we should know something about where he has been—and what it has been like for him to suffer with all those who are hurting and abused. No one will ever *really* know what it was like for me to interview all those orphaned massacre survivors in Rwanda or to roll back a corpse in a Rwandan church and find the tiniest of skeletons under the remains of a mother who had tried to protect her baby with her own body. I would never expect people to totally understand. God doesn't expect this either. He knows that we can never comprehend the smallest fraction of the oppression and abuse that he has had to witness. But we can know him better if we try to understand something about his character and experience as the God of compassion—the God who suffers with the victims of injustice.

If nothing else, it will help us understand why the God of justice *hates* injustice and wants it to stop. If we had to see it and hear it every day like our God does, we would hate it too. To understand where the God of compassion has been is to begin to understand God's passion for justice. Justice, for our Lord and Savior Jesus Christ, is not a good idea, a noble aspiration, a theoretical satisfaction or an impersonal principle—it is his beating heart. He is the "man of sorrows, and familiar with suffering," who weeps with those who weep (Isaiah 53:3; John 11:33-35).

GOD'S BOUNDLESS COMPASSION

God's compassion for the victims of injustice extends to all people, all around the world, without distinction or favor. When it comes to loving the people of the world, God suffers under none of our limitations. He doesn't feel so limited in his resources of compassion that he must establish boundaries for his caring or hierarchies of people, races, communities or nations to love. Rather, as the psalmist writes, "The LORD works righteousness / and justice for all the oppressed" (Psalm 103:6). Indeed God seeks to establish justice "to save all the afflicted of the land" (Psalm 76:9).

The prophet Isaiah said that even the traditional enemy of Israel, the Egyptians, would one day cry out to God because of their oppression under foreign rulers, and he would hear their prayer:

> It will be a sign and witness to the LORD Almighty in the land of Egypt. When they cry out to the LORD because of their oppressors, he will send them a savior and defender, and he will rescue them. So the LORD will make himself known to the Egyptians, and in that day they will acknowledge the LORD. (Isaiah 19:20-21)

God never cuts himself off from those who cry to him in their suffering.

CLAIMING THE HOPE: EXTENDING A CHRISTLIKE COMPASSION

In my natural state my capacity for compassion and love begins with me and proceeds out (or not) to various concentric circles of human relationships with a decreasing fervency. I have a lot of compassion for my family, but by the time my compassion gets out to the remotest concentric circle where people in strange, faraway countries live, I usually don't have much left. Granted, this is quite understandable. The limitations of my mind, let alone the limitations of my heart, do not allow me to embrace everyone in the world in the same way that God does. It seems quite impossible for me to feel the same compassion for people with whom I share very little in common as I do for those with whom I share the same neighborhood, workplace, community, school or country.

While this is quite natural and quite human, it's not particularly godly. Of course, we will never manifest God's all-encompassing love for all people around the world, but the extent to which our compassion extends beyond our immediate circle is the extent to which we are loving more like God and less like our carnal selves. While we can never love the broad world as God does or even love our dearest loved one the way God does, we can at least agree on the ideal toward which we should seek to grow.

While it seems more natural to have compassion for those closest to us, we won't find in the Bible where Jesus asked us to have more compassion for our immediate neighbors or our compatriots than for anyone else. I believe he understands our tendency to do so but is probably eager for us to reach out, as we are able (or as we seek his enabling), beyond our carnal limitations, prejudices, cultural mythologies and convenient stereotypes. Jesus calls us to be witnesses of his love, truth, salvation, compassion and justice "in Jerusalem [at home], and in all Judea and Samaria [nearby], and to the ends of the earth" (Acts 1:8).

Again this is the unique, biblical hope that Christians can offer to a world groaning under the heartache of injustice and oppression: God has compassion on the victims of injustice all over the world, among all people, without favor or distinction. We will, through our acts of compassion, give witness to our belief that what the Bible says is true, or not.

HOPE IN THE GOD
OF MORAL CLARITY

The Bible tells us that the God of justice has compassion for the victims of injustice, and we find hope in this truth. The Bible also tells us how God regards the perpetrators of injustice, and in this there is hope as well. We do not have a God who cannot distinguish between justice and injustice. Rather, Scripture makes wonderfully and dreadfully clear that God judges and condemns those who perpetrate injustice. Quite simply, our holy God has a burning wrath for those who use their power and authority to take from those who are weak.

GOD'S SEVERE HOLINESS

God's wrath is out of fashion. It's not something that we hear about, talk about or even think about. Like animal sacrifices, God's intense and severe anger toward sin strikes us as rather primitive—perhaps appropriate for dense, uncivilized, ancient peoples—something that God has gotten over. As J. I. Packer has observed, such a view probably comes from our habit of "following private religious hunches rather than learning about God from His own Word."[1]

If we truly want to know God, we must endeavor to understand the holy God who has made himself known in Scripture, the God who cannot accommodate himself to the sin of injustice, who can't get used to it, who continually suffers with those who are brutalized in body and spirit by the arrogance of humans. As J. I. Packer has again helpfully commented:

> No doubt it is true that the subject of divine wrath has in the past been handled speculatively, irreverently, even malevolently. No doubt there have been some who have preached of wrath and damnation with tearless eyes and no pain in their hearts. No doubt the sight of small sects cheerfully consigning the whole world, apart from themselves, to hell has disgusted many. Yet if we would know God, it is vital that we face the truth concerning his wrath, however unfashionable it may be, and however strong our initial prejudices against it. Otherwise we shall not understand the gospel of salvation from wrath, nor the propitiatory achievement of the cross, nor the wonder of the redeeming love of God. Nor shall we understand the hand of God in history.[2]

In fact, the knowledge of God's great anger toward and condemnation of injustice is what gives me hope to seek justice in this world. Standing with my boots deep in the reeking muck of a Rwandan mass grave, where thousands of innocent people have been horribly slaughtered, I have no words, no meaning, no life, no hope if there is not a God of history and time who is absolutely outraged, absolutely furious, absolutely burning with anger toward those who took it into their own hands to commit such acts.

In honest humility I understand that as long as I am a member of the human race, I have within me the same base impulse of hatred and violence toward my neighbor, and that I also tremble as a sinner before a holy God. But it is in view of this severe holiness that I come to glimpse the awesome and mysterious mercy of a God who stands ready to forgive not only me but also the genocidal killers of Rwanda. A cheap forgiveness it is not, for it was purchased by God with the life of his own Son.

THE ABUSE OF POWER IS SIN

God's severe judgment flows out of his love for the victims of injustice and from the simple fact that injustice is sin. I, in my humanness, have a way of complicating injustice. I can talk about the abuse of power, especially by government officials, as politically immature, excessively authoritarian, bad policy, real politick and so on. But according to the Bible God takes the abuse of power personally—and he calls it sin. As the prophet Amos declared to the elite of Israel who were abusing their power:

> I know how many are your offenses
>   and how great your sins.
> You oppress the righteous and take bribes
>   and you deprive the poor of justice in the courts. (Amos 5:12)

With the possible exception of idolatry, we are hard-pressed to find any other category of sin for which God's anger burns so bright. We are accustomed to hearing of God's hatred for idolatry, the very denial of who he is as God, but we may be surprised to find that God's hatred of injustice is every bit as passionate. The Bible teaches that everyone "who oppresses the poor shows contempt for their Maker" (Proverbs 14:31). The police officer who beats and robs the orphan, the trafficker who forces little girls into prostitution, the jailer who tortures his detainee—all show contempt for or "insult" (NRSV) the very God of the universe who made the orphan, the little girl and the prisoner.

The prophet Ezekiel makes clear that those who worship idols and those who abuse their power to take from others call down on themselves the most severe holy anger.

> There is a conspiracy of her *princes* within her like a roaring lion tearing its prey; they devour people, take treasures and precious things and make many widows within her. Her priests do violence to my law and profane my holy things; they do not distinguish between the holy and the common; they teach that there is no difference between the unclean and the clean; and they shut

their eyes to the keeping of my Sabbaths, so that I am profaned among them. Her *officials* within her are like wolves tearing their prey; they shed blood and kill people to make unjust gain. Her prophets whitewash these deeds for them by false visions and lying divinations. They say, "This is what the Sovereign LORD says"—when the LORD has not spoken. The people of the land practice extortion and commit robbery; they oppress the poor and needy and mistreat the alien, denying them justice.

"I looked for a man among them who would build up the wall and stand before me in the gap on behalf of the land so I would not have to destroy it, but I found none. So I will pour out my wrath on them and consume them with my fiery anger, bringing down on their own heads all they have done," declares the Sovereign LORD. (Ezekiel 22:25-31, emphasis added)

In this description of the grave sin of Israel, it is the people of public authority (the princes and officials) who are condemned by God for their abuse of power. They are described as wolves and lions—beings of great power—who have no moral excellence to direct their exercise of power. Rather, they simply tear at their prey for "unjust gain." They use their power to take from those who are weaker—to devour their lives, take their loved ones, plunder their treasure and precious possessions. Compounding this sin, the priests and religious officials do not use their influence to stand up for the poor and weak victims of injustice. Rather, they conspire with the oppressors, "whitewashing" their evil works, even dressing them up with false church talk about "the Lord" this and "the Lord" that.

RIGHTEOUS ANGER AGAINST INJUSTICE

God's response to such sin is not dispassionate. It is positively and fiercely angry.

We should not, of course, imagine God being angry like we are—irrational, disproportionate and rooted in fear. For unlike us he does not sin in his anger. But neither should we imagine that God shares our emotional casualness about the suffering of those who are brutalized by the abuse of power in our world. As we might feel about anyone who terrorized our child before our eyes, so we might imagine God's passionate response to those who abuse the people made in his image.

Of course, as Packer points out, God's response is unlike ours in that his indignation is always righteous, always judicial and always accompanied by an offer of redemption for the repentant.[3] But we would be off the mark if we ever got used to an image of God that did not respond to every injustice in our world with a passionate indignation. Such an image would be based on our private hunches about a god who looks like us rather than on what God has chosen to reveal about himself.

In a world despairing under the weight of those who use their power to take from those who are weak, we have a message of hope about the sovereign God of the universe who takes sides, who gets angry, who knows right from wrong.

> But your iniquities have separated
>   you from your God;
> your sins have hidden his face from you,
>   so that he will not hear.
> For your hands are stained with blood,
>   your fingers with guilt. . . .
> The LORD looked and was displeased
>   that there was no justice.
> He saw that there was no one,
>   he was appalled that there was no one to intervene.
>   (Isaiah 59:2-3, 15-16)

> "Their evil deeds have no limit;
>   they do not plead the case of the fatherless to win it,
>   they do not defend the rights of the poor.
> Should I not punish them for this?"
>   declares the LORD.
> "Should I not avenge myself
>   on such a nation as this?" (Jeremiah 5:28-29)

This is what the LORD says:
"Administer justice every morning;
     rescue from the hand of his oppressor
     the one who has been robbed,
or my wrath will break out and burn like fire
     because of the evil you have done—
     burn with no one to quench it." (Jeremiah 21:12)

This is what the LORD says:
"For three sins of Israel,
     even for four, I will not turn back my wrath.
They sell the righteous for silver,
     and the needy for a pair of sandals.
They trample on the heads of the poor
     as upon the dust of the ground
     and deny justice to the oppressed." (Amos 2:6-7)

This is what the LORD Almighty says: "Administer true justice;
show mercy and compassion to one another. Do not oppress the
widow or the fatherless, the alien or the poor. . . . "
     But they refused to pay attention. . . . So the LORD Almighty
was very angry. (Zechariah 7:9-12)

Woe to you Pharisees, because you give God a tenth of your
mint, rue and all other kinds of garden herbs, but you neglect
justice and the love of God. You should have practiced the latter
without leaving the former undone. (Luke 11:42)

Everywhere in the Bible, teachers—Jesus, Moses, King David, the
prophets and the apostles—tell us that our God is a judge who knows
right from wrong and is passionate about the difference.
     Our postmodern mind is often uncomfortable with such a notion,
and not without good reason. We have seen many pretenders to the
throne of divine judgment—inquisitors, witch hunters, imperialists
and self-righteous bigots who know nothing of the Lord in whose
name they have so blithely gone about condemning, expelling and

crushing other people. We are terrified to see what fallible, arrogant humanity can do with the hard steel of the absolute standards of right and wrong. In our revulsion we have lost our love for a perfect, righteous, divine judge who defends the weak, the voiceless and the oppressed with precisely that—an iron sword of truth and perfect moral clarity. As J. I. Packer noted, this adverse reaction to evil is what is necessary for moral perfection.

> The modern idea that a judge should be cold and dispassionate has no place in the Bible. The biblical judge is expected to love justice, play fair and loathe all ill-treatment of one person by another. An unjust judge, one who has no interest in seeing right triumph over wrong, is by biblical standards a monstrosity. The Bible leaves us in no doubt that God loves righteousness and hates iniquity.[4]

CLAIMING THE HOPE: STANDING FAST WITH MORAL CLARITY

Let there be no mistake, evil and injustice thrive on moral ambiguity, equivocation, confusion and the failure to commit. Remembering that injustice is the abuse of *power,* we must know that injustice is strong, forceful, committed. In every case it will prevail against the uncertain, the unsure and the uncommitted.

As a boy I remember puzzling over a proverb of my football coach. He was teaching us how to tackle, and he told us that the best way to get hurt when tackling a big, strong running back was to protect ourselves. In other words, our natural reaction to the sight of a huge, helmeted fullback barreling toward us was to act defensively, but this would end up getting us hurt. Rather than throwing our entire body into the tackle with as big a head of steam as we could muster, we instinctively wanted to slow down the combined velocity of the collision and to make what contact we could by grabbing with outstretched arms.

Using such a cautious approach, we got slaughtered. Inevitably the tackler who tries slowing down gets run over, creamed, lunched. The

running back knows where he is going—the end zone. At the first
hint of a tackler's uncertainty, the running back knows that the best
way to get there is by literally running through his opponent.

   Oppressors also know where they are going, and they are committed. They know that feigning right and then feigning left can introduce moral uncertainty and that this puts them in a perfect position
to run right over their opponents. The Nazis succeeded by moving
about in a society paralyzed by a moral fog. It's hard to believe that
anyone could be morally confused about the Nazis. But Dietrich Bonhoeffer, the great Lutheran minister who was hanged by Hitler's Ge-
stapo for his failure to bow before Nazi idols, said that the failure of
German Christians to resist the Nazi rise to power stemmed from
their lack of moral clarity. "The great masquerade of evil," he wrote,
"has played havoc with all our ethical concepts."[5]

   At the point of moral challenge, Bonhoeffer said, the ones prepared to stand firm against injustice are those who put their trust in
God, the righteous judge of moral truth:

> Who stands fast? Only the man whose final standard is not his
> reason, his principles, his conscience, his freedom or his vir-
> tue, but who is ready to sacrifice all this when he is called to
> obedient and responsible action in faith and in exclusive alle-
> giance to God—the responsible man who tries to make his
> whole life an answer to the question and call of God.[6]

Here then is our hope. In a world where oppressors stand ready to
exploit every moral hesitation, equivocation and complexity, we serve
a God who responds to injustice with a blazing moral clarity and passionate commitment to what is right. In studying Scripture we can
recover the hope and beauty of a holy judge who stands four-square
with the victims of injustice.

HOPE IN THE GOD
OF RESCUE

An Action Plan

The missionaries and Christian service workers churches support around the world see some awful injustice in the communities they serve. At International Justice Mission we hear about it and see it when we meet with them.

Rescuing Rosa

Shortly before writing *Good News About Injustice,* I was in one of Manila's poorest neighborhoods meeting with the director of a center for abused and abandoned girls—a ministry supported by the Christian and Missionary Alliance Church. The director, a gentle Filipino woman in her late forties named Maria, gave me a tour of their small but clean and bright facility and introduced me to some of the thirty orphans and abused runaways who had found the shelter of Jesus' embrace within the center's walls.

Maria and Agatha, a social worker at the center, began to tell me the girls' stories. Agatha left the room to get some papers and came back to tell me about a girl named Rosa. Just thirteen years old, Rosa had given birth to a child a few months before. They let me hold the tiny, precious baby. Her name was May. According to Maria, when Rosa was only twelve, a man in the neighborhood raped her, and May was the child born from that rape. Worse, said Agatha, almost a year later, the man still walks the streets. Agatha sees the alleged rapist in her neighborhood when he stays with his girlfriend down the street.

"Did anyone report the crime?" I asked. "Oh yes," said Agatha and Maria, handing me the documents from the local court demonstrating that a proper complaint had been filed. The local prosecutor's preliminary hearing had led him to seek an arrest warrant from the court. In the file was the warrant—an order from the regional trial court ordering local law-enforcement officials to immediately arrest Rosa's alleged assailant. But as Maria, Agatha, Rosa and all the other girls at the center knew, the man still freely walked the streets. Officials had made no effort to arrest him, apparently because he was a family friend of the local police.

Maria and Agatha had pleaded with the police, and they even contacted the National Bureau of Investigation (the Philippines' FBI) for help. But days went by, weeks, then months, and nothing ever happened.

By the time I arrived at the center, Maria and Agatha had lost any hope of securing justice and lasting protection for Rosa. All the laws in the world will do no good if no one enforces them, and in this poor neighborhood in Manila there was no one to enforce the law for a girl like Rosa.

Under such circumstances, where can Rosa, Maria and Agatha find hope? What hope does God offer in his Word?

GOD'S AFFIRMATION OF ACTION

As we have seen, God makes three clear affirmations about himself in regard to injustices like this. First, he affirms that in Rosa's struggle for justice he stands on her side. He declares himself to be a God of justice who hates the way this man has used his superior physical power not to protect a vulnerable girl but to take from her what personal dignity and sanctity she had. Second, God affirms his compassion for her; he has suffered through this brutal injustice with her, he has heard her cry and sees her suffering. Third, God affirms that he condemns with holy anger this nightmarish act that has been perpetrated against her and that he is prepared in perfect righteousness to punish her assailant for such an act.

God also makes a fourth affirmation: he seeks active rescue for victims of injustice like Rosa. God not only stands at Rosa's side, suffers with her and condemns the assault, he also deeply desires that her assailant be brought to justice and that she be protected from such abuse.

According to Scripture, God's justice, compassion and righteousness move him to an active, real-world response. This is not a God who offers sympathy, best wishes or cruel character-building exercises. This is a God who wants evildoers brought to account and vulnerable people protected—here and now!

> Why does the wicked man revile God?
>> Why does he say to himself,
>>> "He won't call me to account"?
> But you, O God, do see trouble and grief;
>> you consider it to take it in hand.
> The victim commits himself to you;
>> you are the helper of the fatherless.
> Break the arm of the wicked and evil man;
>> call him to account for his wickedness
>> that would not be found out.
> The LORD is King for ever and ever;
>> the nations will perish from his land.
> You hear, O LORD, the desire of the afflicted;
>> you encourage them, and you listen to their cry,
> defending the fatherless and the oppressed,
>> in order that man, who is of the earth, may terrify no more.
>>> (Psalm 10:13-18)

God doesn't glibly spiritualize the suffering of injustice, for he himself has endured it. He knows that the lash is real, that the fist hurts, that torture kills and that injustice can so brutalize our spirit as to make us feel forsaken by the heavenly Father. God knows that, ultimately, lost souls need a Savior and that "our struggle is not against flesh and blood, but against the rulers, against the authorities, against the powers of this dark world and against the spiritual forces of evil in the heavenly realms" (Ephesians 6:12). But he also clearly knows that the powers of darkness and forces of evil can manifest themselves on this earth as real hunger, real nakedness, real imprisonment, real beatings and real injustice. And while never neglecting or subordinating spiritual needs, Jesus called his followers to respond to hunger with food, to nakedness with clothes, to imprisonment with visitation, to beatings with bandages and to injustice with justice (Matthew 15:32-38; 25:35-36; Luke 10:34; 11:42). As the apostle James wrote, "Suppose a brother or sister is without clothes and daily food. If one of you says to him, 'Go, I wish you well; keep warm and well fed,' but does nothing about his physical needs, what good is it?" (James 2:15-16).

Accordingly, our God seeks active rescue for the victims of oppression:

My whole being will exclaim,
   "Who is like you, O LORD?
You rescue the poor from those too strong for them,
   the poor and needy from those who rob them."
      (Psalm 35:10)

I know that the LORD secures justice for the poor
   and upholds the cause of the needy. (Psalm 140:12)

Sing to the LORD!
   Give praise to the LORD!
He rescues the life of the needy
   from the hands of the wicked. (Jeremiah 20:13)

The Spirit of the Lord is on me,
because he has anointed me . . .
to release the oppressed. (Luke 4:18)

This is good news! This is the armor of hope that allows us to do battle in an ugly world of injustice. From God's holy Word we come armed with four powerful affirmations: God is on the side of justice. God sees and cares. God condemns injustice. God seeks rescue for the victims.

HOW DOES GOD SEEK JUSTICE?

But sitting in Maria's office, holding May in my arms and handing Agatha back her worthless arrest warrant, all of this nice theology meets the real world. It is wonderful to know that God is on Rosa's side, that he cares for her, that he condemns such an assault and that he actively seeks to "secure justice for the poor and to uphold the cause of the needy." But Rosa's alleged rapist is being protected by corrupt local officials.

So Rosa could ask a perfectly legitimate question: If God seeks justice for the oppressed, how exactly does he do that? If, as Psalm 10 says, God helps the fatherless, defends the oppressed, "breaks the arm" of evil people and calls them to account for their wickedness—how does he do this? How is he going to do this for Rosa?

A fair question. Do we have an answer? I think we do, and it has everything to do with you and me.

Unless the work of seeking justice is a category of endeavor that is completely different from every other activity on earth that is important to God, the answer to the "how" question has something to do with what God's people do or don't do. If you think about it, two truths apply to everything that God wants accomplished on earth: (1) he could accomplish it on his own through supernatural power, but instead (2) he chooses for the most part to accomplish that which he can achieve through the obedience of his people.

God desires that the gospel of Jesus Christ be proclaimed throughout the earth, and he could accomplish this quite swiftly with an overwhelming trumpet blast from heaven that would leave no doubt about who is Lord. And yet God calls his people to be his ambassadors, to proclaim his good news to the nations. As Paul asked, "How, then, can they call on the one they have not believed in? And how can they believe in the one of whom they have not heard? And how can they hear without someone preaching to them?" (Romans 10:14). Of course, the cheeky answer would be to say, "Well, God could tell them directly." But clearly God has chosen a different plan. By some great mystery and enormous privilege, he has chosen to use his people, empowered by his Spirit, to complete this task. He simply does not have another plan. Indeed, "how beautiful are the feet of those who brings good news!" (Romans 10:15).

The same principle applies to healing the sick, feeding the hungry, clothing the destitute, sheltering the homeless. Through supernatural intervention God could meet all of these needs, yet he has given these tasks to his people. He gives us the great honor and privilege of being his instruments. In response to God's call, Christian ministries like Compassion International, World Relief and World Vision have fed millions of hungry children. Christian medical missions have brought sight to the blind and life to the dying all around the world. In the name of Christ, Habitat for Humanity has brought shelter to thousands of families across the globe. The Salvation Army has shared warm coats and the love of Christ with countless men and women shivering in the cold.

How does God proclaim the gospel and work on behalf of those in need? Clearly he does it through the obedience of his people. True, he has established economies and a fruitful earth to provide for the needs of humankind, and he has created natural physiological processes for healing the body. But when these fail and our neighbor stands before us hungry, sick, naked and vulnerable to the elements, through whose hands does God reach out to meet their needs and show his love? Ours. We are God's hands of mercy and love. Occasions certainly may arise when God intervenes in some utterly supernatural fashion that bypasses all human instruments, but overwhelmingly God chooses to perform those miracles he can through people who are obedient to his call.

So it is with justice. When governments and those whom God has placed in positions of power fail to protect those who are weak, God looks to his people to be his voice of judgment and his hands of rescue.

> So justice is driven back,
>> and righteousness stands at a distance;
> truth has stumbled in the streets,
>> honesty cannot enter.
> Truth is nowhere to be found,
>> and whoever shuns evil becomes a prey.
> The Lord looked and was displeased
>> that there was no justice.
> He saw that there was no one,
>> he was appalled that there was no one to intervene.
>> (Isaiah 59:14-16).

God declared to his people:

> Is not this the kind of fasting I have chosen:
> to loose the chains of injustice
>> and untie the cords of the yoke,
> to set the oppressed free
>> and break every yoke? (Isaiah 58:6).

WHO WILL SEEK GOD'S JUSTICE?

In the twentieth century Christians were quick to understand the ministry God called us to in preaching the gospel. In recent years we have begun to understand that we are to be God's hands in feeding the hungry, healing the sick and sheltering the homeless. But how many of us have thought that when it comes to seeking justice, rescuing the oppressed, defending the orphan and pleading for the widow, God must have some other plan, some other strategy that doesn't depend on his people?

As a million Christian Promise Keepers gathered in Washington, D.C., under the banner of "Standing in the Gap," I wondered how many of us had ever read the context in Ezekiel from which the phrase comes. The passage refers to God's search for a righteous witness amid the brutal abuse of power by government officials (covered up by corrupt religious authorities).

> Her [Jerusalem's] princes . . . devour people, take treasures and precious things and make many widows. . . . Her officials . . . shed blood and kill people to make unjust gain. . . . The people of the land practice extortion and commit robbery; they oppress the poor and needy and mistreat the alien, denying them justice.
>
> "I looked for a man among them who would build up the wall and stand before me in the gap on behalf of the land so I would not have to destroy it, but I found none." (Ezekiel 22:25, 27 29-30)

No thoughtful Christian would say, "Sure, Jesus wants his gospel preached, the hungry fed, the sick healed and the naked clothed, but that doesn't have anything to do with me." And yet many of us have been content to praise God as the God of justice, to extol his compassion for the weak and voiceless and to declare his promises to "rescue the life of the needy from the hands of the wicked" (Jeremiah 20:13)—all the while harboring a suspicion that God generally accomplishes these miracles with mysterious winds or vague, magical forces of history. Worse, viewing a world of injustice from a seat in the grandstand, we may be tempted to shake our fist at God, demanding to know why he's not harder at work blowing those mysterious winds or moving those magical, vague forces of history. Like the Israelites we often weary God with our words, saying, "Where is the God of justice?" (Malachi 2:17).

Meanwhile the Spirit of God stands on the playing field of history saying, "I looked for a person among them, but I found none." To paraphrase Isaiah, "The LORD looked and was displeased that Rosa received no justice. He was appalled that there was no one to intervene" (Isaiah 59:15-16).

There is no question that God grants justice. As Jesus put it, "he will *quickly* grant justice" (Luke 18:8 NRSV, emphasis added). The question is, will God find faith on the earth? Will he find his instruments of mercy and justice, his people, ready for service (Luke 18:1-8)?

Over time I have come to see questions about suffering in the world not so much as questions of God's character but as questions about the obedience and faith of God's people. Given the painful injustice that Rosa endured, it is no wonder that she may be tempted to despair as the psalmist did: "Why, O LORD, do you stand far off? / Why do you hide yourself in time of trouble?" (Psalm 10:1). But gradually it has occurred to me that the problem may not be that God is so far off; the problem may be that *God's people* are far off.

WORKING MIRACLES WITH GOD

A preacher once asked me (and the rest of his congregation) to consider a scene that has stayed with me ever since. He asked us to recall the story about the feeding of the five thousand. The disciples brought complaints about the hungry multitude to Jesus, and he responded compassionately by blessing the bits of food from a boy's lunch—five loaves of bread and two fishes. "Then he gave them to the disciples, and the disciples gave them to the people. They ate and all were satisfied" (Matthew 14:19-20). The speaker then asked us to imagine a scenario in which the disciples just kept thanking Jesus for all the bread and fish—without passing them along to the people. He asked us to imagine the disciples starting to be overwhelmed by the piles of multiplying loaves and fish surrounding them, yelling out to Jesus, "Thank you, thank you, thank you, thank you, thank you, thank you, thank you, thank you!"—all the while never passing along the food to people. And then beneath the mounting piles of food, the disciples even could be heard complaining to Jesus that he wasn't doing anything about the hungry multitude.

This simple illustration struck my heart deeply. How kind of Jesus to include the boy and the disciples in his miracle. Surely he could have done it differently. Surely he could have commanded the heavens to unload manna and quail right on top of everybody. But how beautifully he included the boy's tiny offering. Jesus (the Creator of all things seen and unseen) no more needed those five loaves and two fish than my wife and I needed our toddler children's "help" in baking cinnamon rolls for visitors. But what a wonderful, life-changing day for that boy to be part of Jesus' miracle. How fun for the disciples to go among the grateful, joyful multitudes—to be the hands dispensing Christ's supernatural power and love. How ridiculous, on the other hand, that they should imagine that the vast piles of bread and fish should be given to them for any other reason than to feed those who were in need.

So too with the ministry of God's rescue for the oppressed in the world. *How* does God rescue the life of the needy from the hands of the wicked? Overwhelmingly he does it through those who choose to follow him in faith and obedience. He doesn't need our "help," but he chooses to use us.

Looking at the millions of slaves in India or the thousands of child prostitutes in Asia or thousands of torture victims twisting and bleeding in the world's forgotten jail cells, we can say to God, "Thank you, thank you, thank you, thank you, thank you, thank you, thank you, thank you! Thank you for all the power, protection, freedom and justice you have granted us in sparing us from such fates. Thank you, thank you, thank you, thank you, thank you, thank you, thank you, thank you!"

Or we can ask, What have you given me, Father, that I might help those who don't have power, who don't have protection, who don't have freedom, who don't have justice?

GOD'S PLAN OF ACTION ~ us

This then is the earth-shattering truth with which God yearns to renew our minds and change the lives of those who suffer: The almighty

God of the universe is prepared to use *us,* his people, to seek justice, to rescue the oppressed, to defend the orphan and to plead for the widow. Concretely, he is prepared to use you and me to protect Rosa and others and to bring their oppressors to justice.

How? By using the gifts, resources, relationships, expertise and power that he has given us. The reason he has granted us these things is not merely for our joy (though great joy they rightly bring) but so that we might serve those who lack them.

How does God vindicate Rosa's cause? In her particular case God was prepared to use some of us at International Justice Mission.

GOD'S JUSTICE PREVAILS

When Maria, the director of the Christian center for abused and abandoned girls, referred the case to us, their sense of hopelessness was overwhelming. They had done everything they were supposed to do. They had gone through the trauma and humiliation of filing formal charges. Rosa and the eyewitness had given sworn statements. They had obtained a warrant of arrest for the rapist. They had pleaded with the local police to execute the warrant of arrest. They had even contacted a member of the National Bureau of Investigation to make inquires on their behalf. All to no avail.

When I met Maria at the center to hear their story, more than three months had passed since the court issued its warrant of arrest. Maria and Agatha had come to understand that the assailant was a family friend of powerful local officials and that by comparison they were nobodies.

There I sat, with the nobodies, holding a fading copy of an arrest warrant. But now I could see, really see, what the Bible was talking about. The mandate was always there, but the words had seemed vague and theoretical: "Seek justice, rescue the oppressed, defend the orphan, plead for the widow." Now they spoke very directly, very specifically to me: "Seek justice for Rosa. Rescue Rosa. Defend Rosa. Plead for Rosa."

Given our backgrounds, my colleagues and I knew how to do this. We tracked down her assailant and found out where he was hanging out. We got a photo of him and blew it up into a wanted poster. We obtained copies of the arrest warrant, the preliminary investigation by the prosecutor, the sworn statements and other relevant case documents. A Christian lawyer in Washington, D.C., volunteered his time to package all the materials properly and sent it directly to the commander of the Philippine National Police and to the specific judge who had ordered the arrest of the alleged rapist. Three hours after the national police commander received our package, Rosa's alleged assailant was arrested and behind bars.

Maria faxed to our offices a copy of the local newspaper with its banner headline: "International Letter Leads to Arrest of Rape Suspect." The article described the events of the past few months, concluding that Rosa and those who cared for her "must have surely heaved a sigh of relief, half-thankful that the suspect has been finally arrested. But were it not for a letter from abroad, they may not have anything to be thankful for at all."

We were elated, and we praised and thanked God for his faithfulness in answering our prayers and the prayers of the people at the center. It was awesome to pause for a moment and consider that God had answered those prayers, not through mysterious winds or forces of history but through us. He didn't *need* us, and the steps we actually took were rather elemental. But we were truly, tangibly the hands of God Almighty, the God of justice, as he expressed his compassion and love to Rosa. What an honor! What a privilege!

Indeed, since securing the arrest of Rosa's rapist—International Justice Mission's very first case—we have seen again and again that our God does indeed use his people to answer the urgent prayers of victims of brutal injustice. In 2001, International Justice Mission established a permanent field office presence in Manila, the Philippines, to stand for precious children like Rosa. Staffed by dedicated Philippine Christian professionals—lawyers, investigators and social workers—the office is making a real difference for these children. It is hard for me to fully express the depth of hope I see in all that God has empowered them to do for the "least of these," serving as Christ's hands and feet by bringing the protection of the Philippines' laws against rape, against sexual violence, against brutal abuse to those who urgently need an advocate.

The team has partnered with local authorities to bring tangible relief to hundreds victims of trafficking, sexual abuse and illegal detention; hundreds of precious children, created in God's own image, have known the dignity, the relief and the peace of the justice he intends for them. And perpetrators like Rosa's abuser are no longer free to act with impunity. Over the past several years we have seen dozens of perpetrators of violent abuse held accountable in Philippine court for their crimes.

We are seeing lives changed and hope restored, day by day. God has used the willingness of IJM's Philippine staff to bring peace and dignity to places of loss and despair. And quite incredibly the former victims themselves are now leading a movement of change and hope in their city, through a program called S.T.A.R.s (Standing Together to Advocate Rights), led by IJM Manila's aftercare team. The team empowers and trains former victims of abuse to serve as mentors for others who have faced violent oppression. When IJM Manila partners with local authorities to bring freedom to victims of sex trafficking, one of the first voices of hope the newly rescued girls hear is that of a S.T.A.R. mentor—someone who can come alongside with empathy and let the victims know that, truly, somehow, everything will be OK. I had the opportunity to attend a S.T.A.R.s gathering during a recent trip to the Philippines, and it was an incredible time of joy. I can think of few more powerful images of God's restorative power than of these incredible young women and men, who, as more than conquerors, lead the way to safety and healing for other children who have known their pain.

It's been more than ten years since a letter brought about the arrest of Rosa's perpetrator. I haven't lost the sense of awe that I had when I first saw God use his people to bring justice in her case. More than a decade later, I am amazed at all God does through his people to bring holistic healing and restoration to these victims he so greatly loves. His mercies are indeed new every morning.

THREE PROMISES OF GOD

Through Rosa's story—and the thousands of others like hers that we have seen and lived in Manila and around the world over the past decade—we can see three promises of God on which we base all our hope for bringing about justice: (1) Ours is a God of justice, a God who hates injustice and wants it to stop; (2) God desires to use his people as his instruments for seeking justice and rescuing the oppressed; and (3) God does not give his people a ministry that he won't empower.

Like you, perhaps, I am encouraged by the first promise—the knowledge that God is a God of justice. But frankly, when I look at the brutal and pervasive injustice in our world, the second promise—that he is prepared to use me to seek justice—strikes me as rather overwhelming. Perhaps it does for you as well. But then I consider this third promise, and it changes everything. *God does not call us to a ministry that he will not empower.* Period. And here is where we find real hope.

How pathetic it would be if God said, "Seek justice, rescue the oppressed, defend the orphan and plead for the widow—and good luck to you out there!" But sometimes we act as if that's precisely the way he works, suspecting that he calls us to a grand, godly, utterly impossible work in the world and then doesn't bother to show up. But of course this is not true. As John Perkins explained at a justice forum sponsored by International Justice Mission, Jesus promised that when he left the Holy Spirit would come and we would receive "power" to be his witnesses—witnesses to his gospel, his love, his mercy and his justice (Acts 1:8).

THE JOY IN DOING JUSTICE

Acting by God's empowerment doesn't mean that we will always be safe, that we will find the tasks before us easy or that we will triumph in ways we can always understand or measure. But from the bottom of my soul I believe that God has indescribable mysteries and miracles stored up for his people who seek justice in his name—miracles of a kind and quality that Western Christians, anyway, have not experienced in generations. Truly, "No eye has seen, no ear has heard, no mind has conceived what

God has prepared for those who love him" (1 Corinthians 2:9). I believe that God is prepared to show his faithfulness as the God of justice—through his people and to his own glory—in ways that perhaps only Esther and Gideon could begin to understand.

We will not see heaven come to earth or the world purged of injustice. But we have seen the God of justice being faithful. We have seen him "rescue the poor from those too strong for them" (Psalm 35:10). We have seen that he "secures justice for the poor and upholds the cause of the needy" (Psalm 140:12-13). If we simply and courageously make ourselves available to him, Jesus Christ himself will "release the oppressed" (Luke 4:18)—and we will know the extraordinary joy of watching him do it *through us*. Any childish doubt I clung to, any fear that God would not indeed empower us to do that to which he called us, has been put to rest by over a decade of evidence of God's remarkable faithfulness to us at International Justice Mission. Not to say there haven't been trials. We have met risks and defeats and disappointments, and we have seen how deeply fallen the world truly is. We have been "hard pressed on every side, but not crushed; perplexed, but not in despair; persecuted, but not abandoned; struck down, but not destroyed" (2 Corinthians 4:8-9).

In meeting with difficulties, we simply claim our God, the name of Jesus Christ and the truth of the holy Scriptures.

> For the eyes of the Lord are on the righteous
>   and his ears are attentive to their prayer,
> but the face of the Lord is against those who do evil.
>
> Who is going to harm you if you are eager to do good? But even if you should suffer for what is right, you are blessed. (1 Peter 3:12-14)

PART THREE

REAL-WORLD TOOLS
FOR RESCUING
THE OPPRESSED

ANSWERS FOR
DIFFICULT QUESTIONS

GOD AND INJUSTICE

Vulnerability in the face of an abusive oppressor occurs with different people in different ways every day—all around the world. The reality of these injustices poses some fundamental questions for those who claim to trust in the God of justice revealed in Scripture.

WHY DO SUCH INJUSTICES HAPPEN?

The first question we may ask is, *Why do massacres and other atrocities like Rosa's rape occur?* On one level this is the easiest question to answer.

I don't mean to be glib in stating this so simply, but I believe the reason these offenses occur is because people choose to indulge their selfish and brutal urges to dominate the defenseless. They have chosen to live in rebellion against the God of love and goodness who made them, and now they are left with nothing but their own sinful nature, or whatever you want to call it—the unrestrained will to power, the unmediated libido, the nausea of existence, misogynistic male aggression. Scripture graphically describes such people:

Their throats are open graves;
    their tongues practice deceit. . . .
Their feet are swift to shed blood;
    ruin and misery mark their ways,
and the way of peace they do not know.
    There is no fear of God before their eyes. (Romans 3:13-18)

If people have no respect for God, no love for their Maker, I would ask the question another way: Why *not* pillage, rape, persecute and murder? If it feels good, and they can get away with it, why not? If God is dead or does not exist, as these people believe, why aren't all things permitted? Why should they restrain themselves? Because it's *just wrong*? Because it's *not the way civilized people behave*? Because *what goes around comes around*? Because *they'll end up feeling terrible inside*?

Within tidy circles of properly socialized and reasonable people, such appeals can seem like they actually have the power to restrain people from doing what they otherwise feel like doing. But in the real world outside the philosophy seminar room, oppressors frankly don't care that you think it's *just wrong*. Who are you, they ask, to foist your random moral intuition on them? Who are you to tell them or the lords of the Third Reich what civilized people should and should not do? If what goes around tends to come around, then there's no moral problem, only a practical problem of making sure it doesn't come around to you. They think, *Fine, if being brutal makes you feel terrible inside, then don't do it. But it makes me feel powerful, alive, exhilarated and masterful, so quit whining—unless you want to try to stop me.*

This description of a dark Nietzschean world of self-will—a vacuum devoid of moral authority or spiritual resources for good—used to seem excessively melodramatic to me. But then I got out more. The world is truly full of brutal oppression because humans have rejected their Maker, the source of all goodness, mercy, compassion, truth, justice and love.

Personally, I do not have a difficult time understanding that without God I am as lost as the oppressor. When I don't depend on the

Holy Spirit moment by moment every day, I see the ugliness in me come out: selfishness, pride, insensitivity, anger, gossip, ingratitude, self-righteousness, self-deception, jealousy and covetousness, to name a few.

For most of us these latent forces of great sin are kept in check by various social and cultural restraints, but we should be under no illusions about what exists at the human core. Perfectly *ordinary* human beings are actually capable of being mass murderers. In Rwanda (to say nothing of Eastern Europe during the Holocaust) the killing was not performed by specially trained pathological killers but by ordinary people. When all restraints are released, farmers, clerks, school principals, mothers, doctors, mayors and carpenters can pick up machetes and hack to death defenseless women and children. And this happened in a nation where 80 percent of the citizens identified themselves as Christian. Unless we wish to cling to racist theories about Africans or mythologies of education or civilization (as in Germany in 1933), we must face the objective, historical facts of the matter. The person without God (or perhaps worse, the person without God but claiming "God," "Jesus," "Muhammad," whatever) is a very scary creature.

As I drafted *Good News About Injustice* in 1998, a columnist for the *Washington Post* was asking the same questions. After massacres in Algeria, during which an eight-year-old boy was nearly decapitated while having his throat slit, the columnist asked:

> What could an 8-year-old have done to warrant such a death? What could have been his crime, his ideology, his belief, his threat—and his threat to whom? What explains the murder of a child? Whatever the answer, it must be applied over and over again. The killing of children is an Algerian staple. In some villages, they have been hurled against walls. So, too, is the killing of the women and the aged—and, of course, of men. These people don't seem to be politically involved; nor are they members of the military or police. They are nothing more than peasants and yet they have been murdered by the thousands, often in ways so

gruesome as to be incomprehensible. In the first week of January [1998], as many as 1,000 people were killed in villages about 150 miles from Algiers. The savagery is such that you cannot believe human beings—as opposed to animals—are responsible.[1]

Fyodor Dostoyevsky would argue that the columnist insults animals when characterizing the work of unrestrained human nature as animal-like. In *The Brothers Karamazov*, the brother Ivan comments on the alleged atrocities of the Turks and Circassians

> who, fearing a general uprising of the Slav population, set villages afire, rape women and children, nail their prisoners to fences by their ears and leave them in that state until morning, when they hang them, and commit other atrocities that are hard to imagine. People often describe such human cruelty as "bestial," but that's, of course, unfair to animals, for no beast could ever be as cruel as man, I mean as refinedly and artistically cruel. The tiger simply gnaws and tears his victim to pieces because that's all he knows. It would never occur to a tiger to nail people to fences by their ears, even if he were able to do it.[2]

These are dark discourses on our underlying nature, but at the bottom of this black well is the answer to our hard question about why people like Rosa are oppressed—enslaved, raped, tortured, killed—and why they find no justice. In truth we live in an exceedingly dangerous world in rebellion against its Maker, a world filled with prideful, frightened, willful, violent people who have incrementally chosen to cut themselves off from the Creator's goodness, love, mercy and justice. As C. S. Lewis sums it up, this is the Fall of humanity: "Man is now a horror to God and himself and a creature ill-adapted to the universe not because God made him so but because he has made himself so by the abuse of his free will."[3]

WHY DOES GOD ALLOW INJUSTICE?
Of course, this answer readily begs another infinitely more difficult

question: *Why does God allow humans to so abuse their free will?* Why might God permit someone to hack another human to death? Why does God allow so much injustice in the world?

I believe I've heard most of the neat answers to these questions—a set of answers which in Christian circles often explode in a discussion like an emergency ejection seat, rescuing relieved passengers from a crash-and-burn confrontation with unpleasant mysteries. Frankly, the pat answers don't work, and the insensitivity that I have seen in myself and in others as we have addressed ourselves to Rosa's and others' pain has bordered at times on cruelty. Let's be honest. This is hard. As Irving Greenberg, a writer on the Holocaust, has said, "No statement, theological or otherwise, should be made that would not be credible in the presence of burning children."[4]

We must not be afraid, however, to descend all the way down into the dark well of truth until we find its hard bottom. For there in the dark bedrock, standing ankle deep in muck, we will nevertheless find hard stone underneath our feet—our first immovable foothold for the climb out. Our climb will not take us soaring into the heavens but may be just enough to get us out of the black well, up onto the ground, where we can walk to that place where God is calling us. As we climb, the Scriptures urge us to look for the footholds of humility, the cross, love and eternity.

FOOTHOLD 1: WE START WITH HUMILITY

The wisest and deepest Christian response to the question of why God permits such injustice has always begun with humility. Fifteen hundred years ago Salvian the Presbyter, one of the great fathers of the early church, confronted the question squarely and honestly: "Why does the whole world fall prey to powers for the most part unjust? Perhaps a rational and fairly consistent answer would be: 'I do not know.' For I do not know the secrets of God . . . . I am a man; I do not understand the secrets of God."[5] Job learned firsthand that for people to speak of the first-order motivation or design of the Almighty Creator God is to speak of what they don't understand, "things too wonderful" to know (Job 42:3). In the face of injustice we cannot presume to speak for God beyond that which he has revealed about himself, for even that which we know from God we know only "in part" (1 Corinthians 13:9).

FOOTHOLD 2: WE REMEMBER THE CROSS

Of course, this notion of a lofty, unknowable God who sits beyond the reach of my objections strikes me as infuriating. In the context of human suffering like Rosa's, I find no love for a God who sits on some serene, detached cloud of mystery rolling his eyes and exchanging if-they-only-knew smirks with the angels.

But then I remember Jesus, and I recall what my God, the one true God, is really like—the God of the cross. Even in the midst of the deepest human anguish, I remember why it is that I love Jesus and trust what he says. John Stott expresses my own convictions most beautifully:

> I could never myself believe in a God, if it were not for the cross. The only God I believe in is the One Nietzsche ridiculed as "God on the cross." In a real world of pain, how could one worship a God who was immune to it? I have entered many Buddhist temples in different Asian countries and stood respectfully before the statue of the Buddha, his legs crossed, arms folded, eyes closed, the ghost of a smile playing round his mouth, a remote look on his face, detached from the agonies of the world. But each time after a while I have had to turn away. And in imagination I have turned instead to that lonely, twisted tortured figure on the cross, nails through hands and feet, back lacerated, limbs wrenched, brow bleeding from thorn pricks, mouth dry and intolerably thirsty, plunged in God-forsaken darkness. That is the God for me! He laid aside his immunity to pain. He entered into our world of flesh and blood, tears and death. He suffered for us. Our suffering became more manageable in light of his. There is still a question mark against human suffering, but over it we boldly stamp another mark, the cross

which symbolizes divine suffering. "The cross of Christ . . . is God's only self-justification in a world such as ours."[6]

So when at times I flippantly challenge the Almighty as to why he allows horrendous suffering, I am pulled up in a shudder of humility as I recall that there is no measure of his creation's suffering that he has not been willing to bear himself. Indeed, I stand before a God whose thoughts—and sufferings—are too great for me.

Nevertheless, in all reverence it is right to ask, What, if anything, has God revealed about why he allows evil people to abuse those who are weak?

FOOTHOLD 3: WE RECOGNIZE THAT GOD DESIRES OUR LOVE, FREELY GIVEN

What we know "in part" is that in creating humankind, God would be satisfied with nothing less than a deep relationship of authentic love with each man and woman. He wants us to know the glory of being loved by him. He wants us to experience the glory of knowing him—*truly* knowing him. He wants us to experience the wonder of returning passionate, exultant, personal love to the Maker of the universe, the lover of our souls. The nature of such a relationship, however, requires that he also make us free *not* to love him, free *not* to know him—free to *reject* him and his Spirit.

Consequently, the unfathomable dignity which God has bestowed on each man and woman, the resplendent magnificence with which God exalted those whom he had made in his own image, requires that they be free to turn their backs on him. And as they have done so, all people, to varying degrees, have made themselves a horror—to themselves and to their fellow humans—redeemable only by the ultimate sacrifice of their Maker.

Looking at the human carnage and suffering wreaked by humanity's rebellion against God, we might think that God paid us an "intolerable compliment" in bestowing this "terrible gift of freedom."[7] We might argue with God as Dostoyevsky's Grand Inquisitor argued with Jesus: "You wanted their freely given love rather than the servile

rapture of slaves subdued forever by a display of power. And, here
again, you overestimated men."[8] But in contending so with God we
must be aware that we are arguing about the ultimate value of his
yearning to truly and deeply love us and to be loved by us—and we
are doing so without the benefit of eternity. It's somewhat like arguing whether it's worthwhile to go see the Grand Canyon based on
what one has seen of a drainage ditch in one's yard.

Foothold 4: We Embrace the Hope of Eternity

I do not lightly invoke eternity as a foothold for climbing out of our
paralyzing question about why God allows injustice, but as a convinced Christian, invoke it I must. I believe I have seen, more than
most, something of the magnitude and depth of the pain endured by
the innocent of this earth. I have stood within the walls of a Rwandan
church piled knee high with slaughtered innocence, evidence all
around of the unanswered cries for mercy they raised to God and
humankind. And I can honestly say that, this side of eternity, I walk
away from such a sight with no meaning, no hope, no reason for going on. No words—at all.

But Jesus, whom I have come to trust and respect, asks me to understand that eternity changes everything. He asks me to conceive of
a world outside of time where even those who have lost brothers or
sisters or mother or father or children will receive back a hundred
times as much in the life eternal (Matthew 19:29). He asks me to try
to picture a world beyond the present so glorious in its beauty, goodness and rightness that I should "leap for joy" (his words, not mine)
when I suffer the hatred, exclusion, insults and rejection that accompany the path to such a place (Luke 6:22-23).

According to the apostle Paul, "Our present sufferings are not
worth comparing with the glory that will be revealed in us" (Romans
8:18). Such a dismissive attitude toward earthly suffering might ring
hollow from most people. But I would leave it to more hearty souls to
challenge the credibility of a man who had not only been granted a
peek at the world to come but in this world had been flogged five

times with thirty-nine lashes, beaten three times with rods, nearly stoned to death and imprisoned falsely more times than one could count (2 Corinthians 11:23-28; 12:3-4).

I have every sympathy for those who look into Rosa's eyes or at the lifeless forms piled up in Rwanda and say that nothing in the next world can compensate for the hurt. But I don't honestly know that that's the case.

One could say that the notion of eternity is just pie in the sky, but as C. S. Lewis observed, either there is pie in the sky or there is not.[9] The Scripture's claims about the consolation of eternity are either true or not. Either death will be a black, mocking insult to the injury of life, or we will hear

> a loud voice from the throne saying, "Now the dwelling of God is with men, and he will live with them. They will be his people, and God himself will be with them and be their God. He will wipe every tear from their eyes. There will be no more death or mourning or crying or pain, for the old order of things has passed away."
>
> He who was seated on the throne said, "I am making everything new!" (Revelation 21:3-5).

If such claims are true, it just might change everything. If there were no pie in the sky, Jesus said, "I would have told you" (John 14:2). But if Jesus does not rightly claim absolute divine authority for such statements, then not only is he not a good teacher, he is a cruel liar or a delusional psychopath of the first order. Moreover, if there is no pie in the sky, I frankly don't have any earthly hope that is not immediately crushed under the weight of the empirical data of despair around me.

The pie in the sky is not, for me, a reason to escape from the needs of our world; rather, it offers the nourishment of spirit that has empowered Christians through the ages to serve those needs tirelessly, even unto death.

In the months after I returned from Rwanda, every time I entered a church service I found my mind subconsciously driven to horrible calculations about what it would take, and how long it would take, to murder the entire congregation with machetes—as it happened in scores of churches across Rwanda. I hated thinking it, but there it was. Every time this left me looking to the ceiling, trying to blink back the welling tears so they would not stream down my face. The image of the broken waste of all those Rwandan women and children would overwhelm me, and yet, through nearly clenched teeth I would find my inner soul testify in the words of a hymn that would not stay down: "Crown him the Lord of life / Who triumphed o'er the grave / Who rose victorious to the strife / for those he came to save / His glories now we sing / Who died and rose on high / Who died eternal life to bring / And lives that death may die."[10]

By the grace of God I believe this testimony is true. Somehow, I find the hope of eternity "trustworthy and true" (Revelation 21:5).

When falling into the well of doubt about why God permits injustice on the earth, I scrape my way out by standing first on the limits of my human knowledge. I grab on to the character of the compassionate Creator revealed on the cross. I step up to the mysterious foothold offered by the terrible gift of free will, and lunge up to the dusty ground onto the hope of eternity.

Brushing myself off, I finally get to my feet and face the task before me—preparing my mind and heart to help those like Rosa who suffer because of injustice.

ANATOMY OF INJUSTICE

VIOLENCE AND DECEPTION

We may have experienced occasions when we feel the Spirit of God stirring our hearts to help those who suffer under oppression, but then we immediately feel the undertow of very practical questions. What exactly can we do? How can we actually make a difference? What practical steps are we supposed to take?

These questions leap from our hearts with eagerness, but they most often limp back to us so devoid of practical answers that the inspiration is almost impossible to sustain. Over time a suspicion takes root that incidents of injustice in our world are actually more akin to natural disasters—tragic and sad, but not something we can do much about.

G. K. Chesterton once wrote that "the Christian ideal has not been tried and found wanting; it has been found difficult and left untried."[1] Something similar could be said about the biblical call to seek justice in the world. It's not so much that we have vigorously pursued the call and found God unfaithful in his promises but that we have tended to relegate such matters to the category of things too difficult for us. To be honest, there are any number of projects in my life that I have measured from afar and bracketed as out of my league, silly things like programming the VCR and running a marathon, and deep things like "love your enemies and pray for those who persecute you" (Matthew 5:44).

In the unconscious triage of life in which we sort our challenges into the doable, the conceivable and the incurable, most of us have put injustice in the last category. And understandably so. What in the world is more difficult? What is harder? Whether they are soldiers who murder the innocent, police who torture their prisoners or violent thugs who steal from the poor—violent and deceitful oppressors intimidate us.

DISSECTING INJUSTICE

Nothing is more intimidating than that which we do not understand. And it might be fair to acknowledge that the sin of injustice—the abuse of power—has not always been a well-developed theme of our devotional life. In the hundreds of sermons and Bible lessons we have heard (or preached), how many have dwelled on the sinful abuse of power? The problem is not that injustice has not been a *primary* theme of our devotional life; it has rarely found a place even in our background knowledge of God's Word.

It would strike us as odd if we couldn't really explain what the Bible said about love, forgiveness, idolatry or adultery. If we could only vaguely say that God was generally in favor of the first two and opposed to the latter two, we might consider ourselves mere infants in Christ, feeding only on the milk and not the meat of the Word (1 Corinthians 3:1-2). Yet often our best summation of biblical teachings on justice might run something like this: "God's fair. The world's not. And it's all going to get sorted out in the end." As we might suspect, this is rather thin soup; it just doesn't equip us for dealing with the real world.

Imagine, for instance, that you and I are sitting together in an adult Sunday school class listening to a missionary, home on furlough, as she describes her work with street kids in Manila. We ask her to share what is most urgently on her heart, and she does. She is worried, she says, about three young girls whom she has been getting to know in her ministry. They are between the ages of twelve and fourteen, and they used to come around regularly for a hot meal and to hear Bible stories with the other street children. But she hasn't seen them for weeks. Tragically, when she asked around her ghetto neighborhood she learned that the girls had been abducted into a brothel and were being forced to serve as prostitutes. She wanted to talk to the police about it, but then she learned that the police were running the brothel. Her heart is breaking for these girls, but she doesn't know what to do. She asks us, "Do you have any words of encouragement?"

Somehow in the face of her story it just doesn't seem adequate to say, "Heh. God's fair. The world's not. It will all get sorted out in the end." She just might reply, "Yes, but I love these girls. What am I supposed to do? These children are my neighbors; what would the good Samaritan do?"

As our Sunday school class tries to formulate a godly and loving response, what Scripture would immediately come to mind—verses that tell how God views this situation? What sermons would we recall—sermons about the promises God makes in his Word about such situations? What Bible study lessons would spring to mind—teaching that would help us encourage our missionary about what should be done? How long could our Sunday school class discuss this situation before running out of solid biblical material? Where I come from, most of us simply would express horror at the situation and recommend prayer. But we might struggle to articulate what we should pray for and what Scriptural truths we should base our prayers on.

Of course hundreds of Scriptural references apply to this missionary's situation. It's not that we are not devoted to God or are forgetful of the Bible or are uncaring. Rather, most of us simply don't have ready access to the biblical tools that God intends us to carry as his disciples into an unjust world.

But, praise God, this is a problem with a solution. It is possible to begin moving out of the paralysis of despair simply by coming to a better understanding of what lies in the darkness. If we ask God to give us an understanding of injustice, he will grant our prayer and transform us in the process. As the Scriptures promise:

> The LORD gives wisdom,
>   and from his mouth come knowledge and understanding.
> He holds victory in store for the upright,
>   he is a shield to those whose walk is blameless,
> for he guards the course of the just
>   and protects the way of his faithful ones.
> Then you will understand what is right and just
>   and fair—every good path.
> For wisdom will enter your heart,
>   and knowledge will be pleasant to your soul.
> Discretion will protect you,
>   and understanding will guard you.
> Wisdom will save you from the ways of wicked men,
>   from men whose words are perverse,
> who leave the straight paths
>   to walk in dark ways,
> who delight in doing wrong
>   and rejoice in the perverseness of evil,
> whose paths are crooked
>   and who are devious in their ways. (Proverbs 2:6-15)

Instead of confronting injustice from a blurry distance as something dark, vague and overwhelming, we can examine it, dissect it, lay bare its component parts and demystify its power. Therefore our initial inquiry is a simple diagnosis of the problem: Why is seeking justice so hard?

TWO STORIES OF INJUSTICE

Samson Gahungu is from Burundi, a small African country nestled between Rwanda, Tanzania and the Democratic Republic of the Congo (formerly Zaire). At the tender age of thirteen, he says, "I confessed my sins and obtained salvation." Eventually God's call on his life led him to become the leader of the Evangelical Quaker Church in Burundi. He became a teacher and administrator at a Quaker school in northern Burundi and is the proud father of nine children. Samson's country is torn by the same ethnic conflict between Hutus and Tutsis that erupted into genocide in Rwanda. Samson is a Hutu, but he has worked for unity in his country as head of the peace and reconciliation department of the Burundi Council of Churches. In February of 1996, however, leaders of the Tutsi-dominated military regime sent soldiers to arrest Samson and hundreds of other prominent Hutu leaders throughout the country. Samson was transported to the capital city of Bujumbura and thrown in prison on charges of genocide, flowing from ethnic violence that occurred several years before. Without an opportunity to confront the charges against him or to defend himself, Samson languished in a horrifically overcrowded prison for more than a year and a half.

In a letter from prison Samson described his ordeal:

> To me, prison is stagnation; handcuffed in a cell; crouching in a tiny space, behind walls and bars where you can only see the sky; doing everything in one half-lit, unventilated room, a room enclosed on six sides—fortified walls, roof and floor smoke blackened and filth-stained; deprivation of family and friends; a stream of endless thoughts, monotony, worry, discouragement, loneliness, sickness, hunger, thirst and discomfort.[2]

Perhaps even more painful than these deprivations was Samson's heartache for his wife, who, sick with malaria, was left alone to care for their nine children.

> Recently she [Samson's wife] brought our last born (a three-year-old boy) to visit me. I was extremely happy to see him again, though he was terrified at seeing me in the inmates' uniform behind iron bars. My happiness was mixed with sorrow, because my wife is suffering with malaria. Further she left our children wandering around because of prevailing uncertainty which

maintains them in permanent displacement. Furthermore, they have lost all their belongings in those nomadic-like conditions. They have lost weight because they are homeless and the sadness resulting from our separation oppresses them too much.[3]

Though suffering these overwhelming trials, Samson wrote: "Even though my burden is too heavy, I know that my Lord loves me. I carry my cross imitating the way Jesus carried my sins at Calvary."[4]

Later there was a change in leadership of the military regime, and International Justice Mission was able to make inquiry on his behalf. Finally the Burundi government dropped all charges against Samson and released him to his family.

But as the Jesus of Calvary knows well, Samson and his family suffered deeply under this abuse of power by authorities. Jesus knows all about it because he too was falsely arrested on trumped-up charges and subjected to abuse. Looking at both of their stories will help us dissect the dynamics of injustice.

THE TWO COMPONENTS OF INJUSTICE: VIOLENCE AND DECEPTION

Wherever we find the perpetration of injustice, we will find two components: violence and deception. They may work separately or in combination. Scripture repeatedly affirms this principle.

His [the wicked man's] victims are crushed, they collapse;
    they fall under his strength. (Psalm 10:10)

The wicked draw the sword
    and bend the bow
to bring down the poor and needy. (Psalm 37:14)

The mouth of the righteous is a fountain of life,
    but the mouth of the wicked conceals violence.
        (Proverbs 10:11 NRSV)

The scoundrel's methods are wicked,
    he makes up evil schemes

> to destroy the poor with lies,
>
>   even when the plea of the needy is just. (Isaiah 32:7)

Quite naturally, most of us feel pretty uncomfortable with violence and deception. We don't know much about them, and frankly we don't want to. When was the last time we attended or led a Bible study about violence? When was the last time we heard or preached a sermon series on the way powerful people use deception to hurt those who are weak?

Yet any serious understanding of injustice requires a serious study of these two rather unattractive topics. As a result, even though the Bible repeatedly discusses injustice and oppression, and calls us to be engaged in a godly struggle against these sins, these subjects can feel very foreign to our devotional life as Christians. So although we suspect that injustice is a *major* topic for God, we are so ill-equipped to confront it that we begin to believe that it could only be meant as a *minor* topic for us.

Of course it need not be so. A little understanding can go a long way toward dispelling the intimidating mystique of injustice, and fortunately the Bible is full of teaching material. We can, for example, return to the arrests of Samson Gahungu and Jesus, and discover some specifics about the first component of injustice: violent coercion.

VIOLENCE LAID BARE

Violent coercion is the compelling or constraining of a person to act against his or her free will—usually by physical force, the threat of force or the threat of some other dire consequence. This is the ugly "or else!" wielded by the oppressor. It can be as blatant as a blow to the head or as subtle as a hint of economic destitution. But it is always some sort of force that the oppressor wields to take from those who are in a weaker position. And, it is an incredibly *effective* weapon for oppressors to wield—often not because of their own overwhelming strength but rather because the victims they choose to oppress are so incredibly vulnerable. We are talking not just about corrupt authorities but about bullies who steal from elderly widows, sexually assault small children or enslave the poorest members of their community. We are, in short, talking about those who abuse whatever power they have to harm those who are weaker.

In Samson's case the violence was exercised by soldiers with guns who used the implicit threat of force to detain him and throw him in prison. Similarly, as Matthew describes it, Jesus was arrested by "a large crowd armed with swords and clubs, sent from the chief priests and the elders of the people" (Matthew 26:47). In this brief passage we see three key elements of violent coercion—we find that perpetrators rely on at least one, and often all three, of these elements to commit acts of violence.

The first element: Weapons and brute force. Those who came to arrest Jesus approached with the traditional tools of coercive power: weapons of violence and superior numbers. Injustice is perpetrated by those who are able to force others to submit to their will, usually by hard, physical force. And here is the point: As uncomfortable as it is to face, we need to know that when we see the words *injustice* or *oppression* in the Bible, God is talking about a most untidy sin. This sin has behind it, veiled or unveiled, the forces of physical violence— bullets that tear a body, blows that injure a brain, pressure that crushes a bone. When the soldiers came to arrest Samson and arrest Jesus, they came prepared to physically hurt them or anyone who would stop them. We need to acknowledge this unpleasant reality.

This seems obvious, and in many cases of the most brutal injustice, it is. On the other hand, a great deal of injustice is perpetrated with the realities of coercive violence deeply in the background. At one time in the American South, African American citizens may have seemed to lookers-on as if they were simply uninterested in voting or in sitting in the front of the bus. Nothing about it seemed overtly violent; it was just "the way things are down here." Rev. Martin Luther King Jr. and Rosa Parks exposed the ugly violence that actually kept African Americans from the polls and from front of the bus. To expose the violent coercion that was actually taking place, they did simple but courageous things: they kept trying to register to vote and trying to ride at the front of the bus until the authorities beat them with clubs or dragged them off to jail. These strategies proved very effective; they are a useful lesson for looking at much injustice that we might view as "just the way things are" in this world.

In India, for example, many people look at the fifteen million children sold into slavery and think, *That's just the way things are.* But as I learned from Kumar, the boy enslaved as a seven-year-old whose story I shared earlier, his slavery didn't just happen; it was imposed on him by violent coercion—a coercion more subtle than that which Samson faced but no less brutal. He was not forced into the brick kiln by officers wielding guns but rather by a small debt incurred by a relative.

It's a scheme duplicated over and over in South Asia. At a moment of economic crisis, a family will take a small loan—often as small as just $25—and promise to work for the creditor until it is paid off. But the loan itself was never important to the rice mill- or brick kiln- or salt mine-owner who provided it. It was just the small outlay of ensuring slave labor in perpetuity. For the owner will ensure that repaying the loan is impossible.

Receiving just pennies—barely enough for food—there is no way for the laborer to save enough to pay the owner back. The virtually nonexistent wages are coupled with exorbitant interest rates, by which the owner often swells the sum owed to a hundredfold of the initially borrowed amount. And not only the individual who accepted the loan is ensnared in the ever-growing debt. It gets passed from family member to family member—entrapping entire families in bondage, generation to generation. Even little children, like Kumar, are called to work off the false debt.

Workers laboring under these conditions routinely face physical, verbal and sexual abuse, and violence. A reign of terror makes it impossible for them to leave the facility where they work. Children are kept from school. Women face routine sexual violence and abuse. Families work from sunup to sundown through illnesses and injuries, never coming any closer to freedom. These loan schemes are called many things: bonded labor, forced labor, debt bondage—but the most accurate word is simply *slavery*.

Of course, such slave operations are completely illegal in India, and have been since 1976. But these laws mean little to Kumar, whose young hands are growing hard from the daily stress and heat of the hot clay and heavy bricks.

You may ask, Why doesn't Kumar just leave the kiln? This is the coercive power of violence. Through the coercion of economic desperation, the deception of hidden interest charges and the threat of violence if he does not comply, the kiln owner is able to capture Kumar's income stream in perpetuity, rob him of his childhood and destroy any hope of him ever breathing a breath of freedom in his youth.

Subtle as it may all be, the violence behind Kumar's oppression would be quickly exposed the minute he refused (like Rev. Martin Luther King Jr. or Rosa Parks) to do what was expected of him. He would be violently assaulted—without an advocate to stand on his behalf. On the day Kumar did not begin work at the kiln because he was very sick, the owner came to him where he slept and kicked the little boy in the head, beating him until he returned to his post. Once, a worker escaped from the kiln. The owner quickly found him and brought him back. Kumar and the other slaves were forced to watch him suffer a vicious beating as a warning.

Hidden or not, the blunt fact behind injustice is brute force.

The second element: The powers behind the force. Returning to Jesus' and Samson's arrests, we can see that those who exercised the violent force—the soldiers who made the arrests—were actually *sent* by other people. In Jesus' case the armed men were "*sent* from the chief priests and the elders of the people" (Matthew 26:47). Likewise the soldiers who wielded the actual force that arrested and detained Samson were *sent* by authorities higher up a military chain of command. Violence can be exercised through two very different sets of people: those who actually wield the tools of naked force (that is, soldiers, police officers, thugs) and those who tell them where and when to wield them. We almost always pay attention to the former, those who actually carry the gun or the club. But as we plainly know from Christ's own story, the real players are the equivalents of the "chief priests and the elders of the people." They *sent* the thugs, and without their direction the "large crowd armed with swords and clubs" would likely be a bored group of ne'er-do-wells and lackeys still lounging around the local watering hole waiting for something to do.

There are, of course, occasions when soldiers or police are abusive on their own initiative (and indeed, the land-grabbing thug in Africa or the violent slave owner in India, for example, are generally abusive *entirely* on their own initiatives), but sometimes oppressors are sent on their coercive errands by those who have command over them. Even when soldiers or police use their own initiative to abuse others, those in command have the power to take away their tools of coercion (guns, clubs, handcuffs), and when average citizens engage in violence toward those with less power than they—throwing a widow off her land in the aftermath of a spouse's death, or sexually assaulting a young girl simply because they are bigger and stronger—local authorities have the power to counter their violence or can choose to ignore the abuse.

The third element: A claim to legitimacy. The third element of violent oppression is the perpetrators' claim that they are really doing nothing wrong. The only thing that distinguishes the corrupt police officer arresting an innocent man for personal gain and the kidnapper who seizes is some claim to lawfulness, proper authority or legitimacy. Those who sent the soldiers and police in Sampson's and Jesus' stories did so under a formalized claim of legitimacy or proper authority. The religious elders in Jesus' case felt the need to trump up some criminal charge against Jesus to legitimize his detention and execution.[5] Likewise, the Burundi authorities had to assert some claim against Samson to legitimize his arrest, so they accused him of genocide. Of course, the most abusive governments claim the power to detain *without* charge or trial, as the South African government did when I lived there in the 1980s. Under such circumstances—when the government need not establish *any* legitimate reason for its coercive actions—distinguishing the government agents from common kidnappers becomes difficult.

However, the claim to legitimacy is not a tool used only by authorities engaging in brutality. We see thugs, traffickers and violent bullies appealing to the same spurious claims. Slave owners claim that they have the right to exploit and abuse laborers for generations because of the small loan they have offered the victims, knowing that the laborers will never pay it back with the outrageous interest rates they will apply to it. When confronted about the slaves they hold, many slave owners merely point to the debt and explain that, when you consider *that,* the fact that they are holding children, women and men as slaves is really quite reasonable. Traffickers often tell the young girls that they have kidnapped and forced to submit to serial rapes and violence that actually, *they—the victims*—owe their perpetrators money for the cost they undertook to transport them to this place of terror, and that forcing the child to submit to serial rape is just a way of ensuring that they are repaid for this debt. In our casework in Africa we see violent thugs force widows off their property in the aftermath of a husband's death and explain that "tradition" or some idea of male superiority entitles them to steal from this vulnerable woman all that she has. Each of these oppressors claims that there is some legitimate reason entitling them to commit acts of violence against the weak.

In this brief discussion we can see the three elements of violent coercion that make seeking justice so difficult. First, injustice is difficult to confront because (hidden or in-your-face) it involves the use or threat of physical violence. When we fight violence, violence *fights back.* Second, while the coercive force of injustice is exercised by one person, the actual causal agent behind the violent coercion can actually be someone else—someone who sends those who wield the force. And third, most oppressors will hold tightly to a claim to legitimacy or proper authority—a claim which, if not sustained, removes the distinction between lawful authority and common criminality—one that is often accepted or tolerated in their community. Some oppressors are willing to look like criminals in the eyes of their community, nation or the world, but most are not.

DECEPTION EXPOSED

The other major component of injustice is deception. Sometimes injustice is perpetrated almost purely by deception—that is, when oppressors lie in order to rob victims. In South Africa, the wealthy white landowners would steal their poor black neighbor's plot of land by working in collusion with government officials to raise the land taxes beyond what the poor farmers could pay and then purchasing their neighbor's farm from the government for about one dollar. The prophet Micah described the same deception in Bible times:

> They covet fields and seize them,
>   and houses, and take them.
> They defraud a man of his home,
>   a fellowman of his inheritance. (Micah 2:2)

Isaiah too said that oppressors devise "evil schemes to destroy the poor with lies" (Isaiah 32:7).

More frequently, however, deception is used in combination with violent coercion. As Proverbs observes, "the mouth of the wicked conceals violence" (Proverbs 10:11 NRSV). This is a critical point. The reason that injustice is difficult to confront is that those who perpetrate it almost always lie about it. Most of us are not very comfortable entering into a world where we have to deal with people who do not tell the truth, but if we are going to enter the struggle for justice in the world, we must get used to the idea that we are entering a world where people lie—a lot.

When we are struggling against injustice, we are dealing with people who abuse whatever amount of power they have and lie about it. Sometimes these perpetrators are bullies in a community—using the limited power they have to terrorize those weaker than they. But sometimes these perpetrators are the most exalted and esteemed people of power and authority in the society—these are the liars we are dealing with when we confront injustice carried out from on high. Therefore those of us who have been raised with a respect for authority and a Romans 13 deference to government officials must, if we are going to seek biblical justice, accustom ourselves to the unsettling reality that some of those who have power and authority are not only capable of abusing their power but are capable of going to great lengths to lie about it.

We are not called to gratuitous disrespect for those in authority, quite the contrary. We are to render to them their due, pray for them and submit to their authority as they exercise it in accordance with God's will. But at all times, rulers and authorities remain fallen creatures capable of great and dark sin. King David not only abused his authority to steal Uriah's wife, he also ended up murdering Uriah to cover it up. Nathan, however, had to expose the lie. The "princes" and "officials" of Jerusalem not only "killed people to make unjust gain," but they also used the prophets to "whitewash these deeds" (Ezekiel 22). Accordingly, Ezekiel had to expose the lie. Imagine the context Micah faced among the respected authorities and rulers of Israel:

> Both hands are skilled in doing evil;
>> the ruler demands gifts,
> the judge accepts bribes,
>> the powerful dictate what they desire—
>> they all conspire together. (Micah 7:3)

But God called Micah to expose the lies.

> But as for me, I am filled with power,
>> with the spirit of the LORD,
>> and with justice and might,
> to declare to Jacob his transgression,
>> to Israel his sin. (Micah 3:8)

The obvious need for us to confront deceitful rulers and to challenge unlawful authorities may make us uneasy, but Jesus has never left any wiggle room for divided loyalties. As Peter said, "We must obey God rather than men!" (Acts 5:29). When we hear God's call to enter the struggle for justice, we must remember the profound biblical truth: "Everyone who does evil hates the light, and will not come into the light for fear that his deeds will be exposed" (John 3:20).

DECEPTION IN THE PHILIPPINES

I began to learn some of the hard truths about deception in the Philippines in 1989. I was sent to the Philippines by the Lawyers Committee for Human Rights to try to figure out why the new government, which had taken over from the corrupt dictator Ferdinand Marcos, had not brought any successful prosecutions against the police or military for ongoing human rights abuses. Cory Aquino was president, having recently come to power in a bloodless "people power" revolution that followed after her husband, the nation's leading political dissident, was murdered by Marcos's cronies. When Cory Aquino took over the presidency, she inherited two things from Marcos: an abusive police and military, and a dirty war against a Marxist guerrilla movement in the countryside. President Aquino came to power as a human rights activist—having seen her own husband murdered by an oppressive dictator—but she didn't seem capable of stopping her own army from killing, raping and torturing innocent people as they went about their struggle against the communist insurgency.

When I went to live in the Philippines to find out why this was so, I thought I would start with the most obvious case: the Lupao massacre. Anyone who read the newspapers in the Philippines had heard of the Lupao massacre. Like a smaller version of the American Mai Lai massacre, soldiers from the 14th Infantry Battalion of the Philippine Army murdered seventeen unarmed villagers (including six children and two elderly people) and wounded eight more. A small handful of guerillas had spent the previous night in the village. In the early morning as an army patrol approached the small cluster of huts, the guerillas managed to shoot and kill the leader of the army patrol. By the time army reinforcements arrived, the guerillas were long gone, up the mountains. Out of frustration the army soldiers herded the villagers out of the rice paddies where they had been hiding and began to mow them down with gunfire.

After the incident, the army reported that they had "managed to kill 11 NPAs [New People's Army guerillas] on the spot,"[6] had captured five and had taken two additional wounded NPA members to a hospital. All of this, of course, turned out to be false—for none of the victims were guerillas. They were well-known peasants from the village, their grandparents and children. Later the army claimed that the civilians had been killed in the crossfire during the firefight with the guerillas and added that some of the civilians had been killed when the guerillas destroyed their houses with grenades. But all seven survivors of the massacre told a different story, and the close-range gunshot wounds of the civilian victims proved that the army's second claim was false. As the army's own provost marshal concluded, the villagers "were deliberately killed by the soldiers of the 14th IB,"[7] who were trying to "cover up" the murders. It took some time, but finally the soldiers of that battalion were brought before a court-martial to face charges for the massacre.

To everyone's surprise, however, the court-martial acquitted all the accused soldiers. According to President Aquino, the acquittal resulted from the "noncooperation of certain witnesses."[8] According to the presiding officer of the court-martial, "Twenty witnesses failed to testify which resulted in insufficiency of evidence."[9] The military prosecutors said that they "got little support from the victims, some of whom refused to testify."[10]

This was enormously puzzling to me. On the one hand, I could understand why the victims might not have shown up to testify. First of all, the trial was not held in their province, but inside the army military headquarters in Manila. Testifying at the trial would require a nine-hour roundtrip journey for each day of the trial. More important, when you have seen with your own eyes, as they had, that the army is capable of murdering innocent civilians, it is rather intimidating to walk into *their* headquarters and accuse them face to face. Who knows what will happen to you on your way there or on your way back?

Nevertheless, I also knew that people who had seen their own family members murdered were generally passionate enough about the injustice to do just about anything to see the truth be told. No one in the military could give me very satisfying reasons why the surviving victims of the massacre would not show up, so I decided to go out to Lupao and ask them myself.

UNCOVERING THE SURVIVORS' TRUTH

I traveled the way the survivors would have come. I took a rusted, noisy bus out of the urban sprawl of Manila and headed into the countryside of Tarlac and Neuva Ecija. There is nothing quite as green as the rice paddies that carpet these rural provinces, and it's always so refreshing to get out of the choking smog of Manila. My bus dropped me off in a busy market in San Jose, where I hitched a ride into the village of Lupao. I walked over to the dilapidated municipal hall and asked if anyone knew where attorney Edward Limos lived. They all did, of course, since Ed was just about the only lawyer in the area. The village police corporal gave me a ride on the back of his motorcycle to the lawyer's house. Ed was a shy young man with a soft face and a gentle smile. He was obviously very smart, and amid all the meekness one could clearly see the etched lines of resolution that ran from his eyes to his broad cheek bones. Attorney Limos lived and worked in Manila, but he had grown up in Lupao and had taken a personal interest in supporting the survivors of the Lupao massacre in their search for justice.

Ed introduced me to the mustached mayor of Lupao, and together we took a ride in the village ambulance out to the tiny hamlet of Namulandayan where the massacre had actually taken place. The cluster of huts sat at the feet of sharp green mountains, and I could readily see how the guerillas could make such a quick retreat into the highland mist. I saw the charred remains of the victims' bamboo huts lying flat in the red mud, and Ed showed me where the villagers had been rounded up and shot in the rice paddy.

I talked with several of the survivors. As usual, it was all rather businesslike until I really let my eyes meet theirs. Especially Merissa's—a beautiful eight-year-old girl whose hand had been shot off by the soldiers' high-powered weapons. As old as the story was to Ed, I could tell that he just couldn't stand thinking about what Merissa had been through.

So I asked them, "Why didn't you go to the court-martial and testify against the soldiers who did this?"

"Oh, but we did!" they said. I looked at them puzzled.

"Oh yes," Ed said. "All seven of the survivors testified at the court-martial, and they positively identified at least four of the defendant soldiers."

I showed them the quote of the presiding officer of the court-martial claiming that "twenty witnesses failed to testify," and the statement by the military defense attorney that "the survivors had failed to identify any soldiers involved in the alleged massacre."

Ed, who had accompanied all the survivors to the trial, was stunned by these statements. "We had seven witnesses, and they all showed up. None of the prosecution's witnesses failed to appear."

THE EVIDENCE TELLS THE STORY

There was the proof. Ed handed me the transcript of the court-martial, and sure enough, the testimony of all the survivors was recorded in black and white, along with the names of the four defendant soldiers whom they had positively identified. In fact, the survivors described to me what they had to go through to attend the trial. They woke up at 3:00 a.m. each day to perform their farm chores before leaving for Manila by five o'clock so they could be at the army camp by 9:30 a.m. Unable to afford overnight accommodations in Manila, they had to return each night to Lupao—arriving at around 11:00 at night. In fact, the trial had to be postponed for a time so that Ed could raise some more money to pay for the victims' transportation costs.

One of the survivors, Conchita Carnate, had seen her own husband, Ernesto, bayoneted to death while pleading with the soldiers in the middle of the Lupao rice paddy. She had gone to the court-martial, had broken down under the intimidating presence of all the soldiers, but had gone on to point out her husband's murderer. I showed her President Aquino's statement that the verdict acquitting all the soldiers "was no whitewash since there was no substantial evidence to convict the accused due to the noncooperation of certain witnesses." Mrs. Carnate responded: "We went there to the hearings. We were able to identify the killers. They should be in jail."

I read the entire transcript of the trial many times. There was nothing lacking in the testimony or other evidence against the accused. This is what happened. Initially, the accused soldiers testified that the civilians had been accidentally killed in the crossfire between the guerillas and the army. Then, after the testimony of the survivors and the physical evidence made it clear that this could not be true, they changed their story. Two of the soldiers who had been specifically identified by the survivors took the stand and admitted that their original testimony was false. They admitted that the civilians in Lupao had been deliberately killed by the soldiers. But in a brand-new twist they claimed that the four soldiers who had actually done the killing were not part of their unit, and therefore were not among the defendants before the court. These four soldiers, they said, had been transferred to duty in a remote province.

This patently self-serving testimony was never cross-examined. The four mystery soldiers were never located. And the court-martial heard no further evidence. They simply acquitted the accused and told the public and their president that the surviving witnesses never showed up to make their case.

HOW DECEPTION CONCEALS VIOLENT COERCION
In this painful story we can learn a lot about the deception that makes

the search for justice so difficult. Obviously, it is deception that conceals violence. Out of frustration and anger, these soldiers and their commanders abused their authority and power to take the lives of seventeen innocent and vulnerable villagers. To cover up the injustice, massive deception was applied to the coercive force. To see this, it might be helpful to look at the dynamics of violent coercion reviewed earlier as they apply to this case.

First, the soldiers stole the lives of these victims through the blunt brutality of bayonets and gunfire. Second, the soldiers are part of a chain of command. They were *sent* by others under orders to secure the vicinity. Those who sent them were responsible for equipping them with their bayonets and guns and for supervising how they used them. Third, the soldiers used their bayonets and guns under a claim of lawful authority and legitimacy. Ostensibly, they were protecting the population from the terrorism of the Marxist guerillas and protecting the legitimate government of the people of the Philippines.

All the lies that subsequently flowed out of these events were aimed at obscuring the truth about the nature of the violent coercion involved. With almost every act of injustice there is a natural checklist of lies that tracks the three points above. The oppressor will try to deceive others about three issues:

- the use of violent force—that is, who was hurt, what force was used and who used it
- who was responsible for *sending* those who used the coercive force
- whether the use of force was legitimate or lawful

First, the soldiers deceived people; they lied about *who was hurt,* claiming that it was guerilla soldiers who had been killed. Then, conceding that civilians had been killed, they tried to lie about *who had killed* the civilians, claiming first that the guerillas had killed them with grenades. Later, admitting that the army soldiers had killed civilians, they claimed that these deaths were not unlawful because they were inadvertent consequences of a legitimate firefight with terrorists. When this proved false, they returned to the *who killed* question and claimed that soldiers from another unit had actually done the killing. In the midst of all of this the army never called to account the commanding officers who had sent the soldiers to Lupao, the commanders who equipped them and trained them and the commanders who supervised them at the scene. The whole matter was dismissed as the work of four rogue soldiers from another unit who could never be located and for whom no one could take responsibility.

In every case of injustice the nature of the deception is going to be different, but in almost every case the oppressor is going to try very hard to hide the true nature of the violence under which the victims have been abused. The oppressor will try to deceive others about several issues:

- *What violence, if any, was used?* The slave owner claims that he treats his workers well—and that by employing them, he is actually helping them escape the poverty of their villages.

- *Who, if anyone, was hurt?* The brothel owner in Cambodia lies about the child's age and claims that she works as a prostitute by her own free will and is not being hurt.

- *Who used the violence?* The Philippine Army claims it was the guerillas who killed the villagers.

- *Who sent or exercised authority over the one who used the violence?* The Rio de Janeiro police deny any connection to the death squad that is murdering unwanted street children.

- *Was the application of violence lawful or legitimate?* The Burundi military claims legitimacy for Mr. Gahungu's detention because he is a criminal who has committed acts of genocide.

In each of these cases the deceptions can be exposed, but the lies make it very difficult to seek justice for the victims. Many times even the most senior authorities who exercise power in these situations are *unable* to vindicate the rights of the victims because they themselves are deceived about the nature of the violence. I do not believe, for example, that President Aquino was *unwilling* to seek justice for the victims of the Lupao massacre; rather, she was herself a victim of the lies of her subordinates and thus *unable* to render justice. One might argue that she accepted her subordinates' representations too uncritically, but this is a different point than arguing that she was a coconspirator in the crimes. Again, when we discuss intervention strategies in the next chapters, it will be helpful to remember that injustice can be perpetrated through the ignorance (albeit, often willful ignorance) as well as through the intentional abuses of senior officials and authorities.

VIOLENCE AND DECEPTION: OPPRESSORS' TOOLS TO PREVENT RESCUE

Oppressors use violence and deception as tools not only to carry out injustice but also to keep rescuers from coming to the aid of the victim. Remember that injustice is the abuse of power by the strong over the weak. If victims had as much power as oppressors, they wouldn't be vulnerable and wouldn't be abused. If perpetrators thought that their victims would be protected by the power of excellent, robust law enforcement, they probably wouldn't dare enslave them or steal their property. The rule of law provides a countervailing force that can protect the vulnerable from abuse. Indeed, it can put enough power on the side of the vulnerable that would-be perpetrators will not attempt to abuse them at all.

But what about when the abuse has already happened? When International Justice Mission partners with Cambodian police to enter a brothel where a young girl is being held in forced prostitution, she has a countervailing force on her side that allows her to walk away from the pimp's violent coercion. When the military police arrest and incarcerate soldiers who would shoot unarmed villagers, those villagers have a countervailing force on their side that protects them from the abusive soldiers' violence.

What oppressors must do, therefore, is isolate their victims from those who might come to their aid. As we discussed before, no oppressors are powerful enough to overcome all the forces of truth and justice that humanity could amass against them. So they must keep their victims isolated from those who might bring a countervailing power to bear on the victims' behalf. To do so, they will use their two favorite tools: violence and deception.

If possible, oppressors will use deception. First, if they can, they will make it look like nothing is wrong—like no one's being hurt. Or they will make it hard to figure out who is committing the abuse. Or they will make it seem like the victims deserve the abuse or brought it on themselves. These will all be obfuscation and deceptions designed to keep anyone from coming to the victims' aid.

If necessary, oppressors will use the *threat* of violence to keep their victims isolated. At a minimum they will try to create an atmosphere of intimidation so that everyone is afraid even to ask the questions that will allow others to learn the truth about the victims' plight. Because they are relying on deception, oppressors cannot tolerate open inquiry. If there is one thing they hate, it's questions. People may openly suspect them of abuse and oppression, but if everyone is too intimidated to *prove* it, the oppressors will succeed.

Finally, if people get too close to the truth or to the victim, oppressors may actually use violence to physically stop the intervention. I've had soldiers point their guns at me outside a military detention center and make it clear that they were prepared to shoot me if I kept bugging them about two prisoners who were being held incommunicado within their camp. Sometimes oppressors are indeed prepared to kill, as evidenced by the scores of lawyers and journalists who are murdered every year trying to expose the truth about injustice in the harsher places around the world. Often, however, oppressors simply want to scare people away. They wouldn't seriously hurt them and often they simply couldn't, but if they can deceive people about their violent coercive power, that is often as good as actually having the power. For them the result is the same. Their victims are alone, unprotected, utterly vulnerable. The victims can only cry out in isolation: "Why, O Lord, do you stand far off? Why do you hide yourself in times of trouble?"

God may be asking similar questions—not of himself but of his people:

> The Lord looked and was displeased
> that there was no justice.
> He saw that there was no one,
> he was appalled that there was no one to intervene.
> (Isaiah 59:15-16)

> Then I heard the voice of the Lord saying, "Whom shall I send?
> And who will go for us?" (Isaiah 6:8)

Incidents of injustice are not just something that happen in an unfair world. God is appalled by them and calls us to seek justice. Oppressors can be intimidating, but in studying how they work—through violent coercion and deception—we can prepare ourselves to stand up to them. We *can* do something. The next three chapters offer some specifics about how to investigate the deceptions and how to intervene on behalf of the victims.

INVESTIGATING
THE DECEPTIONS

Let's return briefly to the missionary mentioned in chapter nine, the one who came to visit us in our adult Sunday school class and who was heartbroken over the young girls abducted into a brothel operated by corrupt police in her neighborhood. It doesn't really matter to our story where the brothel is because it could be just about anywhere—Manila, Bombay, Lagos, Rio de Janeiro, Kiev, New Orleans. Regardless of the specific context, the same predictable rules of injustice apply. As we have seen, these girls are victims of violent coercion and deception. The burning question in the heart of the missionary is, Can anyone do anything about it?

OUR SPIRITUAL BUT PRACTICAL CALLING

To provide an answer for her and the many others facing injustice first-hand, we will have to get very practical. To some Christians the discussion of the actual ways and means of fighting injustice might seem, well, too practical. It all might sound rather unspiritual, all-too-human, even unholy. In their discomfort some will want to say, "Our struggle is not against flesh and blood, but against the rulers, against the authorities, against the powers of this dark world and against the spiritual forces of evil in the heavenly realms" (Ephesians 6:12). But Jesus, who was not too spiritual for this world two thousand years ago and still isn't today, knew that the "powers of this dark world" and "the spiritual forces of evil in the heavenly places" are manifested here and now in very real sin, suffering and hurt. And he counteracted those forces with acts of love. Christ has called us to do the same.

Christians of mature faith know that love is both a deeply mystical and a profoundly practical calling. In some mysterious way, when we feed the hungry, visit the sick and clothe the naked, we do it for him also (Matthew 25). Jesus' model for love, a nameless Samaritan, messed up his clothes and his schedule by picking up a stranger who lay wounded and beaten in a ditch (Luke 10). Acts of love like this are so important to God that when the Israelites couldn't be bothered with the workaday practicalities of what it takes "to loose the chains of injustice" and "to set the oppressed free," God stopped listening to their prayers (Isaiah 58:1-6).

It's worth remembering that an entire book of the Bible—the book of Esther—is all about a woman's very practical efforts to stop the violent deceptions of an abusive government official. Christians looking for "spirituality" will want to skip it because God isn't mentioned in the entire book. But anyone who reads it will see why God included it in his divine revelation to humanity. God was not too spiritual to work through the courageous faithfulness of one woman to stop the wholesale slaughter of the Jewish people at the hands of an evil Persian prime minister.

Whatever action God has called his people to do, the giants of the faith have always understood that it is worth doing with real-world excellence. They know that their abilities or gifts depend on the empowering of the Holy Spirit, but whatever they bring to the work in the way of study, of knowledge, of technical expertise, they "work at it with all [their] heart, as working for the Lord" (Colossians 3:23). God is not interested in crosscultural missionaries who are too spiritual to bother preaching in a language that the people can actually understand. He is not interested in missionary doctors too spiritual to bother operating on the organ that is actually diseased. He is not interested in relief workers too spiritual to bother airlifting the food supplies to the country that actually has the famine. He is interested in people who give their all to the tasks before them.

As God calls us to seek justice, he bids us to equip ourselves with some basic knowledge of what it takes to pursue the call with excellence. He does not presume that we are ready but beckons us,

> *Learn to do right!*
> Seek justice,
>   encourage the oppressed.
> Defend the cause of the fatherless,
>   plead the case of the widow. (Isaiah 1:17, emphasis added)

Loving those girls abducted into prostitution by abusive authorities is a very practical, deeply spiritual affair, and something worth learning a thing or two about.

As we saw in chapter nine, rescuing these girls, or any victims of injustice, means overcoming the deception and violence of the oppressor. We overcome the deception of the oppressor through rigorous investigation and asking the difficult questions so that we are armed with the truth. We overcome the violence of the oppressor by bringing this truth to a greater power than the oppressor.

In Cambodia, for example, if our staff receives reports that there are young girls being held in a brothel—we know that the God of justice hears their cries and calls us to see that they are protected. But what does this look like practically? It begins with meticulous investigation to expose the truth. Our team of highly trained investigators uses covert techniques to gather evidence of the crimes. It is only with very specific and concrete proof of the oppression that we can approach local authorities to alert them to the situation and ask them to use their power to bring freedom to these trafficking victims.

In this chapter, we'll explore the process of exposing deception— the investigation that makes intervention on behalf of victims possible. In chapters eleven and twelve, we'll see what intervention can look like. These are practical details. They require meticulousness, precision and rigor. These aren't the traits we're most likely to discuss at our weekly Bible studies—but they are skills that the God of justice uses in his people to answer the cries of the oppressed.

Exposing deception can be described as a process of three steps, and these steps greatly overlap: gathering the facts, substantiating the facts by asking the appropriate questions and collecting all the evidence.

THE FIRST STEP: GET THE FACTS

To uncover an oppressor's deception we must bring the facts of injustice into the light of day. We need to learn the truth about the violent coercion used by the oppressor (the victim, the injury, the method and the perpetrator). We need to learn if there is a sponsor of the oppressor (someone who sends or commands the oppressor). We need to learn what the oppressor's claim to legitimacy is (a claim to lawful authority behind the coercion). We find that oppressors generally tell one of three specific lies about their oppression: it didn't happen; someone else did it; or the abuse was legitimate. Each of these lies can be overcome by the truth, but we must collect the proof. And so the work of justice begins with a factual investigation.

Factual investigation is generally difficult, however, because we have several obstacles to confront: the victims themselves, the need for special expertise and the risk of danger when we challenge oppressors' lies.

The first obstacle: The victims themselves and their advocates. This first obstacle may seem strange, but it's true. Most victims of injustice and their loving advocates, at some level, expect justice without having to supply all the facts. And that's understandable. In fact, there are several reasons why they don't naturally offer investigators the facts of the injustice.

1. *Victims often do not feel the need to carefully note the facts since they have no doubts about what happened—after all, they were there.* To victims, the facts are not in question. Consequently, even though

many of the facts may be known, they are not noted as part of the story and do not come to light. Generally, people feel so passionately about the larger abuse they have suffered or seen others suffer that they simply do not focus on the particulars of the situation—things that seem relatively trivial in the larger tragedy of the story.

If a girl has been abducted into a brothel, for instance, she will probably not think that it matters very much what day of week it occurred. The same is true of a prisoner tortured by a group of police; his first description of the ordeal is unlikely to provide any information about which one of the individual police officers in the group actually struck him in the mouth with his baton. Unless specifically asked, he may dismiss the information as a wholly inconsequential detail—especially compared with the pain of such a blow. Similarly, when we ask an impoverished widow to tell us about the time the gang of armed men sent by the owner of the hacienda destroyed her little house and pushed her off her land, we have a 50 percent chance that she will tell us the whole story—for hours perhaps—without ever telling us the date it occurred. If we don't think to specifically ask, we will walk away with a tragic story but one that never happened in a specific point in time. More broadly, therefore, if we are not very intentional about our investigation, we will miss many pertinent facts.

International Justice Mission's Guatemala field office recently undertook a case in which a young girl had been sexually abused by an Irish national living in her community. But neither the victim nor her mother—nor anyone else in the community, for that matter—actually knew the perpetrator's real name, as he went exclusively by a nickname. So, before they could take any other steps, our investigators had to begin with the very practical—but perhaps surprisingly difficult—task of figuring out the full name of the suspected perpetrator. Only after they had accomplished this task could they partner with local police to ensure his arrest.

2. *The victim's sympathetic advocates generally feel uncomfortable asking the "how do you know" questions.* Uncovering the facts of the abuse from the victims or their advocates requires that we always ask

an awkward question, How do you know what you know?

Imagine again our missionary in our Sunday school class who tells us about "the girls who have been abducted into the brothel." It is quite unnatural for most people to ask the missionary, Well, how do you know that these girls have actually been abducted into a brothel? Your missionary has told you something painful from her heart and you want to express sympathy—which you can't possibly begin to express if you don't communicate that you believe her. And you can't very well express that you believe her if you ask a question that indicates doubt about what she said. Fundamentally, gentle and sympathetic people do not naturally engage in cross-examination of someone who has revealed pain and suffering from their heart. Thus they never ask the questions and never get the answers that are necessary for actually determining the facts of the abuse. This is why our staff undergo rigorous training in communicating with victims and advocates without subjecting them to unnecessary trauma. We *must* ask the questions to get the full facts of the abuse—but we do so with as much sensitivity to the victims and their needs as is possible.

3. *Victims and their advocates easily forget that their story is going to have to be proved to people who don't want to believe it and in the face of vigorous denials from their oppressors.* If we begin with the facts of the abuse as they are relayed through the narration of the victims and their closest friends and supporters, we actually end up with very few of the facts that we need in order to seek justice. So to get the necessary facts, we need to conduct a very intentional investigation, reminding the victims and their advocates of the need for proof—the specific details of the situation, trivial though they may seem. In the end these details will lead to a much stronger case against their oppressors and a greater possibility that they will be brought to account.

4. *There are some facts that the poorest and most vulnerable people in the world simply may not know—like their own birth date or even how to spell their own name.* Many poor and underprivileged people don't have the luxury of keeping track of facts. Most of the Rwandan massacre survivors that I interviewed didn't own a watch, so they couldn't

tell me what time of day or night the worst event of their life occurred. Child prostitution may be illegal, but if the girl doesn't know her own age we don't know if she is legally a child or not. If the bonded laborer can't read or write or do simple arithmetic, then she will not think to obtain a written record of her indebtedness and she will have no idea what rate of interest she is being charged—although it may be more than 1,000 percent a year.

The second obstacle: The need for specialized knowledge and skill. Getting the facts is also difficult because it often requires some sort of special expertise. Without the help of legal, medical and criminal-investigation experts, some investigations would not be possible.

Legal experts. As a preliminary matter, we must know what facts we need in order to prove that the abuse took place. We may have to prove more than we think. Lawyers call this *proving the elements of the crime.* For instance, the crime of rape generally consists of two elements: (1) sexual contact to which the other person (2) did not consent. In different countries there will be different rules about what kind of sexual contact has to be proved, and different rules about what facts establish the absence of consent. Some countries, for instance, require that a girl or woman demonstrate that she actively resisted the alleged assailant. Other countries, however, rightly recognize that a woman might feel too intimidated to resist actively or might think that by doing so she would risk further injury. Imagine a girl being attacked by a man with a gun and then being asked later to prove that she physically resisted her attacker. The absurdity of this has led to the abandonment of such requirements in most Western countries. However, in other parts of the world, especially in those countries with strong cultural biases against the rights of women, the law can be different. So we must know what facts need to be investigated.

Occasionally, fewer facts are required than we might think. In India, for instance, many people concerned about slavery are discouraged when there is no contract or receipt to evidence the abusive loan terms holding a child in a cigarette factory or a salt mine, believing that, without this paper documentation, it will be impossible to prove that the owner was using this debt to hold a victim in slavery. Under Indian law, however, this evidentiary problem is supposed to be the slaveowner's and not the laborer's. According to the law, the burden of proof rests on the owner to prove that the laborer is *not* in bonded servitude. So now the absence of the contract is the owner's problem, not the laborer's. At times some technical knowledge of the law not only frames the question that needs to be asked but also lightens the investigative load.

Medical experts. Sometimes, establishing the fact of the abuse and even the identity of the victim is a challenge. I can remember participating in the exhumation of the body of a woman in the Philippines who had been brutally raped, tortured and murdered by a group of drunken army soldiers on the island of Eastern Samar. An eyewitness to the horror, the victim's brother, had escaped to tell the whole story. But we really needed the body of the victim to prove that the murder actually took place. So the brother led us out to the site where he knew the soldiers had buried her body. But it wasn't there. Apparently, the soldiers had removed it. What were we to do now? How were we going to seek justice for this girl and her family if we couldn't even prove that something bad had happened to her? Fortunately, we had some forensic doctors with us, and they were able to sift through the soil and find more than sufficient tissue samples and other physical evidence to prove the brother's story. Likewise, IJM frequently requires the expertise of doctors and other medical experts to prove the age of minor victims and to document physical or sexual abuse.

Criminal-investigation experts. International Justice Mission has developed and deployed undercover techniques for documenting critically important proof of abuse—in brothels, facilities where labor slaves toil daily and other places of violence. Our investigators enter brick kilns where whole families are held in slavery and covertly record proof of the slaveowner's abuse. When local authorities arrive to bring freedom to the slaves, the owner may claim that they are working for him by choice—but it is hard to argue with undercover footage where he is recorded bragging that he does not pay his laborers, has his thugs beat them if they attempt to leave and fears no consequences because he has a good friend on the local police force.

The third obstacle: The risk of physical harm. In getting the facts necessary to overcome deception, we meet with a third obstacle: the risk of physical danger. Many countries with the most brutal injustices are difficult to access, or they manifest a high level of civil unrest or random violence. Even in relatively accessible and stable environments, however, we may not feel safe asking a lot of questions around people who are violent, deceitful oppressors. We can, however, assess and manage the risks.

Not everyone shares the same vulnerabilities. What may be very dangerous for one person may be perfectly safe for another. It would be very dangerous for the victim of police torture to return to the police station to try to identify the name of the officer who committed the abuse. But it may be perfectly safe for another person, armed with a description of the officer and a plausible pretext for being there, to find out the same basic information.

In most cases, we can determine who is at risk and why; then we can devise a strategy that reduces that risk to an acceptable level. It may be important, for instance, to provide some level of protection for witnesses. In the case involving the woman who had been raped and murdered by the drunken soldiers, we needed to provide protection for the brother who had survived the ordeal. A group of us escorted him to the local prosecutor's office to file the necessary papers, then we drove him and his family to another province where he could find shelter in a safe house until the next step in the proceedings.

There will always be contexts in which it is humanly impossible to operate safely, and in such circumstances there may be nothing we can do. But at least we will be able to distinguish those situations from contexts that simply *feel* unsafe or are unsafe for a particular individual.

The Second Step: Substantiate the Facts by Asking the Right Questions

To overcome an oppressor's deception we must conduct a very intentional and systematic investigation of the facts. This includes making a comprehensive list of questions to be answered. The relevant questions will generally include the following:

- Who is the victim?
- What is the nature of the injury—how has the victim been hurt? Is the abuse or oppression continuing?
- What is the means or method of abuse or injury—how, when and where does the oppressor carry out this injury or abuse?
- Who is the perpetrator, and why does he or she commit the abuse?
- Is the person who actually performs the abuse sent by someone else or under a chain of command or authority? If so, who is the oppressor's commander or sponsor?
- Does the oppressor, the commander or sponsor claim some kind of legitimacy or lawful authority for the abuse? What is the basis for such a claim? Are the oppressor's actions legal in the society?

Generally, these are the questions that need answers. And as we seek answers, we must constantly ask, How do we know what we think we know? Every step of the way this is the most critical question. It's the most important question but the one most people forget to think hard about. How do we *know* the girls were abducted into a brothel? How do we *know* that the armed gang was sent by the landlord? Many times the answer sounds something like this: Well, my brother said his neighbor heard about it from his coworker. Or, Everybody knows it. Or, His mother said she read about it in the newspaper. If so, then we have our work cut out for us.

This question is so important because, generally, when we take the information that we have and seek intervention on behalf of the victim, we are going to present the information to people who are not going to want to believe us—and the perpetrators are going to lie through their teeth to deny everything that we say. They are going to make up an alternate explanation for events. They are going to get their friends to lie in order to back them up. On the basis that the best defense is a good offense, oppressors will even assert some shameful, humiliating, dangerous allegations against us. In such a context it's mighty healthy to have thought a little bit about how we know what we think we know.

THE THIRD STEP: COLLECT ALL THE RELATED EVIDENCE

In a general sense we can know what we know (1) because of what the perpetrator admits, (2) because of what we or others have seen or heard firsthand, and (3) because of what physical things indicate.

Information usually comes in three forms: what people have written down or recorded, called *documentary evidence;* what people say, called *testimonial evidence;* and what is indicated by material things (a scar, a footprint, a bullet hole), called *physical* or *demonstrative evidence.*

Documentary evidence. Usually the most powerful evidence, and the hardest to come by, comes from the words or conduct of the oppressors themselves. While conducting an investigation of slave labor, for instance, International Justice Mission has been able to capture on videotape a slave owner bragging about how he has trapped the dozens of slaves working in his facility. How do we know these people are slaves? Answer: The owner said so. Occasionally we can ask officials very pointed, specific questions about a person or a situation, which compels them to choose between admitting some piece of information or risk being caught publicly later on in a bald-faced lie. Occasionally we can get copies of an oppressor's own records that might prove a fact—like the record books pimps and brothel owners keep of the girls they have trafficked. Sometimes oppressors will say something careless in public that will be recorded by a newspaper or camera.

Testimonial evidence. Most evidence, however, comes in the form

of testimonial evidence or statements from witnesses—either from
the victims or from other observers or participants. For example, if
we can get the girls out of the brothel, they can tell us how they got
there and who put them there. If a missing prisoner was seized from
his home, his family members can tell us who came and got him,
when and how, what they said, and what they looked like. If sources
can be developed within the paramilitary group, they can tell us who
gives them their guns and pays for the gas in the truck.

Physical evidence. After we get the story, the asserted facts will
either be supported or contradicted by "things"—the physical evidence. If the prisoner's wounds match his testimony, then we *know*
he was tortured, not just because he says so but because the medical
examination of his body also says so. If the spent shell casings match
the ammunition that is distributed to the government army, then the
physical evidence *corroborates* the villagers' story that the men who
attacked the ethnic minority village were actually members of the
military, in spite of their civilian clothes.

Thus by various investigative strategies it's possible to establish
the facts of the victim's abuse and overcome the oppressor's deception. The missionary's story about the girls abducted into a brothel by
police sounds hopeless at first. But if I tell you that we are able to
obtain a surreptitious video of the girls in the brothel being offered
for sex by men who can be identified as members of the local police,
bringing about justice doesn't seem so hopeless anymore. Maybe we
can take this information somewhere and get the girls released.

This is the power of factual information. It's usually hard to get,
often *very* hard to get. But once we have isolated the needed information, we can devise a focused plan and mobilize the expertise and
resources that are required to obtain it. Then we can go on to the next
task—intervening on behalf of the victims.

INTERVENING FOR
THE VICTIMS

Injustice is the abuse of power. Oppressors use whatever power or authority they have to take from those who are weak. To do so the oppressor isolates the weaker individual from the protection of the law or from those who might be able to bring power to bear on the victim's behalf.

> I looked and saw all the oppression that was taking place under
>   the sun:
>   I saw the tears of the oppressed—
>   and they have no comforter;
>   power was on the side of their oppressors. (Ecclesiastes 4:1)

Intervention, therefore, is the process by which the isolation of the weaker individual is overcome and legitimate power is introduced on the side of the weaker brother or sister. The term *intervene* literally means "to come in between." So when we intervene, we use the factual information that we have gathered to place a counteracting, protective power between the abuser and the victim, and to ensure that the victim is brought to safety and to hope. So it is that God is able to "rescue the poor from those too strong for them" (Psalm 35:10).

Through more than a decade of IJM casework, we have learned

that the vast majority of victims of injustice in the developing world are not victimized by complicated, knotted violations of human rights, but rather by simple, brutal acts of violence that are already against the law in their own countries. Millions of victims of slavery and trafficking suffer in nations with robust antislavery and antitrafficking regulations. Millions of victims of rape, of illegal land seizure, of police brutality endure violence that explicitly violates their country's laws. This violence persists simply because the victims have less power than those who oppress them. Particularly when they are not effectively protected by the power of rule of law, the poor are incredibly vulnerable to abuse. So, by intervening, we bring power back to the side of the victim, by providing him or her a strong, consistent ally who does not give up.

SEEKING JUSTICE: FOURFOLD METHODOLOGY

At International Justice Mission, when we bring power to the side of the victim through intervention, we have four primary objectives: victim rescue, perpetrator accountability, victim aftercare and structural transformation. Victims of violent oppression and their communities have a host of critical needs that we are able to meet through this fourfold set of objectives. Each facet is a specific and concrete way that we respond to God's scriptural call to rescue the oppressed and to love our neighbor. To successfully accomplish any of these goals, we rely on the investigation discussed in chapter ten. Let's take a closer look at these four components of intervention—four ways to tangibly express God's love for the oppressed.

Victim rescue. "Defend the cause of the weak and fatherless; / maintain the rights of the poor and oppressed. / Rescue the weak and the needy; / deliver them from the hand of the wicked" (Psalm 82:3-4).

This step of the intervention is for the victim presently suffering abuse—the prisoner being illegally detained or tortured, the girl being held in prostitution, the enslaved child. While these victims may have a host of critical needs, including access to education, to medical care or to clean drinking water, their ~~most urgent~~ need is, quite simply, to be *rescued* from the hand of the oppressor. In order to rescue victims from the abuse they are facing, we must bring the results of meticulous and rigorous investigation to those with the power to restrain the oppressor—local authorities. Together, we can ensure that victims are brought out of places of great darkness and harm to places of safety.

Over the past ten years we have seen thousands of victims rescued from situations of horrific, brutal, sometimes unbelievable violence. This work is difficult and can be very dangerous. Indeed, it brings my colleagues and me to absolute dependence on God—for we believe we simply cannot do it without him. But through his mercy and the faithfulness of his people, I have seen the incredible restoration that God brings through rescue. One of the people who reminds me most of this is my friend Stephen.

Ten years ago, as a wave of bank robberies swept Kenya, bank employees like Stephen anxiously wondered if their branches would be struck by the crime. The tense speculation did not last long: Stephen's branch was soon hit by brazen robbers who shot a police officer while making their escape. Shaken by the incident, Stephen and his colleagues wondered if the thieves would ever be found.

Five days after the robbery a police officer investigating the crime arrived at the bank and asked Stephen to accompany him to the station. Stephen assumed that as a trusted employee he would be asked to provide important information that could help solve the case. But in the officer's custody, Stephen quickly discovered how wrong he was: rather than seek his help in the investigative process, the officer intended to force Stephen to confess to a crime he hadn't committed.

The police had determined that the theft had been an "inside job," and, simply because he was an employee, Stephen was falsely accused of robbing the bank and shooting a police officer—a crime that would carry a death sentence if he were found guilty. There was not a single witness or piece of evidence to tie him to the case, but the police were under pressure to show that an arrest had been made, so Stephen was ordered to confess. Stephen had a family: a wife and an eight-year-old son. His first thoughts in the bewildering aftermath of the accusation were of them: *What will they do if I am jailed for a crime I didn't commit? What if I am condemned to death?*

When Stephen refused to confess to the crime, the officers tied his hands to his knees, hung him upside-down and tortured him with clubs, whips and bats. Stephen was threatened, taunted and beaten as the corrupt officers attempted to extract a confession from him.

Stephen was held at the station that night. In pain and in shock, he couldn't sleep. "The second day, I started losing hope. . . . I really took [the officers] seriously that they were going to kill me," Stephen remembers. The men continued to torture Stephen for five days, bringing him to different police stations each night so that his wife couldn't find him.

None of the men torturing him—the very individuals who were charged with *protecting* him—would believe him when he told the truth. Stephen was utterly alone.

Finally, after Stephen had endured days of uncertainty and agony, the officers realized that he hadn't committed the crime and threw him in prison to cover up their abuse. In prison, days, then months passed. Stephen waited, always maintaining his innocence. Corruption had frozen the justice process. Kenya's laws designed to protect wrongfully accused victims were ignored. Months became years, and still, Stephen was not given a chance to prove his innocence despite his wife's efforts to secure justice for her husband. He desperately missed his wife and his son. He feared for his life. Quite simply, Stephen needed *rescue*.

A man of faith, Stephen cried out to God. And the God of rescue heard him. One of the family's neighbors heard about IJM's work on behalf of illegally detained prisoners and reported Stephen's incarceration to IJM Kenya. The Kenya team took on the case. The legal team undertook painstaking research to establish the truth and overcome the lies that had been told by Stephen's oppressors. They brought the information to the authorities with the power to make a difference and stood up for Stephen in court, demonstrating his innocence and proving that there was absolutely no evidence to tie him to the crime. After three-and-a-half years in prison, Stephen was acquitted and released from illegal detention. *Rescue* had come.

"Returning back to my family after the long period was one great moment of overwhelming joy," Stephen remembers. How sweet the moment of rescue can be. But Stephen's story of rescue did not end the day he left prison. Stephen wanted to stand for others enduring injustice. He returned to college to complete degrees in community development, and biblical and religious studies, training he planned to use to seek justice on behalf of others who were suffering. After completing an internship with IJM Kenya and graduating from his university, Stephen returned to IJM—this time as a staff member, working to mobilize communities around Kenya to respond to injustice.

Now Stephen is my colleague. He works every day to bring the rescue he has known to others. He recently assisted IJM Kenya legal and investigative staff to secure the release of eight young boys being illegally detained for interrogation by police. This is the miraculous work of the God of rescue.

Perpetrator accountability. "In arrogance the wicked man hunts down the weak, / who are caught in the schemes he devises. . . . / Break the arm of the wicked and evil man; / call him to account for his wickedness / that would not be found out" (Psalm 10:2, 15).

Perpetrator accountability is the appropriate intervention after the abuse has taken place. The injury can't be undone, but the perpetrators can be brought to account for their abuse, and compensation or restoration sought for the victim. We need to free children like Kumar from slavery and ensure that girls like Rosa are equipped with social services in the aftermath of abuse, but that is not all we must do to seek justice. Kumar's owner needs to go to jail and face financial consequences for the fraud, assault and oppression perpetrated against the child. Rosa's alleged assailant needs to be arrested and forced to face the charges against him. The police operating a brothel need to be identified, dismissed from the police force and tried for the crimes they have committed. The soldiers responsible for the Lupao massacre need to be brought to account for their murders.

When perpetrators are brought to account for their acts of violence, they are stopped from committing them again, and a strong message is sent to the community: Violent abuse against the poor and the vulnerable will not go unanswered. Indeed, by seeking perpetrator accountability, and bringing the law to bear against criminals, we believe that we help to protect other vulnerable people from future abuse. The people have less to fear, and the perpetrators and would-be perpetrators now fear the legal consequences of their activities.

I was able to see the powerful impact that perpetrator accountability has on an entire community during a recent trip to Kenya to see the work of Stephen and his colleagues. During this trip some of my Kenyan colleagues and I were invited to a celebration in a small village outside of Nairobi by a woman named Mary, the mother of an IJM client. On the way to the event Mary led me down a dirt path from the vegetable stall she runs with her husband. This trail was the same that her six-year-old daughter, Geraldine, was walking along with her sister when a man from the village grabbed her. Her sister managed to escape and run for help, but by the time she was able to return with their mother, the man had dragged Geraldine into the brush and sexually assaulted her.

Geraldine was not the first daughter of her small village to suffer the brutality of rape. And her mother was also not the first in the community to discover that justice seemed out of reach, impossible. In the aftermath of the assault, she rushed to the home of the perpetrator; he threatened to kill her. She reported the crime to police; they suggested she simply take some money from the man. She was offered bribes from the perpetrator to stay quiet, but her daughter's dignity was not for sale. She was willing to fight for justice, but alone, she knew she didn't have a chance. Knowing that the perpetrator faced no consequence for the crime—that he was free to harm others—left a wound that counseling and medical care did not and could not heal.

The Christian relief organization World Vision referred Geraldine's case to IJM Kenya, and our legal professionals decided to fight alongside Mary's family. The case was brought to trial and the impossible became possible: Geraldine's rapist was sentenced to twelve years in prison.

And so, on a warm afternoon in July, Mary and her community invited me and my IJM colleagues to celebrate their victory. A generous cup of porridge was pressed into my hands, and I was swept into the joy of their singing and dancing. In a region of the world where it is taboo to discuss sexual violence against young girls, Mary's community had been transformed by hope for justice and a safer community. They had seen what is possible.

Together, we celebrated the ripple effect of hope that the conviction had created. One of the village elders spoke to us through a translator in his quiet, measured tones: "I see now that we have expected too little for ourselves. We did not think justice was possible. We will not make that mistake again."

We will not make that mistake again. This is a community whose little girls will be safer because those who would consider violating them now know that they cannot act with impunity. This is perpetrator accountability—restraining the hand of the oppressor.

It is true that sometimes the process of seeking perpetrator accountability under local laws brings us face to face with some difficult questions. I have met many Christians who have great passion for bringing freedom and dignity to the abused and oppressed, but who struggle with questions about seeking accountability for their oppressors. Would it be more Christlike, they ask, simply to forgive the perpetrator of the crime rather than pursue punishment? Can the judicial structures established by man bring any meaningful accountability? Shouldn't God's ultimate judgment be enough for these perpetrators, who often come from situations of deep poverty and difficulty themselves?

Let's examine what Scripture tells us about perpetrator accountability. Throughout the Bible, we see that God restrains, judges and
exacts punishment on those who abuse others. (For example, read
the Psalms with an eye to this facet of God's character.) Among other
teachings in Scripture, Romans 13 expresses that God carries out his
own accountability against perpetrators of injustice in part *through*
human governments—institutions that God has established as his
servants of justice. Indeed, we see that God chooses to use human
government to bring righteous accountability to wrongdoers. Of
course, those governments can abuse the role God has given them,
but there should be no mistake about the role he *did* intend them to
serve.

Time and again we see in Scripture that God's people are his plan
to bring freedom and justice to those who suffer under the yoke of
oppression and to restrain the arm of the oppressor. The Scriptures
resoundingly show us that God's justice is central to his character;
this trait is reflected through just human magistrates and those who
spur magistrates to upholding justice. Indeed, when human beings
act with justice and fairly punish acts of injustice, while remaining
mindful of the dignity of even the perpetrators of these crimes, we
are living more fully as those who bear God's image.

The restraint of the law provides perpetrators the opportunity to
turn from their ways. Through ensuring that perpetrators of violent
evil are prosecuted for their crimes, we bring safety to others the
perpetrators would have victimized if free to act with impunity. By
seeking convictions under local law, we provide a healthy deterrent
for other men and women tempted to commit the same crimes; we
demonstrate that there are consequences for this abuse. Through
holding perpetrators accountable, we protect vulnerable people—in
response to God's clear call to do so (Isaiah 1:17).

But it is important to remember: We do not take joy in perpetrators' suffering. We are called to pray for them too; Jesus makes this
clear (Matthew 5:44). We pray that their hearts would be softened,
that they would turn from their ways and know the peace of forgive-

ness. Though we do not celebrate any pain the perpetrators face, we do indeed celebrate peace, safety and justice in the lives of those they have harmed. It is also important to note that punishment of perpetrators, however lawful, is never meant to be our final action in their lives. We show godly love toward a perpetrator by restraining him or her from harming others, but also by praying for their reconciliation with their Maker. Perpetrators of even the most violent, dark crimes still bear the image of God and are so loved by him that God sent his Son to die for them as well. Jesus is eager for them to receive healing and redemption if they would turn from their ways. We long not only to protect the vulnerable and restrain their abusers, but to see the very new life we have been given change the lives of those who seem to reject it the most.

Victim aftercare. "He upholds the cause of the oppressed / and gives food to the hungry. / . . . The LORD lifts up those who are bowed down. / . . . The LORD watches over the alien / and sustains the fatherless and the widow" (Psalm 146:7-9).

The effects of abuse do not end the day a victim is rescued from a place of darkness. We seek to provide access to the services necessary to address the effects of the abuse and the vulnerabilities that linger beyond the relief of the immediate abuse. IJM's mission from its inception has been to rescue victims of injustice and oppression. We must not only bring them out of places of great trauma and violence, but ensure that they enter into places of security, hope and goodness. This is what love in its fullness looks like—not stopping until the job is done. Or, as one young girl explained to us, "I know you love me, because you helped me."

Providing excellent aftercare requires a long-term commitment to those we serve. Girls released from forced prostitution, for example, are often without families and need shelter and a place to live where they can experience love and security, as well as critical counseling and spiritual care. It is our joy to partner with some wonderful aftercare homes for these girls, where we see real miracles of life and of transformation. Through the love of these aftercare workers, we see girls who were once abused in horrendous ways grow into confident and joyful young women with dreams for their futures.

I think of a beautiful young woman, Kunthy, who was forced into prostitution at fourteen years old. She was held prisoner in one of Phnom Penh's nastiest slums and locked away in a concrete dungeon that the locals called the Anarchy Building—a dilapidated apartment complex patched together with aluminum and cardboard. Its filthy rooms were infested with rodents and roaches and the drug dealers, pimps, thieves and arms merchants who called it home. It was in this place that Kunthy was repeatedly injected with narcotics that rendered her helpless as she was passed around to be raped by brothel customers. But Kunthy had an ally her perpetrators never expected. Our undercover investigators collected evidence of the abuse at the Anarchy Building, and Kunthy was freed and brought to live in an aftercare home.

Kunthy has come out from the shadow of this abuse to thrive. The loving care of her IJM social workers and the staff of the aftercare home where she lived have resurrected this child. In aftercare she discovered a love of computers and a gift for English. Today, she dreams of opening her own Internet café. She has excelled in school. And she knows what it is to be loved. To be secure. To be listened to. Now, Kunthy assists the staff in welcoming new girls to the center, educating others about trafficking and teaching basic computer skills to other girls in the shelter. With the life given to her, Kunthy now brings life to others.

Though their wounds are deep and unique, it is not only victims of sex trafficking who require excellent and holistic aftercare. When our staff in Africa assist widows pushed off their land, they ensure these women are given the counseling services they need and work to connect them with local microenterprise lenders so they can achieve financial security that will reduce their vulnerability to abuse in the future. And this care extends to all casework types: The prisoner's family needs to be attended to if the primary breadwinner is incarcerated or injured. The torture victim is likely to need basic medical attention, psychological treatment and spiritual restoration. Through the direct provision of these services or through partnerships with trusted, local aftercare partners, IJM staff see light come into dark places. Hope displaces hopelessness.

Nothing is more inspiring to me than to hear my IJM colleagues describe the miracles of transformation they see day after day, and it is our aftercare staff who have the front-row seats. In India, IJM social workers have developed a comprehensive program to ensure that slaves brought from bondage to freedom are not victimized again. Through care, love and practical advice, they see lives once bowed down in abuse—people who have been told that they are worthless, that they are property—transformed into lives of significance and purpose.

Victims of slavery have been forced to depend on their owners for everything they have or will receive. But in freedom, former slaves must learn to live independently. This can be an incredibly challenging transition for those who have struggled under slavery's brutal yoke for years. And because the road from slavery to freedom can be very difficult, IJM's Indian aftercare staff are there to support clients each step of the way.

Our aftercare staff continue to walk with clients for at least two years after they are freed, providing long-term rehabilitation, teaching former slaves how to earn a living as free citizens, providing life-skills training and ensuring formal education for children. After their rescue we may provide a bucket of work tools so the freed slaves can begin new jobs immediately. When victims receive their rehabilitation payments from the government, our staff help them open their own bank accounts and teach them how to manage the funds.

These colleagues care for victims with a tenacious love, ensuring that they are well supported as they navigate freedom. Young Kumar, whose story I shared earlier, is now in school and plans to pursue a career as a police officer so he "can protect the good people of [his] village." And he is joined by thousands more victims of slavery with hope for new lives. Kabithan, once held as a slave in a salt mine, took the knowledge he gained working as a slave for someone else and used his government compensation to purchase a salt-crushing machine to work as a free man for his family. Now he employs ten people in his salt business, pays them all fair wages and provides holiday bonuses and protective foot gear for his team. When his IJM social worker recently visited him, Kabithan told her, "At the salt fields, we were all like prisoners in a jail. . . . I am feeling good now after my release. In the future, I want to provide employment for more people. . . . I want to educate my children, and then it is up to them to choose a career." Chandra, who was born in a rice mill and forced to labor there as soon as she was old enough to work, is now receiving training to become a tailor, the job she dreamed about as a child.

Structural transformation. "[Defend] the fatherless and the oppressed, / in order that man, who is of the earth, may terrify no more" (Psalm 10:18).

As I mentioned earlier, my IJM colleagues and I have seen with our own eyes that the vast majority of abuse suffered by the world's poorest people is not due to complicated, nuanced human rights violations. Rather, the poor are primarily victimized by unvarnished acts of violence that are already against the law in the countries where they live. The widow thrown off her land in Zambia, the sexually abused girl in Guatemala, the trafficked child in India—there are very clear laws on the books designed to protect each of them. But often the public justice system of police and courts is too broken to actually *enforce* the law. In fact, a recent U.N. study concluded that nearly *three out of every five people on earth* are not adequately protected by their own justice systems.[1] The great human rights challenge of our day is to ensure that the poor can count on their own justice systems to protect them. If the poor are not protected by the rule of law, few if any of the other humanitarian investments we make on their behalf will be sustainable. We may provide better food, shelter or medicines, but there will always be another bully to take them away. This is why one of IJM's four core objectives—in addition to victim rescue, victim aftercare and perpetrator accountability—is pursuing structural transformation that will bring sustainable protection to the poor and vulnerable. It was Dr. Martin Luther King Jr. who exhorted us, "We are called to play the Good Samaritan on life's roadside, but that will be only an initial act. One day we must come to see that the whole Jericho Road must be transformed so that men and women will not be constantly beaten and robbed as they make their journey on life's highway."[2] By pursuing structural transformation, my colleagues around the world are partnering with local authorities to bring real change to the highways on which the global poor must travel.

Perpetrator accountability is a key ingredient of structural transformation, for it stops the bad guys from continuing the abuse, and it creates powerful disincentives for others who might be likewise tempted to abuse their power. In fact, without perpetrator accountability it's almost impossible to keep the abuse from occurring again. This is why it is so important not only to set victims of slavery free but to have those who owned them sent to jail. Slave owners must be sanctioned with something more severe than a fine, or else, because of the extremely high profitability of slavery, they may be willing to carry on and simply factor such fines into the costs of doing business. Unfortunately, a recent study conducted by the United Nations Office on Drugs and Crime found that 40 percent of nations affected by trafficking had never issued a *single conviction* for the crime.[3] The truth is, we cannot sustainably combat violent oppression without ensuring that perpetrators face convictions and making sure that would-be perpetrators learn about the convictions, so they can have a deterrent effect.

Of course, perpetrator accountability is not the whole answer for transformation strategies. Many times abuse can happen because of larger, more complicated problems, the solutions to which will require the efforts and energies of a broad coalition: NGOs like IJM, community groups, local governments and the global church. Effective prevention strategies to protect children like Kumar from slavery, for example, might mean ensuring that he and other children like him have access to the education they need, and that his family has access to legitimate forms of microcredit lending, so a debt incurred by a relative does not lead to the enslavement of a child. It may mean making sure local officials in his region are trained on the relevant laws, and it may require building political will so that magistrates are willing to pursue charges against slave owners. It may be necessary to educate the middle and upper classes, who may be ignorant about the abuse, so they too will demand change.

Pursuing structural transformation often means building capacity and political will in local or national government agencies. We may bring to account the individual brothel owner who holds children in forced prostitution, but if the police leadership is not encouraged and assisted in developing better methods for enforcing their country's laws against trafficking children, then it is likely to happen again. Similarly, we may bring the soldiers of the Lupao massacre to account, but if there is no military training in the proper use of force and no accountability within the command structure, the pressures of combating guerilla warfare are likely to lead to further abuses.

International Justice Mission's police-training team is leading an exciting front in the battle for structural transformation that protects the poor. Our team of law-enforcement professionals has provided critical police trainings in several nations around the world, equipping the people responsible for protecting the poorest and most vulnerable members of their communities with the skills they need to serve them with excellence. IJM's police trainers instruct on professional ethics, victim treatment and best practices for ensuring evidence is collected appropriately, perpetrators are apprehended and victims are protected according to internationally recognized law-enforcement standards. What makes IJM's training unique is the way we maintain a long-term presence in the community *with* the police to provide tangible assistance and encouragement in putting the training to work in the streets.

We have had the opportunity to provide training in other arenas as well. A collection of IJM campus chapters recently raised the funds to send a forensic nurse examiner to Guatemala to provide a rigorous training for government doctors and other "first responders" on appropriate treatment for victims of sexual violence. And we see the ripple effect of transformational change. Doctors are committed to training their own communities on what they learned; national police forces have made IJM standards part of their official curriculum. As capacity is built, the poor can begin to count on the systems that are supposed to protect them to actually function.

We can also work to build public demand in the community to see that the laws on the books are enforced and to ensure that all citizens are aware of their rights. We have seen incredible hope in African communities where we have held training sessions on property rights, ensuring that vulnerable people know their legal rights and know what to do if bullies in their community attempt to force them off their land or out of their homes. We have also trained local pastors to use their network of influence to protect the widows and orphans in their communities from this form of violent abuse. Indeed, for some pastors advocacy for widows and orphans begins at the funeral—when, according to local customs, the family gathers together to determine how the deceased husband's property will be distributed. These trained pastors stand up for the widow and ensure that she is able to keep what she is legally entitled to and not be thrown from her land or home. Pastors also have been instrumental in teaching their congregations to make wills that deter interlopers from stealing the widow's property. Long-held superstitions prevent many in these poor African communities from creating wills (in the belief that preparing such a document could hasten a death), but without a will widows and orphans are left to the mercy of thugs and bullies. By changing what the community believes is possible for its most vulnerable members, we see systems transformed.

Obviously, the issues of structural transformation are complicated and often require large-scale, long-term remedies, but every individual case of abuse can provide helpful information about the diagnosis of the problem and the design of the remedy. Structural transformation is a big goal. In fact, it is such a big goal that it may even seem

unrealistic, hopeless or simply audacious. But history teaches us that
it is possible. In fact, *everywhere* there is a reasonably functioning
system of police and courts, there once was a system that was corrupt
and dysfunctional—and someone fought to fix it. Public justice systems don't fall from heaven; they are *built* and fought for. But the
glorious thing is that we have seen God move: we have seen communities change and the vulnerable protected. It is indeed a big goal, but
it is one that *matters*.

I've seen the changes with my own eyes. For example, before beginning operations in Cebu in the Philippines, IJM conducted a base-
line survey to determine the extent to which children were exploited
in prostitution there. The results painted a grim picture of devastat-
ing and pervasive abuse. When we opened our Cebu field office, my
colleagues partnered with dedicated local authorities to bring freedom and safety to minors trafficked into the city's brothels and bars.
Two years later, we conducted a second study, and we discovered that
the number of minors in prostitution had dropped more than 70 percent. In another community in northern Thailand, after several years
of work, brothel owners repeatedly told our investigators that they no
longer used minors because of stricter law enforcement. Injustice in
the lives of the poor is neither inevitable nor unavoidable. These dramatic changes give me great hope. The primary reason the poor in
the developing world suffer from horrific abuse is that the laws on the
books to protect them simply go unenforced. Structural transformation builds rule of law, and with it comes the hope that future generations will not know the same abuse as those past. Transformation
changes lives and brings real hope for sustainable change for the
world's poorest and most vulnerable people.

Praying to the God Who Intervenes

When God calls us to intervene on behalf of those who are suffering
under oppression, he calls us to rigor and to focused excellence. He
calls us to courage. But he also calls us to a prayerful reliance on
him. I believe that any Christian's efforts to do justice must also be

brought humbly before the God of justice. Indeed, it is God who empowers this work. As Christians we readily acknowledge the biblical teachings about the spiritual forces of darkness that often lie behind the evil works of humans (Ephesians 6:12). Thus we engage the spiritual struggle through our prayers in the name of Christ, and through the Spirit who intercedes with God for us (Romans 8:26-27).

It may be important to pause for a moment to remember what Jesus told us about prayer. Amazingly, Jesus taught that our heavenly Father, the Maker of the universe, is actually moved by our requests. This is hard to understand, and to explain it Jesus suggests we picture a strong and loving earthly father who does not always give his kids what they ask for, but neither is he unmoved by their pleas. In fact, he occasionally does something different because they ask.

This is impossible for us to fully wrap our minds around, and so Jesus uses the story of a late-night friend in Luke 11 and a judge in Luke 18 to show us how a person can be moved to act as a result of someone else's persistent pleading. Mysteriously, Jesus says, the sovereign God has positioned himself to be moved by our asking. So Jesus teaches us to ask our heavenly Father for good things, and not give up.

We are called to that persistence in our prayer for victims of injustice. By praying for the victims, every one of us can participate in what our loving Father is doing to help them. In the mysterious ways of God, our prayers—the prayers of the righteous—are "powerful and effective" for those who are "in trouble" (James 5:13-16). When the Israelites cried out for deliverance from their oppressors in Egypt, God heard their cry and delivered them (Exodus 3:7-9). And after the Israelites had entered the Promised Land, they were taken captive and oppressed, but when they asked God for release, he granted it. The Israelites later praised him: "From heaven you heard [our forefathers], and in your great compassion you gave them deliverers, who rescued them from the hand of their enemies" (Nehemiah 9:27). And

David declared, "My prayer is ever against the deeds of evil-doers" (Psalm 141:5).

Through our prayer we become spiritually prepared to see the powerful and merciful hand of God. The intercessory prayer ministry of International Justice Mission finds great inspiration in the wise words of a treasured volunteer prayer mentor, the late Vera Shaw:

> As we recognize many cries for justice, we ask: "Who is sufficient for these things?" We're reminded: "Not by might, nor by power, but by my Spirit, says the Lord." With confidence in God, who loves justice and answers prayer, we can reply, "Not that we are sufficient ourselves to think anything of ourselves, but our sufficiency is of God."

The thousands of prayer partners of International Justice Mission receive a weekly e-mail detailing the needs of IJM clients and staff. Their partnership in prayer has revealed, again and again, the faithfulness of God. The case of Samson Gahungu was a thrilling example, for he had been the object of fervent, focused prayer. Like those faithful Christians gathered to pray for Peter in prison (Acts 12), the prayer partners of International Justice Mission were "overjoyed" and "astonished" to learn of the way God in his sufficiency answered their prayers by releasing Samson from jail.

Of course, our prayers should also lead us into loving action for those who are in need: "Suppose a brother or sister is without clothes and daily food. If one of you says to him, 'Go, I wish you well; keep warm and well fed,' but does nothing about his physical needs, what good is it? In the same way, faith by itself, if it is not accompanied by action, is dead" (James 2:15-17). As we are able, we must seek out those practical interventions on behalf of the oppressed that demonstrate our willingness to love not "with words or tongue but with actions and in truth" (1 John 3:18). For we must remember that *our* obedience is God's plan for answering many prayers of intercession. When the victims of injustice around the world pray as David did, "O righteous God, / who searches minds and hearts, / bring to an end the violence of the wicked / and make the righteous secure" (Psalm 7:9), we, God's people, can be the hands through which God intends to answer their prayer.

CASE BY CASE

STRATEGIES TO STAND FOR "THE ONE"

God's people are his plan to respond to the needs of the oppressed in our world. In answer to God's call, we seek to bring immediate relief through victim rescue, redress through perpetrator account-ability, healing and restoration through loving aftercare. Through our structural-transformation efforts we hope to strengthen systems that will prevent current and future abuse.

But in a world marred by the painful scars of brutal abuse and the laughing evil of violent oppressors, a world where more people are held in slavery than at any previous point in history, the statistics of abuse can feel overwhelming. We look at the massive numbers and are tempted to ask, *How can I possibly do anything to help?* We may even think, *In the face of all the need in the world, my small efforts seem like a cruel joke.* But I believe we can all help meet the urgent—and yes, massive—needs of our world by keeping our eyes fixed on the humanity of the *one* child, the *one* widow, the *one* slave who is before us. For while we may not be able to make the difference for all, *we can make all the difference for one.*

As we explore specific strategies for seeking justice, we remember that the goal of every strategy is to secure relief and restoration for the *one* who suffers. We don't fight for statistics; we fight for human beings created in our Father's own image, and one by one, we can actually make a difference that changes the odds. In this chapter, we'll explore strategies to stand for "the one" by looking at several different ways to seek justice for victims of oppression.

INDIVIDUAL CASEWORK

At IJM we have found that individual casework is the most effective way for us to leverage our skills to accomplish victim rescue, aftercare and perpetrator accountability, and to inform strategies for structural transformation. There are several specific reasons we have chosen individual casework as our approach.

1. *As Christians, we are called to love our neighbor.* God does not call us to love a country, humanity, principles, projects or ideology. Instead, he calls us to something as eminently doable as it is difficult. To love actual, individual people—people made in his image. It is easy to become paralyzed by the massive scale of injustice when we look at the problems in the developing world. And so rather than get caught in what Martin Luther King Jr. aptly called "the paralysis of analysis," we begin to combat injustice through casework the way the Bible tells us to embrace the world—one person at a time. We come face to face with the real and painful struggles of our brothers and sisters around the world.

2. *Casework enables us to make an accurate diagnosis of why the poor are left so vulnerable to violence.* When we begin to think about the reason victims of violent oppression are left vulnerable to abuse, it is easy to attribute the cause of their pain to large concepts—*poverty* or *corruption or lack of capacity.* But these break down into very real and very specific injustices in the lives of the global poor. For example, we could guess at the reasons that rapists who prey on slum residents in one of the African cities where IJM works seem certain they can act with impunity. We might hypothesize that there are cultural elements that make victims less likely

to report the crime or that corruption or bribery keep cases from moving through the system once reported, emboldening would-be perpetrators. However, when our staff actually get down into the streets where the poor live and our lawyers represent their cases one by one, we uncover the facts. Through individual casework we discover, for example, that in this metropolitan area, the police only utilize the services of *one doctor* to testify in court in sexual and physical abuse cases for a population of more than three million people. And this one doctor is also expected to examine every single victim—victims of rape, of physical violence, of sexual abuse, even victims of traffic accidents. Of course, it is impossible for one doctor to do all of this for a city of millions of impoverished residents, and indeed the country's laws never actually state that this specific doctor must provide the injury report. However, despite what's on the books, this doctor's word is the only way police in the region are willing to move forward with a case. So now it's easy to see at least one reason there is no strong record of perpetrator convictions. We have a very concrete problem to solve in order to secure justice for our clients.

Similarly, we may look at Bolivia and attribute the lack of convictions for perpetrators of sexual violence to any one of a number of concepts, like *corruption* or *underdevelopment.* But when our lawyers actually began serving clients in the cities of La Paz and El Alto, they discovered that one of the biggest impediments to securing perpetrator convictions is that jurors often simply do not show up for court. The legal penalties for failing to report aren't significant enough to compel people to appear. This challenge is compounded by the fact that the person responsible for getting the jurors to show up receives no vehicle and no funds for gas, taxi or bus fares to find people. So when jurors don't show, either because they just chose not to or the summoner never tracked them down in the first place, judges often issue a new batch of summons and start the selection process over, creating delays that derail many cases. With this concrete, real-world insight, we have a tangible obstacle to overcome. It won't be easy, but at least we know what we are up against. Solving a defined problem is eminently more possible than overcoming one that exists only in a generalized form. This then is the point: when we conduct casework for individual, specific clients, we discover the real reasons they are vulnerable to victimization, which are concrete problems to solve rather than vague concepts with which to be frustrated.

3. *Casework allows us to dissect* the *real power behind the oppression with specificity.* When we conduct actual cases for actual victims, we come face to face with the forces of violent injustice in their lives. We can intervene for victims of human trafficking by making sure that the individual men and women who traffic children are placed in jail, where they can do no more harm. We can determine who the traffickers may have been working for and how they may have been protected. In short, we can actively confront the structures of injustice in very specific ways. We are not left to guess who may behind a certain type of oppression, because through individual casework we must document and confront the power that is actually there.

4. *Casework allows us to attack the oppressor at his or her greatest point of weakness—lies.* Over the past ten years we have seen many great miracles of justice and restoration as God responds to the cries of the oppressed. And during these years we have heard many lies. Through their lies perpetrators reveal something about themselves— ultimately, they are fearful. They tell lies because they are afraid of judgment, of punishment, of exposure and of the light of truth illuminating their deeds. Perpetrators actually *need* lies to continue in their oppression or else someone will stop them. As Aleksandr Solzhenitsyn explained, "At its birth violence acts openly and even with pride. But no sooner does it become strong, firmly established, than it senses the rarefaction of the air around it and it cannot continue to exist without descending into a fog of lies, clothing them in sweet talk."[1]

Not only do lies reveal weakness in the character of the perpetra-

tors, lies become their Achilles' heel, their point of greatest vulnerability. Perpetrators fear being revealed as liars to those who either
condone their behavior or allow it to pass. By conducting casework
we can counter the lies of oppressors with specific truths. It is one
thing to be known as a dishonest person, but it is another to be
caught in a specific lie with concrete evidence. When a trafficker
claims that the children he held in his brothel were actually adults
there by consent, we can show medical proof of his victims' ages; we
can share their testimony of force and coercion. When the bully
who has forced a widow off her land in Africa claims that her deceased husband would have wanted him to have the property, we
can show the will the husband left behind and point to the national
law that dictates that widows inherit shared property after the death
of a husband. The lies and deception that were once powerful tools
in the hands of the oppressor crumble when confronted with the
truth. Individual casework is a precise, reliable tool to directly respond to this point of weakness, because it allows us to wield the
truth.

5. *Casework gives us concrete intelligence about injustice that can
helpfully inform policy and structural solutions.* At International Justice Mission we view conducting casework like running water
through a hose. You can look at a hose and wonder what condition it
is in; you can study it and guess if there are kinks or holes that would
impede its operation, but the most effective way to locate points of
blockage or damage in the hose is to run water through it. In the
same way, as we conduct casework we find very specific points of
obstruction in public justice systems, and with this knowledge we
can partner with local authorities to bring about real change. We can
discover the specific choke points and holes of the justice systems.
Determining what these obstacles are with specificity gives us concrete problems to solve. And based on specific documentation obtained through individual casework, we can make concrete recom-
mendations, which those in power can actually carry out through
structural reforms.

INDIVIDUAL CASEWORK: IJM'S TEN-STEP
CASEWORK METHODOLOGY

To ensure that we are bringing effective relief to victims of oppression through casework, International Justice Mission follows a ten-step casework methodology, combining the process of uncovering information about the abuse from chapter ten and applying the information to speak truth to power and intervene for the victim, as we've explored in chapter eleven. Now that I've discussed our core objectives and IJM's reasons for using individual casework as our vehicle for pursuing justice, I want to walk us through these ten steps so you can get an idea of how it all fits together in a single case at IJM.

Step 1: Define the case referral. As soon as a case is referred to an IJM field office or our investigators discover evidence of abuse on their own, we begin answering the questions laid out in the chapter ten—questions that may seem simple, but are absolutely foundational to moving forward. What is the victim's name? What is the nature of the alleged injustice? Who is the perpetrator? By answering these initial questions we define the specific case we are undertaking (for example, a specific widow from a certain neighborhood pushed off her land) rather than a general issue (combating illegal land seizure in Africa). This step moves us from staring down a huge problem to the level of "one," where we can make a tangible difference in a real person's life.

Step 2: Conduct a preliminary investigation. The goal of the preliminary investigation is to answer the question, Can we believe it? Do our teams have the basic information they need to believe the case? We must ensure the referral is credible before moving forward.

Step 3: Undertake a violence and deception analysis. As soon as we determine that a case is credible, we must carefully analyze the level of potential violence we are up against. In order to protect the victim from harm, it is extremely important to consider the likely lies the perpetrator will tell and the violence he or she may be willing to use. These are the specific lies we will need to gather information to combat and the specific risks we must prepare to overcome.

Step 4: Define the intervention outcome. In this fourth step we determine whether we are able to take on the case—and we clearly define what success will look like. When a case gets difficult (as they all do), it is tempting to redefine *justice* to something easier; that is, to move the goal line a little closer to where we're standing. Defining at the outset of a case what a "win" will be helps us persevere in seeking authentic, complete relief for the victim. For example, if we have received reports of a young girl held in a brothel, and our preliminary investigation leads us to conclude that the reports are credible and we have decided to take the case on, we determine that a successful intervention on behalf of this victim would be: (1) getting her out of the brothel, (2) getting her into a loving aftercare home where she can begin to heal, and (3) ensuring that the pimp who held her captive and the trafficker who brought her to the brothel are both arrested, charged and convicted. Having carefully defined outcomes, we know we are not finished with the case the day she leaves the brothel. Indeed, in some senses, our work begins on that day.

Step 5: Conduct a power actor analysis. We next need to determine who has the power to stop the perpetrator's abuse and to bring the perpetrator to justice. We call this person the "power actor." In the case described in step four, the power actor would likely be the local police force, a national antitrafficking police force or another crime-specific force. We determine what information we will need to move these power actors to intervene on behalf of the victim and who should present that information to them. This step is critical because to intervene is to put power back on the side of the victim. As a nongovernmental organization, on our own we don't have much official power. But local authorities do; they are the ones who can free the girl and restrain her abusers.

We must determine very carefully to whom we will bring the information, what specific information to present and how it should be presented. This is especially critical if the abuser is in a position of official authority over the victim. If we bring the information to the wrong power actor, we can place the victim in great danger. If the abuser is a public official, then we need to have an excellent understanding of the command structure in which he or she works. We will need to determine who has the power over the official committing the abuse and bring our concerns to *that person*.

Step 6: Conduct an investigation analysis. Our teams consider many specific questions before investigators undertake the often dangerous work of investigation. The most effective evidence—and the safest investigations—arise out of rigorous planning. Before we begin collecting evidence, we ask questions like: In order to mobilize the intended intervention, what do we need to prove, and in what form must we present the proof? Will video, audio or photographic evidence be most effective? Which will we have the highest chance of success in obtaining? What must we prove in anticipation of the lies the perpetrators will tell about the oppression? What operations and operatives will be the most effective?

Step 7: Execute the investigation. With these questions asked, our investigators are able to move into action, executing the investigation and documenting the abuse. I described in chapter ten some of our specific strategies for completing this step in order to collect evidence that we will need to secure justice for the victim.

Step 8: Execute the intervention. With evidence collected, we speak truth to power and partner with the person or people with the authority to bring relief to the victim. This step is the fulcrum in the strategy, it is the point of victim rescue, and it is when healing can begin. This step includes relief for the victim and accountability for the perpetrator. The victim relief may come quickly; the perpetrator accountability will take time, even years.

Step 9: Facilitate aftercare. Once victims have been removed from the situation of abusive violence, we ensure that they are equipped to rebuild their lives, and our social workers begin responding to the complex emotional needs that are often the result of abuse. This step often happens concurrently with the perpetrator accountability component of step eight. For each victim we develop an aftercare plan, detailing goals that will help us ensure that he or she is able to heal and to rebuild his or her life in security, hope and peace.

Step 10: Conduct a postintervention analysis. Once the victim has been rescued, aftercare has begun and the process of seeking their perpetrator's prosecution in the local legal system is complete, we must then ask more difficult questions: What worked well? How must we improve? What lessons can we take from this case to assist other clients? What story do we have to tell? Through asking these questions we learn and grow in our ability to bring effective rescue and restoration to victims in the future.

Additional Intervention Strategies

At International Justice Mission our primary intervention strategy of individual casework—undertaken through the ten-step casework method—enables us to serve specific victims of crimes that are against the laws on the books in their own country. Our work of structural transformation allows us to create sustainable change that benefits not just the clients we have served but other victims and vulnerable individuals we will never meet who will intersect with the public justice system.

But IJM's specific method of individual casework is not the only intervention strategy. In other situations of abuse there are several other strategies that can be used by God to bring relief for victims.

Strategy 1: Personal appeal. In some instances oppressors may relent, largely on the power of a personal appeal to their sense of morality, shame, pride, pity or spiritual convictions. Once one has all the information about the abuse suffered by the victim, it may be possible to arrange a direct, personal encounter with the one responsible for the oppression and seek his or her help in relieving the suffering. If the oppressor is a good person, such as King David, we might, like the prophet Nathan, find success through such an approach.

Sometimes oppressors do not fully comprehend the consequences of their actions and may change their course of action once they learn of their true impact. I can tell you, for instance, that most white South

Africans knew less about the consequences of apartheid for average black South Africans than a reasonably well-informed American who watched the evening news during that era. It may have been willful ignorance, but for many it was ignorance nonetheless. Consequently, successful efforts at introducing white South Africans to the unspeakable, everyday, real-world suffering of their black neighbors (efforts which the government vigorously opposed) often had a ground-shaking effect on whites. The miraculous way in which white South Africans "gave up" the oppressive (and tremendously profitable) structures of apartheid is largely a testimony of the power of appealing to the better aspects of their nature.[2]

In my experience, personal appeals are most effective in stopping oppression when they are made privately (sparing a public loss of face), on the basis of some personal relationship (with shared spiritual convictions often providing a bridge), in a context in which the oppressing party has not been fully exposed to the way his or her actions affect vulnerable people and under circumstances where the oppressor is not fundamentally relying on the oppression to sustain a position of power or affluence.

We must have faith in God's capacity to work through his law, which remains stamped on each person's heart—"their consciences also bearing witness, and their thoughts now accusing" (Romans 2:15). And we must be willing to take risks when we sense God leading us in making such personal appeals. On the other hand, Christians, being generally of good will and often unaccustomed to seeing the ugly underbelly of humanity's fallen nature, can easily overestimate the efficacy of such appeals. Most oppressors in this world are not King David. They are more like the pharaoh who was unwilling to release the Hebrews from oppression until God finally took the life of his son—and even so, he later sent his soldiers into the desert to try to slaughter them.

In most cases, therefore, we must press on to consider the other intervention options, which focus on the sources and limitations of oppressors' power.

Strategy 2: Command discipline. As noted in the discussion of violence in chapter nine, some of the perpetrators who carry out acts of violent injustice use positions of official authority or power to do so and thus are part of a chain of command. This is most obviously true for police and soldiers. Theoretically, they carry the implements of coercive force only because they are authorized to do so by the state. Also in theory they are authorized to use this coercive force only under a very limited set of circumstances and subject to the commands of their superiors. The government gives soldiers and police guns, but they are only authorized to use them when the law says they can and only when their superiors allow them to. So while burly soldiers and police carrying guns often look like they wield tremendous power, usually they are simply the tools of other people and exercise very limited power themselves.

In cases of abuse by the police and military, then, the individuals involved are often either exercising their force outside the limits of their commander's orders or outside the limits of the law. The police abducting girls into a brothel, for instance, are exercising their coercive force not only outside the law but outside their commander's orders—at least their most senior commanders. Thus they are operating as common criminals. Their status as police should offer them no protection. Sometimes at a lower level of the chain of command, their immediate supervisors will protect them—out of loyalty, corruption or mutual protection. If this is the case, we must find a place high enough in the chain of command to make our appeal.

I know of very few places in the world, for instance, where, if we had video footage of officers running a brothel with children, we would be unable to get assistance from the highest level of the police command—the key being the investigative product that removes all doubt of the officers' involvement. Even a corrupt police commander, if senior enough, would generally rather cashier a few low-level police officers than suffer the embarrassment of being seen to openly tolerate forced prostitution of children. The commander can take away his abusive subordinates' instruments of coercive force and their authority to exercise force (by dismissing them from their job), and can subject them to the same legal sanctions that a common criminal would face. So the challenge is to effectively target our efforts at the proper level of the chain of command. The Roman centurion told Jesus: "For I myself am a man under authority, with soldiers under me. I tell this one, 'Go,' and he goes; and that one, 'Come,' and he comes. I say to my servant, 'Do this,' and he does it" (Matthew 8:9). When our initial efforts at confronting violent injustice are unsuccessful, we must find the power actor within a chain of command with the will and the authority to make them successful.

This strategy proved critically necessary for IJM during our first operations in the Cambodian village of Svay Pak, located just a few kilometers away from Phnom Penh. On my first visit to this shanty community, the evidence of the horrific abuse endured by its children was overwhelming: the streets were jammed with brothels openly peddling children for sex. I had seen trafficking before, but no situation as brutal and gut-wrenching as the shameless sale of these young girls— the smallest among them only five years old. The darkness in the village was almost palpable; it was impossible that the local police were unaware of what was happening to Svay Pak's children.

Thanks to the efforts of civil society and government stakeholders, an antitrafficking law had been enacted and an Anti-Trafficking and Juvenile Protection Unit of the Cambodia National Police had been formed. But in Svay Pak, brothel owners were paying the local police to protect them and their trade in children. There was no way to bring rescue and safety to these children and ensure that those harming them would be prosecuted for their crimes without the participation of law enforcement. But we presented detailed evidence of the abuse to local police officials, and they repeatedly ignored it. To bring freedom to these children, we would need relationships with Cambodian officials, and we knew we needed to get higher on the chain of command than those who had not responded to the compelling evidence we had already provided. We needed to find officers of good will and commitment to their country; these power actors could make all the difference for the children of Svay Pak.

We worked tirelessly to develop relationships of trust, calling upon all the support we possibly could. In this instance we didn't have relationships high enough on the chain of command within Cambodia to effect the change the victims needed. So we approached the U.S. ambassador to Cambodia, who did have these relationships. We shared the evidence we had collected with him and asked for help. Through the advocacy of the ambassador and much persistence on the part of my colleagues, we got word that the deputy prime minister of Cambodia had ordered his people to work with us to get these girls out. Finally, we had the support we needed to conduct the operation.

In a single day of operations in 2003, dozens of Cambodian police partnered with our team on the ground to rescue thirty-seven girls and arrest thirteen perpetrators. Among those arrested was the former district police commander of Svay Pak, who was dismissed from the police force for his complicity in the crimes. Through collaboration with local authorities and appeals further up on the chain of command when we initially were unsuccessful, we were able to secure relief for victims of brutal injustice and ensure that the perpetrators of this crime faced just consequences so they could not harm others. And this operation in Svay Pak marked the beginning of a radical transformation in Cambodia. Through political pressure and technical help, Cambodia started to turn serious attention toward combating trafficking. Among countries afflicted with serious trafficking problems, it remains one of the most active in its commitment to bring the abuse to an end. In the years since that operation in Svay Pak, IJM Cambodia has partnered with local authorities to bring rescue to hundreds more victims of trafficking.

Of course, more serious difficulties arise when the abusive police or soldiers are conducting their abuses with the explicit support of government institutions. Some countries do not prohibit torture during interrogation. When I lived in South Africa, it was not illegal to detain someone without charge or trial. It was technically illegal to torture them, but it was tolerated and even ordered by commanders of the security forces. Under these circumstances, interventions within the chain of command will generally not be effective. So we use a different strategy of intervention, one that takes into account the sources and limitations of the government's power.

Strategy 3: Social demand. When the government authorities are unwilling to stop abuse through domestic legal sanctions or to bring the perpetrators to account through their chain of command, then advocates for the victims must seek other means. If the Philippine government, for instance, is unwilling to bring to justice the soldiers who perpetrated the Lupao massacre through its own court-martial system, then other measures must be considered. If the regime in Zimbabwe is unwilling to cease the disappearance and detention of political dissidents, then other methods must be considered for bringing an end to the abuse.

One way to devise such a strategy is to consider the government's own sources of power and its dependent relationships. Governments and authorities can always look very powerful, but their power is always derivative—it's derived from relationships with other people, institutions and resources. Who do the leaders of this country depend on for their power to rule? Do they rule because of their popularity and legitimacy among the people of the country? Do they rule by the force of arms? If so, how do they pay for their guns and their soldiers? Do they depend on economic relationships with major corporations or other governments?

If a government rules significantly because of its popularity or legitimacy with the country's broader public, then one of the most powerful ways to intervene on behalf of the victims of abuse is through an appeal to the public. Thus, effective efforts at publicizing the documented abuses through the media, public demonstrations, educational events and conferences can cause the government to lose its popularity and legitimacy.

President Aquino, in the Philippines, was very sensitive to public opinion, especially on human rights matters. Thus she would be very responsive to a broad public outcry over the Lupao massacre. But

President Aquino did not rule purely because of popular support. In fact, she remained president largely because a significant block of the nation's military leaders *allowed* her to rule. Since this was the case, if those military leaders didn't want to bring the Lupao massacre perpetrators to justice, then an appeal to President Aquino purely through popular opinion would not work.

Discovering that the government's power rests with military leaders rather than popularly elected civilian leadership requires a shift in intervention strategy. The focus must turn to the relationships of the military leaders. Among other things, we may find that these leaders depend heavily on relationships with foreign governments for funds, arms, legitimacy or economic prosperity. In the case of the Philippines there was a strong relationship between the military and the United States government. Knowing this, we could bring the information about the Lupao massacre to the attention of U.S. government authorities so they could use their influence with the Philippine military leaders—through the State Department, congressional inquiries, the U.S.'s presence at the United Nations and so on. Of course, if U.S. government leaders do not wish to act on behalf of the victims of Lupao, then the case can be taken to the relationships that those leaders depend on, that is, their relationships with the American public.

Observing this chain of dependent relationships, we can see the various points at which it is possible to influence the power actors who can bring relief to the victims. Seeing how this chain of relationships works explains why it might be extremely important that documented evidence of events in a little village in a country of Southeast Asia reaches the eyes and ears of a caring public in the United Kingdom or Canada, for example. A lot of rulers and authorities around the world depend quite heavily on their relationships with donor nations, including the European Union states, the United Kingdom, Canada and the United States. At their best, these relationships can function to benefit the world's poorest and most vulnerable people, who may never get a chance to share their own stories in the halls of power.

International diplomatic tools can play an important relational role. For example, the U.S. Department of State's Trafficking in Persons Office, created in 2001, issues an annual "Trafficking in Persons Report." This document is growing into a powerful diplomatic tool to fight slavery. Countries are assigned a ranking on a tri-level tier system depending on the level of their commitment to combating slavery and the active steps they have taken to combat the slave trade within their borders. With placement on tier three comes sanctions and other negative consequences—diplomatic penalties that can have a real effect on governments' willingness to respond to slavery and other human rights abuses.

Nearly all governments remain very sensitive to questions of legitimacy, and this is one reason why international law (like the Universal Declaration of Human Rights or the Geneva Conventions) and international institutions (like the United Nations and the International Labor Organization) can be very important. It's not so much that the system of international law and the United Nations have effective instruments for enforcing international codes of conduct, because for the most part they don't.[3] Rather, they provide objective standards against which the actions of governments can be measured and a forum through which information about abuses can be publicized thoughtfully and broadly. We can have tremendous facts of abuse, but if we don't have a forum to publicize it and a shared standard to illustrate it, then our facts may do us no good. Of course, these forums have serious limitations, as we have seen with regard to the humanitarian crisis in Darfur this decade, for example.

The effect of public and international opinion can be very powerful. It doesn't always result in immediate action, as we've seen this decade with regard to humanitarian abuse in Burma and Zimbabwe, but public opinion can sometimes be a forceful ally on the side of vulnerable, powerless victims of oppression. And as Nathan the prophet knows, there is nothing ungodly about presenting the facts of abuse boldly and truthfully before rulers and the public; it is an act of courageous love on behalf of those who are victimized by the abuse of authority. Conversely, we learn from Jonah's story that there are circumstances when failing to speak the truth to abusive and sinful rulers is an act of open rebellion against God.

Strategy 4: Economic interventions. Under circumstances in which the oppressors seem impervious to the powers of public shame and the chain of command or authority, we may consider other strategies to bring power to bear on behalf of victims. Sometimes an analysis of the oppressor's sources of power and dependent relationships leads us to consider methods of intervention that affect the oppressors' economic interests.

The military regime that ruled Nigeria from 1983 to 1999, for instance, did not seem to mind being viewed as criminal thugs by much of the world. They executed their critics, tortured their political prisoners and stole their country's public wealth—all the while remaining unimpressed by the verbal condemnations of the United Nations and various national governments. The U.S. State Department bluntly described conditions in Nigeria in 1997: "All branches of the security forces committed serious human rights abuses. . . . Security forces continued to commit extrajudicial killings and use excessive force to quell antigovernment protests. . . . Security forces tortured and beat suspects and detainees."[4]

The United Nations Human Rights Committee commented:

> The Committee is deeply concerned by the high number of extra-judicial and summary executions, disappearances, cases of torture, ill-treatment and arbitrary arrest and detention by members of the army and security forces and by the failure of the government to investigate fully these cases, to prosecute alleged offences, to punish those found guilty and provide compensation to the victims or their families. The resulting state of impunity encourages further violations of Covenant rights.[5]

The heads of state of the Commonwealth countries were meeting in New Zealand in 1995 and threatened to expel Nigeria from the Commonwealth if it proceeded with the execution of nine prominent political dissidents. The Nigerian government killed them all anyway. Human Rights Watch reported: "Africa's most populous country [Nigeria] became a full-fledged human rights outlaw in 1995."[6]

Clearly the power of public shame was insufficient to protect the victims of the Nigerian government's abuse of power. It's safe to say that the Nigerian government remained in power through the force of its military and the support of a ruling clique that siphoned off the country's natural resources for handsome profits. Of course, to pay for this military force and these powerful friends, the rulers needed money. Over 80 percent of the military regime's revenues came from the sale of oil—about ten billion dollars a year. Close to half of that was purchased by Americans at the gas pump, especially through Shell Oil. If the military regime were seriously threatened with an end to its oil revenues, would they have been so cavalier about their brutal abuse of power?

Given Nigeria's transition to democracy in 1999, these questions are hypothetical. But it is possible under certain circumstances to intervene on behalf of the victims of injustice by creating negative economic consequences for the perpetrators. For example, the economic sanctions imposed on South Africa during apartheid are often cited as having applied constructive pressure upon the government for change.

However, imposing economic sanctions on abusive governments is not appropriate in all circumstances. Sanctions may further isolate a rogue regime from any moderating contact with other nations. Many times the common people are hurt by the sanctions while the ruling clique continues to prosper. Often some other countries will simply replace whatever economic partnerships other countries have withdrawn. Finally, if not surgically targeted at the point of true economic vulnerability for the oppressors, the impact of the sanctions will be defused throughout the society and prove ineffective.

Nevertheless, oppressors do have economic vulnerabilities, and occasionally they can be powerfully influenced by a thoughtful and consistent combination of pressures, including economic pressures.

And economic pressure can be very successfully utilized to respond to human rights abuses that are part of or result from market processes. After public outcry at the abusive conditions of overseas shoe factories in the mid-1990s, American-owned shoe manufacturers began to take serious steps to address some of the abusive child-labor conditions of their overseas suppliers because they saw the economic threat in being associated with the oppressive "sweatshop" suffering of children. In the past decade the diamond industry has taken steps to remove conflict diamonds—diamonds whose sale directly funds armed conflict and civil wars—from their supply chains after consumer outcry became a legitimate business concern. Christians should think critically about what we are supporting with our consumer dollars, which can be a powerful tool to bring a voice to those who have none.

Strategy 5: Military force. Under the most extreme circumstances, in which the oppressor is in political power and cannot be influenced by the pressures of public shame or negative economic consequences, and where the quality and magnitude of human rights abuses is extraordinarily grave, then military force may be considered as an intervention tool on behalf of the oppressed. There are, of course, numerous serious complications that accompany the decision of one country to intervene militarily in the affairs of another, and some Christians from the peace-church tradition oppose the use of such force under any circumstances.

I, on the other hand, believe that there are a limited number of cases when the use of military force can be effective and godly. I believe that short of military force, there was no other way to stop Hitler's slaughter of the Jews in Europe. More recently a consensus of 20/20 hindsight has been reached in American foreign policy circles that the United Nations or powerful Western nations could have saved hundreds of thousands of lives in Rwanda through a brief and overwhelming deployment of military force. Such a deployment would not have solved Rwanda's long-term problems of ethnic violence, but it could have quickly brought a halt to the orgy of genocidal murder.

The dynamics of international military-police action are far too complex to discuss here, but suffice it to say that there are times when a loving response to the victims of the world's most horrendous and determined oppressors requires prayerful consideration of forceful action. But there are other situations in which military intervention may actually contribute to or exacerbate situations of injustice. These debates are complex and could fill (and have) many books, but I think it is enough to say here that Christians should be at the forefront of these discussions and debates. These issues are far too important and urgent for God's people to follow passively.

PUTTING AN INTERVENTION STRATEGY IN ACTION: DETERMINING THE MOST EFFECTIVE AGENT

When considering these intervention strategies, we must wisely consider the best *agent* of intervention. The method tells us *how* to seek it. Questions about the agent of change focus our attention on *who* should be the one to implement the intervention strategy. To determine the best choice, we can ask five pertinent questions.

1. *Who is in the most secure position to seek the intervention?* Those who intervene on behalf of the oppressed frequently face risks of retaliation, but not everyone faces the same level of risk. As a foreigner from the United States, I was in a much safer position to ask the Philippine Army hard questions about the Lupao massacre than were the vulnerable villagers. Occasionally it may be safer to funnel a Christian ministry's information about abuses through a well-known, local advocacy group in a way that does not draw unwanted attention to the expatriate Christian ministry. Also a prominent leader of high social standing may be less vulnerable to recrimination than an impoverished and vulnerable squatter—and thus he or she might be a more secure agent of intervention.

2. *Who will have the most efficient and effective access to the victims?* The variety of intervention types and methods may require access to the courts, to government leaders, to international organizations, to the media, to social and economic elites, and so on.

Consequently, it is worth considering the different kinds of people who might gain quickest access to the targeted audience.

3. Who has the best relationship or basis for a relationship with the power actors whose assistance is most critical? The intervention generally requires not only access to the right people but also their cooperation. Such cooperation is most likely to come from people who connect at a personal level because they share common backgrounds, interests or communities.

4. Who has the required expertise? There are some interventions that require specific expertise. Courtroom interventions are generally limited to practicing lawyers. Media and public-relations interventions and campaigns require yet another set of skills. Interventions with the United Nations and other international bodies also may require specific expertise. Obviously, when choosing an agent for a specialized intervention, we should choose one with the appropriate expertise.

5. Who has the greatest credibility? The agent of the intervention must have credibility with the one to whom the intervention is targeted. The sources of personal credibility vary; they frequently include the elements already mentioned—preexisting relationships, job specialty, expertise. But credibility also may be a matter of political background, ideological tradition, family background, social status, ethnicity, and professional or educational background. Evaluating the relevant personal credibility factors will help us choose the best agent for the intervention.

In all these matters, as we try to obey God's call to intervene on behalf of the oppressed, we will surely need his wisdom and guidance. As Jesus advised his disciples when facing abusive officials, we must be "as shrewd as snakes and as innocent as doves" (Matthew 10:16). Fortunately, God *promises* to grant us wisdom if we only ask him for it in faith (James 1:5). May he then grant us the wisdom to pursue life-giving intervention by selecting the best method and the most effective agent as we rescue victims of abuse.

THE BODY OF CHRIST
IN ACTION

What We All Can Do

God is in the business of using the unlikely to perform the holy. To declare his glory God worked through an old man with few relatives and no children, and established a nation whose descendants would outnumber the stars and through whom "all peoples on earth will be blessed" (Genesis 12:3; 15:5). To slay an oppressive giant who terrorized entire armies of Israel, God worked through a scrawny shepherd boy who didn't even know how to dress for battle. To build the church of Jesus Christ and to turn the world upside down, God worked through the most unlikely crew of humble women and common fishermen—not many wise, not many powerful, not many noble (1 Corinthians 1:26).

We Are All Qualified to Seek Justice

God has chosen to use the "foolish" and the "weak" to accomplish his divine will on earth, and that simply means that I am qualified to be on his team. We all are. And when it comes to seeking justice for the hurting in our world, he doesn't have a special roster. He intends to use you and me. He doesn't have any other plan. In fact, it was precisely for such good works that we were created; they don't save us or make us righteous before God, but they allow us to fulfill the godly purpose for which God created us. As Paul wrote, "For we are God's workmanship, created in Christ Jesus to do good works, which God prepared in advance for us to do" (Ephesians 2:10). And what are *good* works?

> He has told you, O mortal, what is good;
> and what does the Lord require of you
> but to do justice, and to love kindness,
> and to walk humbly with your God? (Micah 6:8 NRSV)

Again, when the prophet Isaiah tells us to "learn to *do good*," he follows with the more specific exhortation to "seek justice, rescue the oppressed, defend the orphan, plead for the widow" (Isaiah 1:17 NRSV).

When it comes to seeking justice in a world of vulnerable men, women and children, all of us are privileged to play a role. You may be wondering, where do I fit in? I'm not a lawyer or an investigator, but I want to be part of what God is doing to rescue the oppressed. As with all of the good works at the core of God's priorities, this is an all-hands-on-deck proposition. When it comes to sharing the good news of Jesus Christ, for example, all of us do what we can. Some of us will preach to stadiums full of people, some will translate the Scriptures for a whole language group, some will stand and give a testimony to a sparsely attended prayer breakfast and others will share their faith over a cup of coffee with a friend. Still others will support each of these endeavors with prayers, financial resources or simple words of encouragement. But *all* of God's people are privileged to "give the reason for the hope" (1 Peter 3:15) that is in them and can do *something* to advance Christ's commission to make disciples among all the nations.

Our calling does not stop with sharing the good news. All of us are also called to do something to care for the poor. If we aren't, then, asks the apostle John, how can the love of God be within us (1 John 3:17)? And we are all called to do something to seek justice for the oppressed. Why? Because along with mercy and faith, justice, Jesus said, is one of the "more important matters," one that none of us can neglect (Matthew 23:23).

Besides, why would we want to neglect it? We would miss out on the many opportunities to express our love for God and for our neighbors. In so doing, we also would miss out on the fullness that God intended for our life. For this is, after all, the abundant life for which Christ came to earth and died for us—a life of godly significance, of divine importance (John 10:10).

Truly we can't share the gospel with everyone, feed all the hungry, comfort all the afflicted or rescue all the oppressed, but *all* of us can, praise God, do *something* to advance these priorities of God. There certainly are different seasons of activity, different gifts and different needs and opportunities in the life of a follower of Christ, but if we ever look at the works that God asks us to do—proclaim the gospel, help the poor, defend the abused—and say, "Well, you know, that's really not *my* thing," then we have simply made a conscious decision to impoverish our spiritual life. Christ in his holiness abhors injustice. As we grow into his character and image, we not only grow in our passion to seek justice, we are also led into those concrete good works for which we were created.

Each member of the body of Christ has a very tangible role; Christ in his grace has shut none of us out of his glory. Clearly, not everyone has the same role, and an appreciation of the special gifts and expertise that God has granted for the work is extremely important. But Christ accepts every offering and often counts the most humble offering as the greatest.

Seeking justice is the task of bringing truth and power to bear on behalf of those who are oppressed, and here the diverse gifts of the body are called out in glorious array. In this chapter, we'll first explore how several specific groups of people can use their particular areas of giftedness and positions of service to seek justice. Then we will explore steps that any Christian can take to follow God's great and urgent call to his people.

SEEKING JUSTICE THROUGH THE BODY OF CHRIST: YOUR LOCAL CHURCH

In his call to us to seek justice for victims of violent oppression, God has given us a task that requires the great energy stored in the global church. The work of justice can be difficult and even scary—but it is not work we are asked to undertake alone. As we follow his call to bring victims of injustice the relief they urgently need, God frees us from the fear and triviality that can stifle our faith. His call is for all Christians—and he will equip us in our churches and Bible studies and community groups to pursue this call to protect the most vulnerable of our global neighbors.

One great challenge for churches beginning to wade into this work has been a lack of clear examples of what church engagement in justice actually looks like. We are blessed with strong models of churches engaged in evangelism and mercy ministry, but in the past century, churches have had few established examples to look to for engaging in the hands-on work of justice. Christians who had caught the vision of justice for the poor often simply didn't know how to start their own churches in this work. But over the past ten years, we at IJM have had the immense joy of witnessing a sea change, as churches of all types and sizes have discovered God's call to justice and dived into the work. These churches are now becoming models of how the local body of Christ can engage in the hands-on work of justice in a significant and meaningful way. A church in California, moved by the need for more resources for victims of violent abuse, partnered with International Justice Mission in Huànuco, Peru, to create a safe and loving home for victims of violent abuse. A church in Georgia has introduced International Justice Mission to its extensive network of contacts in Thailand, equipping our frontline team there for greater ministry. In Ohio, a church moved by God's call to love the least of these has engaged the resources and energies of its people to support IJM's aftercare work for sex trafficking victims. Churches around the country have begun to stand on behalf of victims of trafficking and other forms of injustice in their own communities. (Visit IJM's website to read the stories of some churches leading the way in justice work.)

The engagement of churches in the work of justice flows naturally out of communities of spiritual health and leadership committed to acting as if what Jesus tells us is indeed true. It is true that the work of justice has been unfamiliar to much of the church for so long that the initial steps into this call can sometimes be difficult or scary. However, I believe that Scripture makes it clear: our engagement with the work of justice is no more and no less than an extension of our desire to follow our God and Savior. Thus the entire army of God can remain disengaged from the battle if they do not know their Lord well enough to hear his voice. Or worse, they can be led off into a passionate struggle for justice following only the carnal call of humans, a struggle that ends up knowing only the voice of raw power. But if our leaders—the pastors, seminary professors, ministry trainers, Sunday school teachers, Bible study leaders, and educators of our churches and organizations—teach us about the God of justice, we can, and will, follow *him* in the struggle against injustice.

Our shepherds and teachers must lead us in the authority of the Word of God to know God's passion for justice, Christ's compassion for the oppressed, God's holy condemnation of the sinful abuse of power and his deep desire to rescue the vulnerable. From the Word of God we learn that God's plan for seeking justice in the world is to use his people to work acts of love and rescue. Spiritual maturity will equip us with a hope that will withstand the inevitable trials and suffering that accompany obedience to Christ. Our spiritual disciplines and God's own Spirit will prepare us to be witnesses for Christ's love and holiness in a hurting world of oppression. And confronted with the violent oppression that terrorizes the most vulnerable people in our world, fed by spiritual health, we will act on God's call to justice.

Or—we won't.

Some Christians will be so shocked by the unfamiliarity of this God of justice, that they will, like the Pharisees of Jesus' day, return to a rigorous and passionate worship of a different God—their familiar God of tithes and sacrifices—and neglect the God of the Bible, the God of justice, mercy and faith. A heavy responsibility and glorious opportunity is in the hands of the global church. Jesus called the faith community of his own people back to their Scriptures, to rediscover this God who had become unknown to them. At least one teacher came secretly to Jesus in the night to learn more (John 3:1-17), but most teachers simply grew angry at the suggestion that they had veered from the God of the Scriptures. They closed their ears to the voice of Christ.

Other believers, however, will, like Saul of Tarsus, hear Jesus. They will see that even in their zealousness to serve God, they have missed out on a full knowledge of him. The Scriptures will come alive for them with a freshness that they have not known in years. They will rediscover Christ's simple and straightforward proclamation:

> The Spirit of the Lord is on me,
>   because he has anointed me
>   to preach good news to the poor.
> He has sent me to proclaim freedom for the prisoners
>   and recovery of sight for the blind,
> to release the oppressed,
>   to proclaim the year of the Lord's favor. (Luke 4:18-19)

Yes, Christ has come to set us free from sin and death through his sacrifice on the cross, but he has also come to deliver the poor, the prisoner and the oppressed. The prophet Isaiah made this clear to the leaders of Israel who were tiring God out with their prayer meetings and their spectacles of fasting in sackcloth and ashes.

> Is not this the kind of fasting I have chosen:
> to loose the chains of injustice,
>   and untie the cords of the yoke,
> to set the oppressed free,
>   and break every yoke?
> Is it not to share your food with the hungry
>   and to provide the poor wanderer with shelter—

when you see the naked, to clothe him,
and not to turn away from your own flesh and blood?
(Isaiah 58:6-7)

"*Then*," says the prophet,

your light will break forth like the dawn,
and your healing will quickly appear;
then your righteousness will go before you,
the glory of the LORD will be your rear guard.
Then you will call, and the LORD will answer;
you will cry for help, and he will say: Here am I.
(Isaiah 58:8-9)

The teachers and shepherds of today's church have a huge task before them in helping Christians come to know the God of justice. Our Bible scholars, theologians, pastors, Bible study leaders and historians need to dig deeply into the Scriptures to help us understand how God in his holiness relates to the sinful abuse of power and how we can do our part in "setting the oppressed free." In the twentieth century we grew in our understanding of evangelism, world mission, care for the poor, healing of the sick. We also learned how to be a voice of moral integrity within an idolatrous and promiscuous society. But we have a wonderful journey ahead of us in understanding a Christian's role in a world where power is used to abuse the weak. And the body of Christ cannot take up its rightful ministry of justice if its mind has not been thoroughly renewed by and rooted in the Word of God.

Thus every Christian—and particularly those Christians whom God has placed in positions to lead and nurture his people—has a tangible place to start: searching the Word of God to know the God of justice.

The LORD will guide you always;
he will satisfy your needs in a sun-scorched land
and will strengthen your frame.

You will be like a well-watered garden,
   like a spring whose waters never fail.
Your people will rebuild the ancient ruins
   and will raise up the age-old foundations;
you will be called Repairer of Broken Walls,
   Restorer of Streets with Dwellings. (Isaiah 58:11-12)

Frontline Global Workers

The next most critical role in developing a Christian witness for justice in the world will be played by frontline workers in the field—the tens of thousands of missionaries and relief-and-development workers who minister throughout the globe. After all, they represent the very incarnation of the body of Christ within the communities where the victims of abuse actually live. Living and working among the poor, the marginalized, the minorities and the isolated peoples of our world, these frontline workers are the eyes and ears, the hands and feet of the body of Christ. They hear from the prisoner's family after their father is dragged away by security forces. They notice—as few others do—when little girls disappear, having been abducted into sexual exploitation. The widow dispossessed of her land is actually a member of their congregation. The minority tribal group members being harassed by the army are the people for whom the missionary has been translating the Scriptures. The missionary doctor is the one who stitches the wounds of the student tortured by the police. The child sold into slavery or raped by a town councilor is actually a sponsored child of the Christian relief-and-development agency.

Many Christians are tempted to make the mistake, however, of expecting these global workers to provide direct intervention on behalf of the victims of abuse. In many cases this is unwise. As we have seen, seeking justice for such victims requires overcoming the oppressor's powers of deception and violence through a careful investigation of the facts and a tactical intervention with appropriate authorities. Taking on such a task requires a number of resources of which, in my experience, global Christian workers are in short supply.

1. Emotional energy. Taking on the cause of a victim of abuse requires substantial emotional energy as we interact with the victim's pain and the relentless frustrations of seeking vindication for their cause. The emotional drain of it all can quickly run a missionary down, and if he or she starts the process with depleted emotional resources, it's very difficult to persevere.

2. Time. A careful accounting of the facts and a persistent intervention with authorities can require extensive expenditures of time. Stepping with conviction into the complicated and frustrating world of the oppressed, a global worker can find many days swallowed up by the endeavor.

3. Finances. These efforts can also require significant expenditures of financial resources. To ministries already feeling the strain of limited funds, the expenses that accompany a proper investigation and intervention can prove a great burden.

4. Security. Most critically, perhaps, intervention on behalf of a victim requires a certain level of security against personal or governmental retaliation. Often guests in a foreign country, global Christian workers are particularly vulnerable to governmental retaliation if the authorities are unhappy with the questions workers are asking or the cause they are pleading. The trouble-making worker or ministry can be kicked out of the country. Necessary permits or licenses can be denied. Legal and civil protections or privileges can be withdrawn. Worse, missionary workers who live in the community may be vulnerable to personal, physical retaliation from the oppressive forces in the community.

5. Expertise. Most global Christian workers simply don't have the expertise that these cases require. Very few missionaries or relief-and-development workers have professional backgrounds in criminal investigation, risk assessment, legal intervention, government relations and other areas of expertise that are frequently required in such matters.

Thus when the special needs of abused children, widows, prisoners or refugees come to their attention, these workers are gener-

ally not in a very strong position to directly intervene on their behalf. Nor is it fair to expect them to do so in most cases. The victim
of oppression is worthy of the expenditure of emotional energy,
time, resources, personal security and expertise that their cause
requires, but it does not follow that, in the fullness of the body of
Christ, all of this should fall on our frontline workers in the field,
who for the most part have been sent and equipped for very different tasks. When the missionary who teaches theology at the Bible
school in Ethiopia sees signs of famine in the community, we don't
expect him to become an expert in emergency humanitarian relief.
When the church planter in Southeast Asia finds mounting conditions of drought, we usually don't expect her to become a hydraulic
engineer. When a woman in the village needs cataract surgery, we
don't expect the Bible translator to do it. Rather in each case we
look to the broader body of Christ and call on the surgeons, the
well-drillers and the famine fighters.

We can expect the missionary at the seminary to share some rice
with a next-door neighbor. We might expect the church planter to
teach the villagers about boiling water. And we might expect the
Bible translator to bandage a simple wound. Similarly, on occasion
international workers will be in a reasonable position to seek justice for a victim of abuse in their community and can make a con-
tribution toward the elimination of oppressive conditions. But we
are mistaken if we think that seeking justice—overcoming violence
and deception—is a simple task that the average caring person is
equipped to do on his or her own. This is simply not the case, and
we should adjust our expectations for global Christian workers
accordingly.

However, we should not make the mistake of thinking that just
because the Christian worker in the field can't do what is required
in a given case that there isn't anyone in the body of Christ who can.
There will be occasions when there is nothing anyone can do, but
we must not confuse this very narrow category of cases with the
broader category of cases in which there is nothing that the field-

worker can do. Between the list of cases where *no one* can help and the list of cases where the *fieldworker* cannot help is a long list of cases where *someone* can help. The average fieldworker, for example, stands utterly powerless before the elderly woman in the community who has grown blind from cataracts. But for the Christian surgeon, a miraculous healing of her sight is just a routine surgery away. Likewise, the case of injustice that seems utterly hopeless to the Christian engineer who has come to a community to dig a new well may be a straightforward piece of work to a Christian public justice professional.

What we need, then, is to make sure that global Christian workers have access to such resources and expertise. We must ensure that the full body of Christ is tending to the needs of the world rather than piling yet another unfair burden on missionaries and relief-and-development workers.

MISSION TEAMS

It's fair to say that within a stone's throw of just about every victim of oppression in the world, there is a Christian who God has called and placed in the community to share the love of Jesus. Around the world God's people are called to seek justice in their own communities—and in many communities in the developing world, the local church carries the battle for justice at the frontlines, ministering to victims of violent abuse in their congregations and bringing their needs before God in prayer. These believers from every nation are also joined by those God has called to serve him outside of their own communities—from long-term missionaries who share God's truth, to doctors who practice medicine in impoverished communities to create a tangible picture of God's healing and his goodness, to those engaged in the life-giving work of mercy ministries, providing food and other vital services, to frontline workers God has given a vision of change for the world's poor through educational or microfinance opportunities.

But these long-term international workers do not labor alone. Churches often send short-term teams to the developing world to build homes, work with orphanages, engage people in evangelism, provide medical care and enact other live-giving affirmations of God's goodness alongside local churches in the community they are serving. These trips provide the opportunity to engage in the work of justice on the frontlines alongside the global body of Christ. Identifying injustices in the communities the team serves provides a holistic picture of what God desires for that community. In the process, the team may discover an issue that its congregation can assist with. Interested individuals can visit the IJM website to acquire *As You Go,* a mission-training DVD developed to assist with this very purpose. After viewing the DVD, an individual or group can speak with their church leadership to see whether they might add the ministry of justice to the ministries of compassion and mercy they will engage in on the trip.

Remember, the key to oppressors' power over victims is isolating them from those who might be able to intervene on their behalf. As long as victims are cut off from those who might be able to expose oppressors' deceptions and introduce a counteracting power to protect the victims, oppressors are free to abuse the weak. God's first step in enabling the body of Christ to seek justice for the oppressed, therefore, has been to break down the isolation of the vulnerable by deploying his witnesses into their communities—into every city, village, hamlet, nook and cranny of this broad world. What an amazing thing God has done through those who have obeyed the call of Christ to international service—whether on a lifelong commitment to international mission or a short-term trip! He has sent his disciples into the far reaches of the world, and the oppressed are not alone. As we go into the field to serve the poorest, we must ask God to help us and our team to develop the eyes to see and ears to hear about injustice in the community we serve.

Both short-term mission teams and long-term fieldworkers can do a great deal to bring real help to victims of violent injustice: they can share what they know with the larger body of Christ. There are two key tasks in this process.

1. *We must develop the eyes to see and ears to hear about injustice.* Jesus is sensitive to the abuse of power among his people, so global Christian workers need to ask God for Christ's tenderness. By conversation and demeanor we will convey to the community that we are interested in listening with a careful ear to the injustice that our neighbors endure. Or we will give the impression that such matters really aren't our concern. In many communities the most powerful way to heed the biblical injunction to bear each other's burdens (Galatians 6:2) is to hear the stories of those who are burdened by the oppressive abuse of power. With love and courage we can communicate to our neighbors that stories of injustice are of urgent, passionate concern to God and therefore of compelling interest to God's people. IJM's training for short-term teams provides several resources to equip them for this task.

2. *We must tell the story.* Short-term teams and long-term field-workers can share the information they learn with those who might come to the victim's aid. The team might know people in the community—the local church it's connected with, civic leaders, lawyers or advocates—who could investigate the matter and help the one who is suffering abuse. IJM provides a justice assessment resource for teams headed into the field to help them to document what they have seen as part of our *As You Go* mission-training resource. This justice assessment is used by our staff as we consider how we might respond to the justice needs of communities around the world. Whether it is with IJM, with local contacts or people in the church body who have particular expertise, the goal is to share the story with those who can provide help and rescue. Sometimes workers don't know who to turn to with information about violent injustice—and in some situations, turning to the wrong person might have dire consequences. International Justice Mission can identify trustworthy Christian agencies to which global ministries can tell their stories. IJM will consult with the ministry about where to turn or, if possible, take on the matter as a case referral and independently pursue an investigation and intervention on behalf of the victim.

Both short-term teams and long-term fieldworkers can also share these stories with the churches and individuals that support them back home. Mobilizing the full body of Christ as a witness for justice in the world will only happen when Christians come to know the heart of their God—the God of justice—and when they understand some of the needs around the world. No sources are more qualified to provide such a ministry to a church community than the workers they have sent into the field.

In taking these two basic steps, short-term teams can participate in God's call to justice—loving their neighbors as the good Samaritan did. The good Samaritan's great act of love consisted of two similar parts (Luke 10:25-37). First, he refused to walk obliviously on the other side of the road when he encountered the injured man; he got close enough to assess the man's needs. Second, he offered what aid he could by bandaging him and taking him to an inn, and he referred his hurting neighbor to the innkeeper—a professional who was equipped to meet the man's needs in a way that the Samaritan could not. The good Samaritan was *good* not because he was able to meet all of the hurting man's needs but because he had mercy on the man and cared for him, and then referred him to someone else who could help him.

Global Christian workers can obey Christ and tangibly love their neighbors who suffer abuse by turning compassionate eyes and ears toward them, listening to them, recording their story, and referring them to local or international entities that might help them.

COUNTRY AND CULTURE EXPERTS

Apart from its frontline workers in the field, the Christian agencies of world mission and international relief and development have also developed an extraordinary body of experts on countries and cultures around the world. Name a nationality, an ethnic group, a language group or any other cultural or political subdivision of humanity and we can find a Christian scholar, researcher or fieldworker who has spent the better part of a lifetime studying their history, culture, mores, traditions, communal dynamics, governance, social systems, religion, worldview, language and leadership.

Over the last few generations the leaders of international mission have committed vast amounts of resources to the study of various countries and cultures. The theory of modern mission in the past couple of generations has focused on the task of conveying the gospel to communities in forms that are readily accessible to the existing culture. The notion of Western missionaries seeing themselves as purveyors of Western culture was abandoned long ago.[1] Instead, today's Western missionaries largely see themselves as students of the culture they enter. And in the educational and training institutions of the church and the mission community worldwide, this study has reached a level of sophistication, comprehensiveness and depth that rivals or exceeds the expertise of secular educational institutions, foreign policy institutions, governmental agencies and international business groups.

All of this intelligence and expertise within the worldwide Christian community is tremendously helpful in seeking justice where needed. The experience and know-how of fellow Christians in the practical matters regarding access to a country, logistics, security, geography, transportation and language can be indispensable for conducting investigations and interventions. Particularly when it comes to making interventions, the cultural, social and political expertise and relationships of the broad body of Christ can be extraordinarily helpful. An analysis of a society's power structure, communal dynamics, cultural sensitivities and historical context is extremely important for the development of a surgical and effective intervention, and much of this analysis is readily available within the networks of Christian agencies and institutions.

Alongside IJM's national staff members—local Christians with a deep understanding of their own countries and cultures—the global Christian community can provide invaluable expertise and understanding, with the goal of bringing relief to the most vulnerable among us. Thus in the work of seeking justice, there is a tremendous role to play for all Christians in mission, academia, international service, global business and other vocations wherein expertise in multiple countries and cultures is acquired. These experts simply need to recognize the value of their wisdom, knowledge and experience, and share it with those who are pursuing interventions on behalf of the oppressed. Obviously International Justice Mission is most grateful to add such expertise to its councils of international consultants.

PUBLIC JUSTICE PROFESSIONALS

Christian public justice professionals can play a critical role in answering God's call to the entire body of Christ on behalf of victims of oppression. Over the past ten years, I have seen God work incredible miracles through men and women with specialized training willing to be used by him. As we have seen, the first task in seeking justice for the oppressed is to overcome the deception behind which oppressors hide their coercion and abuse. When we think of professions to which God calls believers, many of our minds jump to pastors, missionaries or Christian counselors. And God does call many people to serve him through ministry in these careers. However, I have also seen God use the years of training and skill of IJM's corps of undercover investigators to his glory in marvelous ways.

Perhaps we are not accustomed to thinking about law-enforcement professionals, lawyers or government-relations experts using their skills in Christian ministry. If so, we need to rethink such a view. If we are called to seek justice as part of building the kingdom of God, then we need to make full use of the gifts of those who possess the skills and experience to deal with violence and deception.

Around the world, from IJM's Washington, D.C., headquarters to each of our field offices in the developing world, God works through the professional skills of IJM's investigators and lawyers. In Guatemala he uses the training of our field office director, a Guatemalan attorney who practiced family law and taught at the local university before joining IJM to represent in court child victims of sexual violence. In the United States, God uses one of our vice president's decades of tactical police experience to lead the investigative efforts of our staff around the globe—investigations that bring freedom and relief to victims of violence.

At International Justice Mission, Christian public justice professionals with top-level technical skills from developing nations as well as from the West have proven that they can be used of God in miraculous ways to protect the vulnerable. Certainly, this ministry requires a specific combination of gifts and experience. The sensitivity and serious risks associated with work in these contexts requires an uncompromising standard of professional excellence and technical skill. The circumstances afford no generosity for those who bring only good intentions, the best of motives or tender hearts. Without a fierce commitment to the sharpest standards in operational and tactical excellence, we honor neither God nor those we serve. But such professional excellence must be ruled by the fruit of the Spirit. The ministry of International Justice Mission—and of those seeking to serve God by serving victims of violent oppression—requires, first and foremost, great spiritual resources of faith, courage, humility, and a self-effacing and sacrificial spirit of service. It requires a capacity to work with meekness, love and honesty among people of other cultures, a heart that listens first and speaks last. It requires discretion, wisdom and a special measure of self-mastery and self-denial. Ultimately, it depends on a life of urgent, unceasing prayer.

And of course God is not only working through the professional training of International Justice Mission's employees. Christians working in law-making bodies, foreign service, the United Nations, the military, the diplomatic corp or international human rights agencies may be called on to render assistance based on the skills, experience and relationships God has given them. Christian law-enforcement professionals enforce the rule of law so people around the world know safety and security. God has, in his mercy and mystery, equipped the body of Christ with men and women uniquely skilled to bear witness to justice and overcome deception and coercion. The body must deploy what God has given to defend those who are vulnerable in our world.

INTERNATIONAL BUSINESS PROFESSIONALS

God's deployment of his ministers around the world also includes the large numbers of Christian business professionals who have developed extensive expertise and influential relationships around the globe. There are occasions when this wisdom and these relationships can be leveraged not only for successful business development but also in service to those who are weakest in society. Occasionally, business professionals can make direct inquiries of government authorities and business partners about specific cases of alleged abuse that come to their attention. When done respectfully, with humility and with accurate, specific facts, such inquiries can have a dramatic effect on local authorities or elites who otherwise might not have such matters brought to their attention—primarily because the victims are far from the social and economic circles in which such leaders move.

Christian business executives and professionals can seek out personal relationships with members of the local church community in the country where they are working. Better still, like Christ they might seek relationships with indigenous Christians outside the socioeconomic circles in which their business relationships move. Through personal relationships with the indigenous Christian community, business people working abroad can bring a Christlike sensitivity to the influence of corporate power in that community—an appreciation for the economic opportunity that can come from international investment, as well as an appreciation for the negative consequences that otherwise might go unnoticed in the formation of corporate business strategy.

International business professionals may also be able to serve the work of justice by providing introductions into the extensive networks of in-country contacts they may have developed. Christian business executives can provide IJM field office staff with personal introductions to government or business leaders who may be able to help facilitate relief for the victims we serve. Many times we can find powerful people in the country's senior business and government circles who are eager to help when the issue is presented to them with discretion, respect and accuracy. Christians working globally as business professionals are frequently in a position to access these relationships on behalf of those who are weak. These relationships can be critical in lending status and power to the cause of the vulnerable.

Finally, international business professionals are frequently in the position to provide financial support to undergird the work of seeking justice. Obviously, although the poor frequently need the assistance of public justice professionals, they cannot pay to retain the services they desperately need. Business professionals can participate directly in God's work by making it financially possible for public justice professionals to provide specialized services to those who cannot pay for them. Therefore those God has prospered in their international business dealings can render back to God something of his graciousness by supporting Christian efforts to seek justice for victims of oppression in the very nation where God has granted successful business endeavors. There may be instances in which such support might be the very reason God has granted special prosperity to a member of the worldwide Christian family. God pours out great joy on those who bring rescue to the hurting in this way!

THE STORYTELLERS AND COMMUNICATORS

In the work of seeking justice there are two stories that deserve to be told with passion and excellence: the stories of the victims of abuse and the stories of what God has done to bring rescue. The boy sold into slavery, the girl held in prostitution, the student tortured by soldiers, the widow pushed off her land—all deserve to have their stories told with honesty, authenticity, power and life.

In doing so, we can provide an indispensable service of love to the victims of injustice. We provide a voice to the voiceless. We tell the truth about injustice. We affirm the dignity and worth of those who have been told in a thousand ways that their suffering does not matter. We overcome the humiliation, loneliness, indignity and despair of those who suffer under not only the oppressor's abuse but also the oppressor's aggressive lies—the lie that no one will believe their story, that no one cares about their story, that nothing can be done about their story.

By vividly telling the stories of victims, we not only lend their stories the dignity and honor they deserve, we also provide an essential service of love to fellow Christians and citizens who are isolated and alienated from the hurting neighbors God created them to love. Through the stories of victims we can render the reality of injustice in a way that overcomes the barriers of distance, vagueness, remoteness and emotional numbness, and we connect them to the intimate human drama of their suffering neighbor.

The writers, producers, artists and media professionals in our Christian community can play a vital role in bringing deliverance by telling the stories of the oppressed with all the conviction, clarity and vividness their special gifts of communication allow. And where God in his mercy and power has brought rescue, the story of his faithfulness needs to be told—with every tool of communication and artistic expression at our disposal. Such stories inspire hope, encourage the afflicted and give witness to God's glory.

Over the past ten years, IJM's artist partners, and other Christian artists committed to using their creative gifts to share with the body of Christ the struggle for justice in our world, have shown the church the beauty and the hope of God's call to restorative justice. International Justice Mission's frontline casework stories have inspired beautiful musical expressions of God's call to justice, haunting artistic renderings that impart deep truths about oppression, documentaries that show the reality of violence against the poor, and concert series held to raise funds and awareness for this vital work. From singer-songwriter Sara Groves's evocative melodies and profound lyrics exploring the struggle for justice in our world to the urgency of the messages communicated by filmmakers awakening passion in a new generation of abolitionists, we have seen God accomplish marvelous things through the skills of gifted communicators.

And all Christians have the opportunity to serve as a voice for the oppressed in their own communities—through sharing stories of hope, redemption and justice. I hope that the stories of changed lives in this book will resonate with thousands of people. And IJM's website is packed with more—as well as video and audio tools for sharing these stories. We need to use the platforms God has given us to share this urgent call to all his people. As we witness to God's work of restoring hope, dignity and life to victims of violent oppression, we truly share in his goodness—and we mobilize those around us to join in this incredible work.

WHAT EVERY CHRISTIAN CAN DO

God can use our careers, our artistic expression and our words to bring relief to victims of injustice. But you may be wondering, *where do I start today?* There are some practical pathways for involvement in this work—steps we can take that, as IJM has seen over the past decade, truly can make a life-or-death difference for victims of injustice.

God in his graciousness has provided a role for every Christian in the work of seeking justice. Rescuing the oppressed is meant to be an integral part of our life of Christian devotion simply because it is how we share in the fullness of the character of God. What a joy, what a privilege to be used by God to transform the lives of those broken by the crushing abuse of power! What poverty, what sadness, what regret to have never known the profound joy and satisfaction in being used of God to redeem a life from oppression and violence.

When it comes to the biblical work of seeking justice, every thoughtful and compassionate Christian can know the exhilaration, significance and challenge of being the instrument of our almighty God. At IJM we see this journey in three parts: Educate, Explore, Engage.

EDUCATE

Raise awareness. Our communities need to know the truth about violent oppression. We can share with our church, school and family about the abuse faced by the poor, and about God's gracious plan to include us in bringing relief to these victims. In order to undertake this task effectively, we'll need to become familiar with our global neighborhood. From keeping up with the international section in our daily paper and conducting focused research on specific topics of injustice, to seeking out friends of different cultural backgrounds from our own, we must familiarize ourself with the hard truths of violent oppression. It is with this knowledge that we can begin to raise awareness of justice issues within our family, church, school and community.

Awareness creates the social demand necessary to bring change. Imagine what would happen if every Christian in America called their representatives in Washington, D.C., to discuss how we might end slavery in our lifetime? It would dramatically change the political landscape. But because only a handful of Christians are cognizant of the crisis of modern-day slavery, little is accomplished.

Indeed, awareness also helps us raise the resources necessary for growth. The two greatest needs for IJM to expand its mission are qualified professionals to join the team full time and for financial resources so IJM can continue to show up in the places where the poor urgently need an advocate. Without increasing awareness, the growth of justice ministry will be limited.

I believe that without the knowledge of the abuse faced by our brothers and sisters around the globe, our own spiritual lives are simply impoverished. If all the work God has done in our own lives, our churches, our Bible studies and our youth groups is to be used *for* something, we must begin by learning about the massive and urgent needs in our world, and we must educate our communities of faith about these vital issues and God's call on our lives.

Build up the justice generation. In the last fifty years an incredible shift in the North American church has resulted in the emergence of many Christian relief-and-development agencies dedicated to ministries of mercy and compassion. Over the past decade we have seen a seismic shift in the North American church regarding the need and opportunity to be engaged in God's call to justice. God is doing an incredible work of mobilizing the church to bring justice for those suffering from violent oppression, and the coming generation is positioned to have the greatest effect in continuing to bring about this shift. When speaking at youth events we have discovered that those in attendance are already convinced that God seeks justice for the oppressed. We are so inspired by and take such great hope in their commitment that we refer to this generation as the "justice generation." It is our desire to nurture this God-given passion in the coming generation, but we need the assistance of the entire body of Christ. Visit the IJM website for resources to educate and encourage students in the work of justice. Students can learn about starting or joining an IJM campus chapter at www.ijm.org. IJM's campus chapters have been a strong voice of education and advocacy in their schools.

Explore

Become a part of the IJM Institute. Join the IJM Institute, a web-based community where Christian leaders share ideas and engage in dialogue about concrete action for overcoming injustice. It is a source for leaders to gain access to urgent rescue updates, global news, cutting-edge tools, best practices and technological reflection as they seek to draw others into the work of justice. To join the IJM Institute, visit www.ijminsitute.org.

Incorporate justice on a short-term trip. IJM's *As You Go* mission-training DVD was described earlier in this chapter (see p. 222). This tool is a great way for a church community to explore the work of justice as it engages in ministries of compassion and mercy internationally. Visit IJM's website for more details.

Engage

Seek God. When confronting violent oppression, we become aware of our limitations. We are desperate for God's assistance to move the cases forward and to protect victims and IJM staff who are on the front lines. As a result IJM staff around the world stop work each day for corporate prayer, as well as a time of individual stillness and silent prayer. We would love to have you as a partner in seeking God for assistance as well. Every Christian can bring before God the urgent needs of a prisoner illegally detained, the numbing despair of a child held in prostitution, the wounds of a torture victim or the suffocating burdens of a child held in bonded servitude.

Those who commit to serve as an IJM prayer partner receive weekly prayer requests from IJM related to specific cases. We covet your prayers and believe that the God of justice longs to hear your voice. International Justice Mission's vast network of prayer partners take the concerns of justice to the throne of our heavenly Father each day. They experience the glory of stepping into the very heart of what the Creator of the universe is doing in history. They participate in the divine redemption of the orphan and the widow as God rescues their lives from the pit. Over time, these partners come to know and love our staff members, and they uphold us and our families in prayer. They come to know the victims of abuse in tiny villages or megacities, and they challenge God to manifest his character of compassion and justice.

Followers of Christ who step with him into the work of justice through intercessory prayer experience the glory of stepping into the very heart of what the Creator of the universe is doing in history. They participate in the divine redemption of the orphan and the widow as God rescues their lives from the pit. They come to know God. They see his faithfulness, his loving kindness, his mysterious ways. In this way every Christian who loves Jesus can proclaim his character of love and justice around the world.

Consider joining us for the annual Global Prayer Gathering in Washington, D.C., which is a unique event in the life of IJM. It is the one time each year when all of IJM's field directors—the real heroes who spend each day fighting for justice on the frontlines—join us to share firsthand stories of rescue as well as current challenges they are facing. It's a time when IJM prayer partners and supporters are invited to gather with us for a focused time of prayer and worship, asking God to intervene on behalf of the victims of injustice throughout the world. We have seen remarkable answers to prayer through this time together. Please visit the IJM website to learn more about joining us at the Global Prayer Gathering or becoming an IJM prayer partner.

Become a Freedom Partner. Enable IJM to stand up, speak up and show up on behalf of the oppressed through a monetary commitment to the work of justice. Every person has the capacity to bring a miracle in the lives of those who suffer injustice.

IJM's Freedom Partners select where to invest their monthly gift of $50—either in a region where IJM does casework or to overcome a specific injustice, such as sex trafficking. IJM provides rescue stories and updates from the area where our partners choose to invest. Learn more at IJM's website.

Join IJM's justice campaigns. The U.S. government has significant capacity to influence world leaders in the area of human rights abuse. You can learn how to partner with IJM to encourage our government representatives to take action on behalf of the global poor through getting involved in our justice campaigns. At the time of this book's updating, IJM supporters have sent thousands of postcards to their senators and representatives, asking them to commit to supporting the abolition of slavery worldwide. We eagerly anticipate the response to these actions in the coming months and years. With the knowledge that slavery is a priority for their constituents, we will see our leaders take further steps to bring protection to victims of violent oppression.

Work to unite the global church. It is vital for the future of the justice movement to have the local church in the developing world at the forefront of this work. Their communities are affected by the violence, and out of their congregations God will create the social demand for change, raise up leaders to pursue justice for the community and enable connections with Christians in positions of influence. IJM continues to hire church mobilization staff for its field offices worldwide to build bridges with local churches and church leaders. We also are seeking connections with overseas church leaders eager to participate in IJM's mission. Please visit the IJM website to learn more about job opportunities to unite the global church.

Consider a career in human rights. IJM constantly needs qualified interns, fellows and full-time professionals. Christians pursuing these career paths have a tremendous opportunity to use their careers to follow God's call to justice. For college students, graduate students, law-school students and recent graduates, IJM has a top-notch internship program. It is a wonderful opportunity to explore a career in human rights through hands-on experience and a mentoring relationship with one of the IJM staff. IJM also has a fellowship program for professionals interesting in volunteering for an extended time in one of our field offices, and we need qualified professionals from the United States and around the world who are interested in seeking justice full time. And in addition to lawyers and criminal investigators, professionals in other disciplines make IJM's human-rights work possible—we succeed through the commitment of IT professionals, administrators, communications and accounting professionals, donor-relations specialists, and social workers. Visit IJM's website to learn more about these opportunities.

God Accomplishes the Miraculous Through the Ordinary

It is indeed incredible that our God chooses to accomplish the miraculous through the ordinary—that he calls us to be part of his glorious work of justice on behalf of those who cry out for an advocate. And that we can each actually make a difference for victims of injustice through "ordinary" actions—by contacting our government representatives, by financially supporting those working on the front lines, by lifting up the needs of the oppressed in prayer. Our individual actions may feel small—but over the past ten years, I have seen the compound effect of God's people standing together and demanding something different for our brothers and sisters around the world.

God longs to use us, his people, do to something good, something real, something significant. And, quite marvelously, he has. I have seen widows rejoice at the return of land stolen by local thugs. I have seen a victim of police brutality and torture leave his jail cell and lead his community in the work of justice through joining IJM's staff. I have seen girls victimized by the brutality of sex trafficking heal and grow into remarkable young women, mentoring and leading other former victims in the process of hope and healing. I have seen former slaves start their own businesses and glory in the goodness of providing stable jobs within their own communities. Along with the staff at IJM and the churches and individuals who have come alongside us, I have seen these miracles and more thousands of times over. And we have seen these miracles *because* of the concrete, practical, courageous and sometimes scary steps that Christians around the world have taken in response to God's call to us.

Together, we can answer God's call to us. A child in Texas leads a fundraising campaign at her elementary school because she wants to see slaves freed. A veteran criminal investigator decides to leave a smooth career in Chicago so he can provide rigorous and excellent training for law-enforcement officials half a world away. A Bible study leader in Guatemala City commits to mobilize his congregation on behalf of child victims of sexual violence in his city. A mother in London pauses from the frenetic pace of raising her young children to pray for child slaves she will never meet face to face. A college student rallies her friends to embark on an awareness and fundraising campaign, eventually sending a sexual-assault forensic examiner to Latin America to train medical professionals. Each step God's people take in obedience to his call propels his movement around the world. And it is glorious: slaves go free, victims are vindicated, abusers are put behind bars, believers find deep meaning and purpose in their faith.

God is moving his people to the work of justice. He is creating a movement—but this movement is not monolithic. It's ordinary people—you and me—taking one step at a time to follow God's holy and good call to us: *Seek justice.* We have seen God do mighty things through the willing hearts of his people. And we will see him do much more. For there is a world awaiting hope—and the God of justice longs to use us as his eyes and ears, his hands and feet. There is much work to do, but our God has shown us the goodness and life he longs to give to victims of oppression through his people. What an honor! What a call! May we join him in this work with ever-deepening faith, courage and joy. As with every miracle God has prepared for his earth, he waits for us to turn our hearts toward Jesus—to persevere in one holy devotion as we offer ourselves to him: "Here I am, LORD. Send me."

REFLECTION AND
DISCUSSION GUIDE

CHAPTER 1: THE RAGE IN RWANDA

Prior to reading this book, how would you have defined *justice* and *injustice*? What sources may have influenced your definitions? Consider the following factors: education, media, books, personal experience, culture and so on. Are there any sources that should have influenced your definition? What conclusions can you form about the way your definitions of *justice* and *injustice* have been formed? If it's helpful, make some notes about your thoughts.

- Describe a story of injustice you have seen, heard or experienced.
- Now, read Zechariah 7:9-10. Based on your current understanding of justice, what does it mean to "administer true justice"? Reflect on a time when someone has "administered justice" on your behalf. What did that require? What did you learn or understand as a result of that experience?
- For those of us who have only witnessed injustice through media, it may seem "true" but hardly "real." On the scale of 1 to 3 (see fig. A1 on p. 242), how real does injustice seem to you every day? Discuss or write down your response.
- What steps might you take to help this seemingly distant concept become more real to you?
- What does it look like to respond to God's call to seek justice? What barriers do you face personally? What cultural barriers do you face? What barriers do we face as the body of Christ globally?

1	**2**	**3**
Global injustice does not seem like a reality to me because . . .	I am only beginning to understand the reality of global injustice because . . .	Global injustice seems very real to me because . . .

Figure A1.1. Global injustice scale of reality

What would it look like for us to be people who choose to act—now?

> **Let us not become weary in doing good, for at the proper time we will reap a harvest if we do not give up. (Galatians 6:9)**
>
> How can we pursue justice without "growing weary"? List a few ideas, or write a short prayer asking God to sustain you and others as you seek to make the truth of global injustice a reality in your life. Consider praying that God would deepen your understanding of what it means and looks like to "render true justice."

CHAPTER 2: PREPARING THE MIND AND SPIRIT THROUGH SCRIPTURE

Reflect on a time when you received genuine compassion from another person. As a victim of injustice, how might it feel to be the recipient of compassionate action?

- Read the following passages: Deuteronomy 10:18; 24:19; Jeremiah 22:3. What does biblical compassion require? How does biblical compassion differ from worldly compassion?

- What are a few practical ways to cultivate what Haugen calls "compassion permanence"? Why is this necessary for those who desire to heed God's call to seek justice?

- Over one million women and children are taken into forced prostitution every year. Over twenty million people live as slaves in our world today. These statistics are helpful and underscore the reality of injustice in our world today—but statistics can be hard to grasp as reality and will often leaving us feeling numb with despair. What ideas do you have for making these numbers more real as you share them with others?

- In what ways might knowledge of Scripture transform you as you seek to make the daily choice of action over paralysis, the choice of hope rather than despair in the face of injustice? Read Romans 12:2. How might you use Scripture to prepare your mind for action?

I have hidden your word in my heart . . . (Psalm 119:11)

Consider the Scriptures listed below. Select some or all of these Scriptures and begin to "hide" them in your heart by writing them down, memorizing, or reading them frequently:

Micah 6:8, Proverbs 14:31, Psalm 11:7, Psalm 33:5, Isaiah 1:17

CHAPTER 3: CHAMPIONS OF JUSTICE

Begin by reflecting on the following quote by C. S. Lewis: "Despair is a greater sin than any of the sins that provoke it." Do you agree with this quote? Why or why not?

- Describe a time when you responded to a situation of injustice with hope. Describe a time when you responded to a situation of injustice with despair. Why do you think you responded differently in these two situations? What could you do to build your capacity for hope?
- Read Hebrews 6:19. Why is hope essential to your journey of living God's call for justice? How might you cultivate this hope?
- When you consider slavery, sex trafficking, sexual violence, illegal detention, police abuse, land-grabbing and other forms of violent injustice that are a daily reality of the global poor in our world today, are you tempted to believe that these crimes are unbeat-

able? Do the stories of Kate Bushnell, Edgar Murphy and Jessie Daniel Ames reframe or expand what you believe to be possible? If so, how? If not, what might?

- Have you ever heard a sermon preached or a Bible study taught on the ways that the powerful use force and lies to oppress the poor? If not, why do you think this reality is not explored from the pulpit or the podium?

- Do you agree with the author that this aspect of our biblical witness—seeking justice—has been missing throughout most of the twentieth and twenty-first centuries? What will it take to grow and deepen Christian conviction of the truth that justice is central to discipleship?

Chapters 4-7: Hope in the God of Justice, Compassion, Moral Clarity and Rescue

> **Read John 13:1-17.** Based on this passage, what does our responsibility to others look like? How might you respond to the needs of others in ways that stretch beyond your current inclinations? How might you anchor your response in hope?

Begin by reading Proverbs 14:31. What is the relationship between worship and justice? Reflect on a time when you have experienced a connection between the two, or think of how you could experience that connection. Describe that experience out loud or on paper.

- Which of the following statements best describes your understanding of God's character as it pertains to justice?

  1. I am beginning to understand God's character as it relates to justice.

  2. I am continuing to investigate how justice is central to God's character.

  3. I understand God's attribute of justice and try to reflect that

understanding in my daily life.

4. I understand that injustice is important in the Bible, but I'm not sure what it means for God to be a "just" God.

- What do you believe it means that God is the God of justice? What Scriptures are most helpful to you in understanding this aspect of

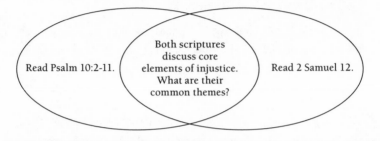

Figure A1.2. The core elements of injustice

God's character? (For Scripture ideas, see appendix 3.)

- Do you or others you know experience discomfort at the idea that God expresses wrath toward perpetrators of injustice? Why or why not?
- How might the reality of God's holy intolerance of injustice help us understand more fully God's gift of forgiveness?

Frederick Buechner said, "The place where God calls you is the place where your deep gladness meets the world's deep hunger." Reflect on how your service to the oppressed contributes to your gladness. How might this manifest itself in worship?

To further experience God's heart for justice through worship, consider downloading the following music:

"I Saw What I Saw" or "When the Saints" by Sara Groves
 "Come Away" or "Over the Room" by Ten Shekel Shirt
Abolition Strategy, album by The Wrecking

CHAPTERS 8-9: DIFFICULT QUESTIONS
AND THE ANATOMY OF INJUSTICE

Haugen reminds us of this G. K. Chesterton quotation:

"The Christian ideal has not been tried and found wanting; it has been found difficult and left untried."

Think of a difficulty you have faced and overcome. How might your life—or that of another—be different today had you left the challenge untried?

- Why is the calling to seek justice difficult? Scary? Messy? Daunting? Consider the following attributes of God's character. How do these truths about God's character provide hope and motivation to wade into the challenge? Which of these truths motivates you the most right now? Why?

  1. God is omnipotent: he is all powerful and has unlimited authority and influence.

  2. God is omnipresent: he is in all places at all times.

  3. God is omniscient: he possesses perfect knowledge and wisdom.

  4. God is faithful: what God has said about himself is true and everything God promises will come to pass.

- Based on your understanding of this section, how do you grapple with the weighty and pervading question, Why does God allow injustice?

- Haugen describes four "footholds" on which we can stand when answering why God allows injustice. Which of the following footholds is most helpful in framing your understanding of how to develop a response to this question? Why?

  Foothold 1: We start with humility.

  Foothold 2: We remember the cross.

  Foothold 3: We recognize that God desires our love, freely given.

Foothold 4: We embrace the hope of eternity.

- Do you believe that ordinary people, if free of basic restraints, are capable of committing violent acts of injustice? What restraints exist in our society? In what ways is a reconciled relationship with God a restraint against our inclination to commit violence against our neighbor?

- Perpetrators are both those who actively commit injustices and those who actively choose ignorance or avoid standing up for those being treated unjustly. Do you agree with this statement? Why or why not?

- What is the difference between violent coercion and deception? Based on the stories in the book, identify and list some ways each was used to oppress victims.

- In what ways might you use coercion and deception to assert influence or power? How might God be revealing these behaviors through your study of injustice?

> What steps can you take to encourage your pastor or other teachers in your life to give voice to the anatomy of injustice and God's plan to overcome it? How can you give voice to these issues in your life?

CHAPTERS 10-13: INVESTIGATING AND INTERVENING
Begin by reading Romans 12 in its entirety. Now consider the following quote from chapter thirteen:

> It's fair to say that within a stone's throw of just about every victim of oppression in the world there is a Christian God has called and placed in the community to share the love of Jesus.

- How would you describe your responsibility to meet the needs of the poor and oppressed? Imagine some things that you can do locally and globally to fulfill that responsibility. (See appendixes 2-4 for ideas and resources.)

- How does our action (or inaction) toward the oppressed make it believable (or not) that God truly is good, that God has great compassion for those who are suffering?

- The author describes IJM's fourfold intervention plan and highlights the stories of several IJM clients as he discusses victim rescue, perpetrator accountability and victim aftercare. From the following list, which victim's story did you most connect with? How might you share this story in order to educate others about and engage them in the need for intervention?

  Stephen (pp. 173-75)

  Geraldine (pp. 176-77)

  Kunthy (p. 180)

  Kabithan (pp. 181-82)

- The author says, "When it comes to seeking justice in a world of vulnerable men, women and children, all of us are privileged to play a role." Look at the following four words and decide which best describes you. Based on your choice, how might you be uniquely qualified to seek justice?

  ambassador

  teacher

  rescuer

  shepherd

Think about and remember a time when you intervened on behalf of someone who was experiencing coercion, deception or injustice in another form. What was that like? After reading this book, how are you better equipped to advocate or intervene on behalf of the oppressed?

Taking Action

> Try summarizing, aloud or on paper, what you have learned about combating injustice in fewer than 100 words. Then use this skill to briefly, but effectively share the need to combat injustice with others. Consider posting your 100 words to an online blog or social networking website and encourage readers to respond.

- Read 1 Peter 1:13. As you move toward action, prepare your heart and mind through prayer. Consider praying for the following five things, which are essential to discerning injustice and acting accordingly:

    1. *Humility.* As you engage with victims of injustice, remember that you do not have all of the answers. If you are battling injustice in another country, pray that you will conduct yourself well and humbly in your host country.

    2. *Wisdom.* Pray that God will provide wisdom as you encounter and think about injustice.

    3. *Love.* Ask God to cultivate in you love for people who are far away, unfamiliar or unlike you.

    4. *Hope.* Pray against the temptation to despair in the face of injustice.

    5. *Guidance.* Pray for people that may help and guide you as you seek to do God's work of justice.

- Identify one area of action from the following list that you can reasonably commit to today.

    Tell the stories

    Go

    Send

    Pray

- Which did you select and why?

- Think about injustice that may occur in your local area. Because we believe that God hates all injustice, how might you apply the truths of this book to respond to these injustices in your own community?

Conclude your time of study and reflection by developing a simple action plan for yourself. Use table A1.1 to determine how you can best equip yourself and others to fulfill the unique role that God has for you in seeking justice. Select some action steps from one or more of the boxes. For practical ideas and resources to help you educate, explore and engage, visit IJM's website and see appendixes two through five of this book.

Table A1.1.

Educate	Explore	Engage
Raise awareness	Open your eyes to injustice around you	Seek God
Raise resources	Become a part of the IJM Institute	Commit with at least one other person to pray weekly for the work of overcoming violent injustice globally
Build up the "justice generation"		
Start an IJM campus chapter	Incorporate justice issues into a short-term mission trip using the *As You Go* mission-training tool	Receive weekly IJM prayer partner updates
Create a justice-centered ministry		Participate in the IJM Global Prayer Gathering
Start a Bible study organized around these issues	Visit the IJM website for tools and information (www.ijm.org)	Become an IJM Freedom Partner—raise resources
Create a blog	Explore other human rights websites	Join IJM's justice campaigns
Tell the victims' stories		Explore a career in human rights
		Engage in advocacy on the local level

As you move forward responding to God's call to act on behalf of the oppressed, may you know God's presence and power. May you know your identity as a follower of Christ, who himself proclaimed

> The Spirit of the Lord is on me,
>> because he has anointed me
>> to preach good news to the poor.
>
> He has sent me to proclaim freedom for the prisoners
>> and recovery of sight for the blind,
>> to release the oppressed,
>> to proclaim the year of the Lord's favor. (Luke 4:18)

SUGGESTED INTERNET SITES

Each of the following sites is an excellent starting point for research on current developments and issues in human rights.

International Justice Mission
www.ijm.org

Amnesty International
www.amnesty.org

Freedom House
www.freedomhouse.org

Department of Labor
www.dol.gov

U.S. State Department
www.state.gov

University of Minnesota Human Rights Library
www.umn.edu/humanrts

United Nations Treaty Collection
http://untreaty.un.org

U.N. High Commissioner for Human Rights
www.ohchr.org

The International Criminal Court
www.icc-cpi.int

Human Rights Watch
www.hrw.org

Human Rights First
www.humanrightsfirst.org

International Labour Organization
www.ilo.org

UNICEF
United Nations Children's Fund
www.unicef.org

UNIFEM
United Nations Development Fund for Women
www.unifem.org

U.S. Department of Justice
www.usdoj.org

U.S. Department of Health and Human Services
The Campaign to Rescue and Restore Victims of Human Trafficking
www.acf.hhs.gov/trafficking

U.S. Department of State
Office to Monitor and Combat Trafficking in Persons
www.state.gov/g/tip

Bureau of Democracy, Human Rights and Labor
www.state.gov/g/drl

World Health Organization
www.who.int/en

JUSTICE SCRIPTURE VERSES

It is exceedingly strange that any follower of
Jesus Christ should ever have needed to ask whether
social involvement was their concern.

JOHN STOTT

These verses from the Scriptures begin to lay out the meaning of biblical justice and the reason God requires his people to seek it.

Then the LORD spoke to Job out of the storm: / "Brace yourself like a man; / I will question you, / and you shall answer me. / "Would you discredit my justice? / Would you condemn me to justify yourself?" (Job 40:6-8)

He will judge the world in righteousness; / he will govern the peoples with justice. (Psalm 9:8)

The LORD is known by his justice; / the wicked are ensnared by the work of their hands. (Psalm 9:16)

For the LORD is righteous, / he loves justice; / upright men will see his face. (Psalm 11:7)

The LORD loves righteousness and justice; / the earth is full of his unfailing love. (Psalm 33:5)

Your righteousness is like the mighty mountains, / your justice like the great deep. / O LORD, you preserve both man and beast. (Psalm 36:6)

He will make your righteousness shine like the dawn, / the justice of your cause like the noonday sun. (Psalm 37:6)

Your throne, O God, will last for ever and ever; / a scepter of justice will be the scepter of your kingdom. (Psalm 45:6)

No, in your heart you devise injustice, / and your hands mete out violence on the earth. (Psalm 58:2)

They plot injustice and say, / "We have devised a perfect plan!" / Surely the mind and heart of man are cunning. (Psalm 64:6)

I will sing of your love and justice; / to you, O LORD, I will sing praise. (Psalm 101:1)

The LORD works righteousness / and justice for all the oppressed. (Psalm 103:6)

Blessed are they who maintain justice, / who constantly do what is right. (Psalm 106:3)

Good will come to him who is generous and lends freely, / who conducts his affairs with justice. (Psalm 112:5)

I know that the LORD secures justice for the poor / and upholds the cause of the needy. (Psalm 140:12)

It is not good to be partial to the wicked / or to deprive the innocent of justice. (Proverbs 18:5)

When justice is done, it brings joy to the righteous / but terror to evildoers. (Proverbs 21:15)

The righteous care about justice for the poor, / but the wicked have no such concern. (Proverbs 29:7)

Learn to do right! / Seek justice, / encourage the oppressed. / Defend the cause of the fatherless, / plead the case of the widow. (Isaiah 1:17)

Of the increase of his government and peace / there will be no end. / He will reign on David's throne / and over his kingdom, / establishing and upholding it / with justice and righteousness / from that time on and forever. / The zeal of the LORD Almighty / will accomplish this. (Isaiah 9:7)

Yet the Lord longs to be gracious to you; / he rises to show you compassion. / For the Lord is a God of justice. / Blessed are all who wait for him! (Isaiah 30:18)

Here is my servant, whom I uphold, / my chosen one in whom I delight; / I will put my Spirit on him / and he will bring justice to the nations. (Isaiah 42:1)

Listen to me, my people; / hear me, my nation: / The law will go out from me; / my justice will become a light to the nations. (Isaiah 51:4)

My righteousness draws near speedily, / my salvation is on the way, / and my arm will bring justice to the nations. / The islands will look to me / and wait in hope for my arm. (Isaiah 51:5)

This is what the Lord says: / "Maintain justice / and do what is right, / for my salvation is close at hand / and my righteousness will soon be revealed." (Isaiah 56:1)

Is not this the kind of fasting I have chosen: / to loose the chains of injustice / and untie the cords of the yoke, / to set the oppressed free / and break every yoke? (Isaiah 58:6)

Truth is nowhere to be found, / and whoever shuns evil becomes a prey. / The Lord looked and was displeased / that there was no justice. (Isaiah 59:15)

For I, the Lord, love justice; / I hate robbery and iniquity. / In my faithfulness I will reward them / and make an everlasting covenant with them. (Isaiah 61:8)

O house of David, this is what the Lord says: / "Administer justice every morning; / rescue from the hand of his oppressor / the one who has been robbed, / or my wrath will break out and burn like fire / because of the evil you have done— / burn with no one to quench it." (Jeremiah 21:12)

Woe to him who builds his palace by unrighteousness, / his upper rooms by injustice, / making his countrymen work for nothing, / not paying them for their labor. (Jeremiah 22:13)

I will search for the lost and bring back the strays. I will bind up the injured and strengthen the weak, but the sleek and the strong I will destroy. I will shepherd the flock with justice. (Ezekiel 34:16)

I will betroth you to me forever; / I will betroth you in righteousness and justice, / in love and compassion. (Hosea 2:19)

But you must return to your God; / maintain love and justice, / and wait for your God always. (Hosea 12:6)

I hate, I despise your religious feasts; / I cannot stand your assemblies. / Even though you bring me burnt offerings and grain offerings, / I will not accept them. / Though you bring choice fellowship offerings, / I will have no regard for them. / Away with the noise of your songs! / I will not listen to the music of your harps. / But let justice roll on like a river, / righteousness like a never-failing stream! (Amos 5:21-24)

He has showed you, O man, what is good. / And what does the LORD require of you? / To act justly and to love mercy / and to walk humbly with your God. (Micah 6:8)

And the word of the LORD came again to Zechariah: "This is what the LORD Almighty says: 'Administer true justice; show mercy and compassion to one another. Do not oppress the widow or the fatherless, the alien or the poor. In your hearts do not think evil of each other.' " (Zechariah 7:8-10)

Here is my servant whom I have chosen, / the one I love, in whom I delight; / I will put my Spirit on him, / and he will proclaim justice to the nations. (Matthew 12:18)

Woe to you, teachers of the law and Pharisees, you hypocrites! You give a tenth of your spices—mint, dill and cumin. But you have neglected the more important matters of the law—justice, mercy and faithfulness. You should have practiced the latter, without neglecting the former. (Matthew 23:23)

Woe to you Pharisees, because you give God a tenth of your mint, rue and all other kinds of garden herbs, but you neglect justice and the love of God. You should have practiced the latter without leaving the former undone. (Luke 11:42)

This righteousness from God comes through faith in Jesus Christ to all who believe. There is no difference, for all have sinned and fall short of the glory of God, and are justified freely by his grace through the redemption that came by Christ Jesus. God presented him as a sacrifice of atonement, through faith in his blood. He did this to demonstrate his justice, because in his forbearance he had left the sins committed beforehand unpunished—he did it to demonstrate his justice at the present time, so as to be just and the one who justifies those who have faith in Jesus. (Romans 3:22-26)

I saw heaven standing open and there before me was a white horse, whose rider is called Faithful and True. With justice he judges and makes war. (Revelation 19:11)

BOOK RESOURCE GUIDE

"The arc of the moral universe is long,
but in the end, it bends toward justice."
MARTIN LUTHER KING JR.

The following books are excellent starting points to continue your own study of God's call to justice, the importance of rule of law for the global poor and the human rights challenges of our history and today.

Bonhoeffer, Dietrich. *Ethics.* New York: Simon & Schuster, 1995.

————. *Letters and Papers from Prison.* New York: Simon & Schuster, 1997. (I recommend reading these two selections by Bonhoeffer together for comprehension.)

Haugen, Gary. *Just Courage: God's Great Expedition for the Restless Christian.* Downers Grove, Ill.: IVP Books, 2008.

Labberton, Mark. *The Dangerous Act of Worship: Living God's Call to Justice.* Downers Grove, Ill.: IVP Books, 2007.

Lewis, C. S. *God in the Dock.* Grand Rapids: Eerdmans, 1994.

GENERAL HUMAN RIGHTS

Bales, Kevin. *Disposable People: New Slavery in the Global Economy.* Berkeley: University of California Press, 2004.

Batstone, David. *Not for Sale: The Return of the Global Slave Trade—and How We Can Fight It.* New York: HarperCollins, 2007.

Dallaire, Roméo. *Shake Hands with the Devil: The Failure of Humanity in Rwanda.* New York: Da Capo Press, 2004.

Hochschild, Adam. *Bury the Chains: Prophets and Rebels in the Fight to Free an Empire's Slaves.* New York: Houghton Mifflin, 2006.

————. *King Leopold's Ghost: A Story of Greed, Terror and Heroism in Colonial Africa.* New York: Mariner Books, 1999.

Human Rights Watch. *Human Rights Watch World Report.* Published annually.

Kara, Siddharth. *Sex Trafficking: Inside the Business of Modern Slavery.* New York: Columbia University Press, 2008.

Kidder, Tracy. *Mountains Beyond Mountains: The Quest of Dr. Paul Farmer, a Man Who Would Cure the World.* New York: Random House, 2004.

Paton, Alan. *Cry the Beloved Country.* New York: Simon & Schuster, 2003.

Perkins, John. *Let Justice Roll Down.* Ventura, Calif.: Regal Books, 2006.

Power, Samantha. *A Problem from Hell: America and the Age of Genocide.* New York: Harper Perennial, 2007.

U. S. Department of State. *The Trafficking in Persons Report.* Published annually.

Wiesel, Elie. *Night.* New York: Farrar, Straus and Giroux, 2006.

ADVICE TO STUDENTS CONSIDERING AN INTERNATIONAL HUMAN RIGHTS CAREER

The secret of success in life is for a
man to be ready for his time when it comes.
BENJAMIN DISRAELI

International Justice Mission receives a tremendous number of inquiries from Christian students who are interested in a career in the field of international human rights. The passionate interest of these students is a great encouragement to us at IJM, and it represents immeasurable hope for those who suffer injustice in our world and for those who are yearning to see a courageous and authentic witness for Christ in dark places. Equally encouraging is the thoughtful way these students are pursuing practical questions about how they might prepare themselves for effective service. God is glorified by missionary doctors, famine fighters and church planters who demonstrate a rigorous commitment to excellence through careful, thoughtful preparation for service. In the same way, those who seek to serve God by bringing rescue to victims of oppression begin their journey of excellence by thinking hard about how they might prepare themselves for their work.

Accordingly, we would like to offer a few candid words of guidance that we hope interested students will find helpful. It is, of course, impossible to chart the right course for any specific student, and in the end we rely on God's promises for direction (Proverbs 3:5-6) and wisdom

(James 1:5-6). God has already given clear guidance to *all* Christians: they are to be engaged in the work of justice (Isaiah 1:17; Micah 6:8; Matthew 23:23). For those who are exploring a career in international human rights, we would like to provide the following food for thought.

Students who are interested in a career in human rights would be well served by educational preparation that focuses on the foundations of faith, professional skill and crosscultural training for effective service in the field.

A *Christian* witness for justice is built on a relationship with Jesus Christ, the One Christians regard as God and the source of all justice, compassion, power, truth and goodness. Accordingly, the strength and ultimate usefulness of our Christian witness for justice flows from the grace of God and our investment in the intimacy and quality of our relationship with our Maker. Accordingly, we advise those most zealous for justice to begin their journey by deepening their companionship with the God of justice. For a Christian, a career in justice brings power, joy and sustainability when it is built on a strong spiritual foundation in Christ (Psalm 127:1).

Knowing that engagement in human rights corresponds to God's command to seek justice for the oppressed, the strength of our resistance to evil comes directly from our complete reliance on God, the One who is most offended by evil. Sincere study, prayer and worship are the channels through which God builds this foundation. When we begin to understand how our heavenly Father feels about the world we live in, we are more able to act in ways that honor him. Service to the oppressed finds its unyielding determination in a life focused on Christ, seeking his glory and following his example of love. As Oswald Chambers writes, "Service is the overflow which pours from a life filled with love and devotion. . . . Service is what I bring to the relationship and is the reflection of my identification with the nature of God."[1]

PUBLIC JUSTICE SKILLS: INVESTIGATION AND INTERVENTION

Building on a foundation of devout faith, the human rights profession is built on two unique disciplines: investigation and intervention. As deception and violence are tools of the oppressive perpetrator, investigation and intervention expose the deception and bring protective power to bear on behalf of the victim.

Investigation is the tool necessary to address the deception used by oppressors to cover up their deeds. Proverbs 10:11 affirms this principle: "The mouth of the righteous is a fountain of life, / but the mouth of the wicked *conceals* violence" (NRSV). Vocationally, training in the legal or law enforcement professions provides a particular focus on the hard work of exposing the truth and finding the facts amid confusion, conflict and lies. Lawyers and law enforcement professionals are trained specifically in fact finding, exposing lies and demonstrating *with proof* the innocence or guilt of the accused. Since the human rights field requires this same skill, the student would be well served by experience and education in the fields of law or law enforcement. Another critical path is that of social workers, who help victims of abuse uncover some truths as well: that victims are *valuable,* that they deserve *justice*, that they can *heal*. Their role in supporting the victim through the justice process is invaluable.

The discipline of intervention relates to the oppressor's use of violent coercion to dominate the victim's environment and decisions. To combat this misuse of power, students must learn how to access power on behalf of those who are vulnerable. An expertise in social, political, economic and governmental power—a knowledge of where power resides and how it is exercised—is important. From a broad perspective the academic disciplines of government, international relations, politics and history can provide a strong foundation of study. More specifically, a background in law enforcement (through law enforcement academies, investigative training and experience), as a lawyer or as a social worker are three ways to equip oneself for international human rights work. There are certainly other paths students can follow into this work; however, we will focus this discussion on these vocations, as each of them offers a fairly structured path to gain experience.

A student who wants to pursue a career in international human rights work must develop the capacity to translate his or her professional skills into a crosscultural, developing-world context. The ability to function, solve a problem and live in the developing world transforms the student-as-tourist into a problem-solving participant in a foreign and economically underdeveloped society. Every bit of time spent overseas helps, but opportunities that extend beyond two months are generally more significant. Specific experiences might include summer or semester mission trips in the developing world, study-abroad programs conducted with a foreign university, the Peace Corps, nongovernmental organization volunteer opportunities and business start-ups in a developing context.

These experiences allow students to develop and test their capacity to contribute in the difficult environment where the poor spend each day, which includes dirt, inconvenience, sickness, bugs, risk and physical discomfort. More important, such experiences test students' capacity for the deeper and indispensable qualities of humility, attentiveness, compassion, patience and faith.

Career in Law
For those who are interested in pursuing a law degree, we offer the following suggestions. First, we must confront the brutal truth about the way the legal profession allows law schools to sort graduations of promising legal talent. There is a clearly understood ranking of law schools by reputation (published in magazines and books), and the legal profession doles out its introductory opportunities largely on the basis of the reputation of the school an applicant comes from. There are exceptions to the rule, of course, but students should not underestimate the general power and pervasiveness of the rule. In addition, most law students will get a better education at a better-ranked law school, not because the law professors are so much better or the course content much different, but because the caliber of students will be better. Accordingly, students will be pushed to think harder and get more out of their education by the peers around them.

As a general matter, students should try to go to the highest-ranked law school they can. Many schools advertise special offerings such as international law and human rights, but for students seeking to optimize their career options these advertised areas of special interest do not generally make up for the institutions' less-esteemed reputation. If a higher-ranked school is an option, a student would be ill-advised to attend a law school on a lower tier because of advertised specialties, "quality of student life" or geography (unless you know you want a job in that particular locality).

Once in law school, students interested in a career in human rights would be well-advised to take available courses that focus on (1) the battle over facts (litigation, civil and criminal procedure, evidence, etc.), (2) governmental institutions and processes of power (constitutional law, administrative law, government relations, legislative process, public policy, etc.) and (3) substantive international and human rights law. Clinical opportunities for litigation service and relationships with professors who can open doors for research, job experience, clinical experience or clerkships in the three areas mentioned previously are good investments of your time.

It will be important to develop a long-term vision of a job or place of employment that is most appealing. Human rights work is accomplished at human rights NGOs, public law institutions (such as the Department of Justice) and private firms (using the vehicle of pro bono legal work). During law school use the first summer to experiment, the second to establish a "foot in the door" and the third to gain employment.

Finally, a student interested in pursuing the special joys and holy calling of human rights service must be undergirded with perseverance and a long-term commitment to a vocational pursuit of justice. The gifts of advocacy are extremely valuable. There will be many bidders for your service, and you must find a way to stay committed to the clientele you want to serve with your gifts. The poor and oppressed will have the least to offer in terms of the compensation normally tendered to the profession—the least money, the fewest perks, a lower professional status and little renown. So, what will sustain your commitment as the bidding war increases, as your training makes you more valuable? Only one thing: a clear understanding, in advance, of what you want in exchange for your services.

Consider students who head to medical school with the vision of becoming missionary doctors in the developing world. Over time their training makes them very valuable, and they find themselves in a bidding war of opportunities. Generally, anything a doctor does is good and noble, but there definitely is a spectrum of need, both in terms of the urgency of the suffering and the availability of those who can meet the need. There are those who need surgery for a gunshot wound in the inner city, those who need a cure for their cancer, those who need knee surgery to play next season, those who need a tummy tuck. Various clientele will make aggressive bids for the service of medical students. What will sustain these medical students in their vision for overseas ministry among the poor?

Likewise the legal profession offers a variety of perfectly honorable opportunities, but they exist on a spectrum of moral and monetary urgency. Some in the legal profession put violent criminals behind bars and keep the innocent free, some help a business play by the rules, some give an offending corporation its best argument in court, and some (very few) actually lie and cheat for whoever will pay. It will be easier, more lucrative and safer for law students to offer their gifts of advocacy to serve these clientele than to serve the victims of oppression overseas, those who are most in need of a witness of Christ's love and God's justice. What will sustain these law students in their vocational vision to "the least of these"?

Only a clear, advance conviction: the students who equip themselves with the tools of advocacy to follow Christ in service to the most needy in our world and are prepared to receive the compensation that Christ alone offers—joy, peace, meaning, love, holiness and a treasure that is eternal.

CAREER IN LAW ENFORCEMENT

A career in law enforcement enables you to bring the protection of the rule of law to the weak and vulnerable. If you are interested in pursuing an international human rights career, a law enforcement career should include all aspects of policing. This would be tremendously helpful in future interactions with the victims of various types of crimes and in probable encounters with government officials. Students should focus on active criminal investigative experience and seek a high level of professional training.

Most law enforcement agencies will not hire anyone under the age of twenty-one. Use that to your advantage. Course study involving the police sciences will help you understand how investigation and reporting affect judicial procedures. Courses in technical writing, public speaking, psychology and sociology with an international emphasis give you insights into the cultures around you. Some local programs such as explorer posts, ride-alongs and citizen neighborhood watch organizations allow you to observe law enforcement in action. Most state agencies maintain similar programs. At the federal level there are employment options that allow you to interact with law enforcement indirectly in portions of an investigation. All of these will allow you to look at the inner workings and see how the systems of law enforcement function in reality.

IJM needs to interact with various facets of law enforcement in the communities we have been called to work in. There is a need for law enforcement professionals committed to ensuring that all people are protected by the rule of law at the federal, state and local levels. Deciding where to work will involve your personal preferences, adaptability and ultimately God's will in your life.

CAREER IN SOCIAL WORK

Due to the wide range of issues involved in providing aftercare to victims of violent abuse, the most practical course of study for someone wishing to pursue an international aftercare career is social work.

A master's degree in social work, with concentrations of study in both community development and clinical practice provides the student with knowledge and experience on a macrolevel, but within the context of the needs of individuals and families. A graduate school offering an international concentration combining fieldwork, courses on advanced policy and advanced practice courses is highly recommended. Experience-based academic programs incorporating international internship opportunities into the curriculum are a vital part of the learning process.

Seek a graduate program that equips you to learn how to build partnerships and collaborative relationships while learning the principles of human rights and global justice. Crosscultural studies, program design, monitoring and evaluation are invaluable as well. Most important, discover what you are most passionate about through reading, research and continuing-education programs. God has put this in your heart for a reason, but passion alone is not sufficient to provide healing care to clients of injustice.

Choose a reputable, ranked graduate school with a commitment to international social work. Ensure professors are doing research in international issues, engaged with international forums or professional societies, and are willing to accommodate your special interests and mentor you. Also inquire as to whether the graduate school has international students in the program each year. The greater the number of international students, the more opportunity you will have to learn from them, establish contacts with international social workers around the world, and engage in international student group activities.

Every social work graduate student participates in two fieldwork experiences, one each year of graduate school. Find out what fieldwork opportunities are offered in the program to ensure that you have choices that would give you solid experience related to your field. You don't necessarily have to have an international-oriented field placement to gain experience that will help you if you pursue international social work in the future. For example, if you want to work in aftercare with trafficking survivors overseas, doing your field practicum at a local rape crisis center would give you credible experience in crisis response, rape trauma, counseling, legal services and the healing process. If you want to work with slavery or police-brutality issues overseas, doing your field practicum at a local refugee resettlement

center would provide you invaluable experience working with transla-
tors and understanding grief and loss issues, the process of transition
and resettlement, torture and war trauma issues, resiliency and recov-
ery, community development and healing, and more.

OTHER CAREER CONNECTIONS TO GLOBAL JUSTICE

Though you may not be pursuing a career in law, law enforcement or
social work, you can play a vital role in global justice. IJM and other
justice-oriented groups rely on the expertise of people with extensive
training in international relations, government relations and human-
rights program monitoring and design. In order to secure rescue for
victims of oppression, we also rely on the skills of excellent administrators, accountants, human resources and IT professionals. Pastors,
seminary professors and ministry trainers expose people to God's
passion for justice and his plan to use his people to rescue the oppressed. Missionaries and frontline relief-and-development workers
play an instrumental role in reporting cases of injustice and oppression. Writers, producers, artists and media professionals who tell the
stories of God's work in rescuing the victims of abuse are critical in
advancing the cause of justice in the world. We invite you to pursue
a lifelong vocational journey in the ministry of justice, a journey of
excellence, creativity, adventure and joy.

ADDITIONAL RESOURCES
FOR STUDY AND REFLECTION

Please visit International Justice Mission's website—www.ijm.org—
to access many more resources to equip you on your journey into the
work of justice. There are tools to help you engage your church, your
school, your community and your own heart in the work.

NOTES

Preface to the Tenth Anniversary Edition

[1]Commission on Legal Empowerment of the Poor, *Making the Law Work For Everyone*, vol. 1 (New York: United Nations Development Programme, 2008) <www.undp.org/legalempowerment/report/index.html>.

[2]Deepa Narayan et al., *Voices of the Poor Crying Out for Change* (New York: Oxford University Press; Washington, D.C.: World Bank, 2000) <http://siteresources.worldbank.org/INTPOVERTY/Resources/335642-1124115102975/1555199-1124115201387/cry.pdf>.

[3]Bono, "Transcript: Bono remarks at the National Prayer Breakfast," *USAToday.com*, February 2, 2006 <www.usatoday.com/news/washington/2006-02-02-bono-transcript_x.htm>.

Preface to the First Edition

[1]C. S. Lewis, *The Screwtape Letters*, rev. ed. (New York: Collier, 1982), pp. 137-38.

Chapter 2: Preparing the Mind and Spirit Through Scripture

[1]"The Progress of Nations," UNICEF, 1997 <www.unicef.org/publications/files/pub-pon97-en.pdf>.

[2]"Justice Not Excuses," *Stop Violence Against Women*, Amnesty International <http://asiapacific.amnesty.org/actforwomen/justice-index-eng>.

[3]Deepa Narayan, *Voices of the Poor: Can Anyone Hear Us?* (New York: Oxford University Press), 1:278.

[4]Michael Wines, "The Forgotten of Africa, Wasting Away in Jails Without Trials," *The New York Times*, November 6, 2005.

[5]"The Small Hands of Slavery: Bonded Child Labor in India," Human Rights Watch Children's Rights Project, 1996 <www.hrw.org/legacy/reports/1996/India3.htm>.

Chapter 3: Champions of Justice

[1]C. S. Lewis, *The Screwtape Letters*, rev. ed. (New York: Collier, 1982), p. 138.

[2]Dana Hardwick, *Oh Thou Woman That Bringest Good Tidings: The Life and Work of Katherine C. Bushnell* (St. Paul: Christians for Biblical Equality, 1995), p. 27.

[3]Ibid., pp. 30-31.

[4]Ibid., p. 32.

[5]Irene Ashby-MacFadyen, "Child Life vs. Dividends," *The American Federationist*, May 1902, p. 215.

[6]Hugh Bailey, *Edgar Gardner Murphy: Gentle Progressive* (Coral Gables, Fla.: University of Miami Press, 1968), p. 83.

[7]Ibid., pp. 85, 88.

[8]Ibid., p. 108.

[9]NAACP advertisement in the *New York Times*, November 1922, cited in *Who Built America*, ed. Roy Rosenzweig (New York: Pantheon, 1992), 2:303.

[10]Jessie Daniel Ames, *Southern Women and Lynching* (Atlanta: n.p., 1936), cited in Harvard Sitkoff, *A New Deal for Blacks* (New York: Oxford University Press, 1978), p. 274.

An important precursor to the ASWPL in exposing the horror and injustice of lynching was the Southern Committee on the Study of Lynching (S.C.S.L.), which counted among its leaders W. J. McGlothin, president of the Southern Baptist Convention (Sitkoff, *New Deal for Blacks*, p. 271).

[11]Jessie Daniel Ames, "Reminiscences of Jessie Daniel Ames: 'I Really Do Like a Good Fight,'" interview by Pat Watters, *New South* 27 (spring 1972): 35.

[12]Sitkoff, *New Deal for Blacks*, p. 275.

[13]C. Van Woodward, *The Strange Career of Jim Crow* (New York: Oxford University Press, 1974), p. 143. Lynching did return on a diminished scale during the tensions of the civil rights movement of the 1960s.

[14]Jacquelyn Dowd Hall, *Revolt Against Chivalry: Jessie Daniel Ames and the Women's Campaign Against Lynching* (New York: Columbia University Press, 1979), p. 163.

[15]Dr. Martin Luther King Jr., "Where Do We Go from Here?" commencement address to Springfield College, Springfield, Mass., June 14, 1964 <www.indiana.edu/~ivie web/mlkwhere.html>.

[16]David Bosch, *Transforming Mission* (Maryknoll, N.Y.: Orbis, 1996), p. 426.

[17]Ibid., p. 510.

[18]Ibid., p. 508.

[19]John Gregg Fee, *Autobiography* (Chicago: n.p., 1891), cited in Sydney E. Alhstrom, *A Religious History of the American People* (New Haven, Conn.: Yale University Press, 1972), p. 653.

[20]Alhstrom, *Religious History*, pp. 637-40.

[21]Bosch, *Transforming Mission*, p. 509.

[22]Carl F. H. Henry, "A Summons to Justice," *Christianity Today*, July 20, 1992, p. 40.

Chapter 4: Hope in the God of Justice

[1]Katherine C. Bushnell, *God's Word to Women: 100 Bible Studies on Women's Place in the Divine Economy*, 2nd ed. (Oakland, Calif.: K. C. Bushnell, 1930), paragraph 13.

[2]"Hidden Apartheid," Human Rights Watch, February 12, 2007 <www.hrw.org/en/node/11030/section/10>.

Chapter 5: Hope in the God of Compassion

[1]Some may be troubled by the theological notion of an all-sufficient God who suffers, but like the Reverend John Stott, I believe it is inherent in God's willful commitment to love: "The best way to confront the traditional view of the impassibility of God [i.e., the notion that God is incapable of suffering], however, is to ask 'what meaning can there be in a love which is not costly to the lover.' If love is self-giving, then it is inevitably vulnerable to pain, since it exposes itself to the possibility of rejection and insult. It is 'the fundamental Christian assertion that God is love,' writes Jürgen Moltmann, 'which in principle broke the Aristotelian doctrine of God' (i.e., as 'impassible'). 'Were God incapable of suffering . . . then he would also be incapable of love,' whereas 'the one who is capable of love is also capable of suffering, for he also opens himself up to the suffering which is involved in love.' That is surely why Bonhoeffer wrote from prison to his friend Eberhard Bethge, nine months before his execution: 'only the Suffering God can help.' " (John Stott, *The Cross of Christ* [Downers Grove, Ill.: InterVarsity Press, 1986], p. 332.)

Chapter 6: Hope in the God of Moral Clarity

[1]J. I. Packer, *Knowing God* (Downers Grove, Ill.: InterVarsity Press, 1973), p. 144.

[2]Ibid., p. 142.

[3]Ibid., p. 136.

[4]Ibid., p. 128.

[5]Dietrich Bonhoeffer, *Letters and Papers from Prison* (New York: Macmillan, 1972), pp. 4-5.

[6]Dietrich Bonhoeffer, "Who Stands Fast?" in *The Martyred Christian: 160 Readings from Dietrich Bonhoeffer* (New York: Collier, 1983), p. 157.

Chapter 8: Answers for Difficult Questions

[1]Richard Cohen, "Savagery in Algeria," *Washington Post,* January 15, 1998, A23.

[2]Feodor Dostoyevsky, *The Brothers Karamazov* (New York: Bantam, 1981), p. 286.

[3]C. S. Lewis, *The Problem of Pain* (New York: Collier, 1962), p. 69.

[4]Irving Greenberg, quoted in David P. Gushee, *The Righteous Gentiles of the Holocaust* (Minneapolis: Fortress, 1994), p. xii.

[5]Salvian, *The Governance of God,* in Fathers of the Church, ed. Harold Dressler (Washington, D.C.: Catholic University of America Press, 1947), p. 3.

[6]John Stott, *The Cross of Christ* (Downers Grove, Ill.: InterVarsity Press, 1986), pp. 335-36.

[7]The phrase "intolerable compliment" is from Lewis, *Problem of Pain,* p. 42; "terrible gift of freedom" is from Dostoyevsky, *Brothers Karamazov,* p. 309.

[8]Dostoyevsky, *Brothers Karamazov,* p. 308.

[9]Lewis, *Problem of Pain,* p. 144.

[10]Matthew Bridges, "Crown Him with Many Crowns" (1852).

Chapter 9: Anatomy of Injustice

[1]G. K. Chesterton, *What's Wrong with the World* (San Francisco: Ignatius Press, 1994), chap. 5.

[2]Samson Gahungu, "Letter from Burundi," *The Friend,* April 19, 1996, p. 21.

[3]Samson Gahungu, "Letter from Burundi," *The Friend,* January 17, 1997, p. 11.

[4]Ibid.

[5]When Saul persecuted the church, he based it "on the authority of the chief priests" and "tried to force them to blaspheme" so he would have legal authority to throw them in prison (Acts 26:10-11).

[6]*Manila Times,* February 11, 1989, quoted in *Impunity: Prosecutions of Human Rights Violations in the Philippines* (New York: Lawyers Committee for Human Rights, 1991), p. 31.

[7]"Provost Marshal General Report to Chief of Staff of AFP," *Manilla Chronicle,* July 14, 1989, quoted in *Impunity,* p. 51.

[8]*Manila Chronicle,* July 14, 1989, quoted in *Impunity,* p. 127.

[9]*Manila Journal,* July 14, 1989, quoted in *Impunity,* p. 126.

[10]Ibid.

Chapter 11: Intervening for the Victims

[1]Commission on Legal Empowerment of the Poor, *Making the Law Work for Everyone,* vol. 1 (New York: United Nations Development Programme, 2008) <www.undp

.org/legalempowerment/report/index.html>.

[2]Martin Luther King Jr., "Beyond Vietnam: A Time to Break Silence," speech delivered to the Clergy and Laity Concerned, New York City, April 4, 1967 <www.americanrhetoric.com/speeches/mlkatimetobreaksilence.htm>.

[3]Global Report on Trafficking in Persons (New York: United Nations Office on Drugs and Crime, 2009) <www.unodc.org/documents/Global_Report_on_TIP.pdf>.

Chapter 12: Case by Case

[1]Aleksandr Solzhenitsyn, "Nobel Lecture in Literature, 1970," The Nobel Foundation <http://nobelprize.org/nobel-prizes/literature/laureates/1970/solzhenitsyn-lecture.htm>.

[2]The South African story is clearly more complicated than this; it was a struggle strewn with the corpses and casualties of violent white resistance to change. The international sanctions and the violent pressures of the black political struggle definitely had an impact. But had the white South Africans had the *will* to use all the force at their disposal and to endure the relatively mild consequences of international sanctions, they certainly would have had the power to maintain their apartheid way of life well into the twenty-first century. The power of personal appeals to spiritual convictions, morality and notions of common human decency is beautifully chronicled in Michael Cassidy's *A Witness Forever* (London: Hodder & Stoughton, 1995).

[3]There are exceptions, of course. It was a U.N.-sponsored force that threw a horrible military clique out of power in Sierra Leone. The U.N. is bringing the perpetrators of genocidal crimes in Rwanda and Bosnia to justice.

[4]Bureau of Democracy, Human Rights, and Labor, "Nigeria Country Report on Human Rights Practices for 1997," U.S. Department of State, January 30, 1998, pp. 1-2 <www.state.gov/www/global/human_rights/1997_hrp_report/nigeria.html>.

[5]Human Rights Committee, Comments on Nigeria, U.N. Doc. CCPR/C/79/Add.65 (1996).

[6]Human Rights Watch, "Human Rights Watch Africa" <www.hrw.org/hrw/about/divisions/africa.html>.

Chapter 13: The Body of Christ in Action

[1]Of course, the exportation of Western cultural baggage does continue to some extent, but when it does, it happens contrary to the missionary's own best theory and training. Missionaries rightly believe in the power of the gospel to *transform* the cultural (as in mitigating cultural traditions of headhunting or bride burning), the way Christians in America believe that the gospel should be a force of transformation within their own culture of materialism, arrogance, hedonism, etc. But most international Christian workers have traveled light-years in understanding the difference between exporting the idiosyncrasies of their own cultures and allowing the transcendent verities of the gospel to affect each community in its own indigenous culture.

Appendix 5: Advice to Students Considering an International Human Rights Career

[1]Oswald Chambers, "The Call of the Natural Life," *My Utmost for His Highest* (Grand Rapids: Discovery House, 1992), January 17.